# Journeys at the Margin

## Toward an Autobiographical Theology in American-Asian Perspective

*Peter C. Phan*
*Jung Young Lee*
Editors

*A Liturgical Press Book*

THE LITURGICAL PRESS
Collegeville, Minnesota

1    2    3    4    5    6    7    8

**Library of Congress Cataloging-in-Publication Data**

Journeys at the margin : towards an autobiographical theology in
    American-Asian perspective / Peter C. Phan, Jung Young Lee, editors.
        p.    cm.
    Includes bibliographical references.
    ISBN 0-8146-2464-2 (alk. paper)
    1. Asian Americans—Religious life.    2. Theology, Doctrinal.
I. Phan, Peter C., 1943–   .   II. Lee, Jung Young.
BR563.A82J68   1999
230'.089'95073—dc21
                                                                98-47088
                                                                CIP

*Dedicated to the memory of our beloved companions on the journey*
*Jung Young Lee (1930–1996)*
*and*
*David Ng (1934–1997)*

# Contents

Preface   vii

Introduction: An Asian-American Theology: Believing and Thinking at the Boundaries   xi
*Peter C. Phan*

Five Stages Toward Christian Theology in the Multicultural World   1
*Choan-Seng Song*

A Life In-Between: A Korean-American Journey   23
*Jung Young Lee*

The House of Self   41
*Julia Ching*

A Japanese-American Pilgrimage: Theological Reflections   63
*Paul M. Nagano*

A Path of Concentric Circles: Toward an Autobiographical Theology of Community   81
*David Ng*

"But Who Do You Say That I Am?" (Matt 16:15): A Churched Korean American Woman's Autobiographical Inquiry   103
*Jung Ha Kim*

Betwixt and Between: Doing Theology with Memory and Imagination   113
*Peter C. Phan*

From Autobiography to Fellowship of Others: Reflections on Doing
Ethnic Theology Today   135
   *Anselm Kyongsuk Min*

Church and Theology: My Theological Journey   161
   *Andrew Sung Park*

Selected Bibliography   173

Contributors   177

# Preface

This preface should have been a joint effort of Dr. Jung Young Lee and myself. Sadly, Professor Lee's sudden and premature death on October 11, 1996, has left me as the sole person responsible for this preface, as well as for the editorial work on this book, deprived of his gentle wisdom and whole-hearted support.

The idea of a book on Asian-American theologians was conceived by Jung. In his proposal for the book, Jung wrote:

> I have discovered that theological students are interested in reading stories, particularly the personal stories of theologians. Life experience seems to be a key to the undertaking of one's own theology, and it has powerful and practical implications for young theologians and lay people because it provides the framework of one's life story rather than describing ideological speculation. . . . I am, therefore, proposing a book that tells the life stories of several well-established Asian Americans.

When the Committee on Research and Scholarship of the Association of Theological Schools, of which Jung and I were members, met in the fall of 1995, we had the chance to talk about the projected book. Jung was fascinated by my own story of how I left Vietnam and asked me to contribute to the book and to seek a publisher for it. After The Liturgical Press expressed interest in it, Jung asked me to be co-editor with him. Jung already had a list of contributors, and I suggested a few more.

The essays Jung had in mind for the book were not to be mere autobiographies; he did not believe in the virtue of public self-disclosure, even when done by theologians. Theology for him is autobiographical, but not all autobiography is theology. Rather, he and I were looking for reflections by Asian-American theologians on how being an Asian and a North American has shaped the way they understand the Christian story and develop their own theologies.

For Jung, who has written a book on marginality as the key to multicultural theology,[1] the common thread knitting the diverse stories of Asian-American theologians together is their immigrant status, or to use his expression, their "marginality." There are, says Jung, many different kinds of marginality. Marginal persons are (1) those living in substandard urban areas; (2) the jobless or unemployed; (3) those who are at the periphery of economic or political structure; (4) migrants from one location to another; (5) deviants or nonconformists; and (6) ethnic or racial minority persons who have difficulty integrating into the dominant ethnic group.

Most Asian-American theologians belong to the last group. As immigrants they live and work "in-*between*" the two societies, their native and their host, far from centers of power, even though they occupy positions of influence and even prestige. Paradoxically, because they do not belong exclusively to either society, they belong to *both,* so that in addition to being "in-*between*" they are also "in-*both*." Furthermore, out of the resources of both societies and cultures they can build not only bridges between the two worlds but also a new, different world with a new center; in this sense they are "in-*beyond*" these two worlds. How Asian-American theologians understand their task in their peculiar social situation and how they carry it out is the concern of the book.

Let it be unambiguously stated here that the authors of the essays in this book are by no means the only nor the most representative nor the most influential Asian-American theologians currently working in North America. The contributors were chosen on the basis of our professional acquaintance and friendship. We did try to have all ethnic groups and denominations and genders among Asian-American theologians represented; unfortunately, two contributors were prevented by various circumstances from completing their essays. It is our fervent wish that collections of essays by other Asian-American theologians will be published soon to complement ours.

It is my sad duty to inform readers that during the composition of this book, another contributor was called to eternal life. Professor David Ng passed away unexpectedly on April 29, 1997, a great loss for the world of Christian education. Jung and David were close friends during their earthly lives; may their friendship continue to bloom in the presence of the Triune God and in the company of the saints. To their

---

[1] Jung Young Lee, *Marginality: The Key to Multicultural Theology* (Minneapolis: Fortress Press, 1995).

memory this book is dedicated by all their friends, deeply grateful for their legacy in the development of an Asian-American theology.

Peter C. Phan
The Catholic University of America

# Introduction

# An Asian-American Theology: Believing and Thinking at the Boundaries

*Peter C. Phan*

Why a book on the personal, intellectual, and even spiritual odysseys of a handful of Christian Asian-American theologians?[1] If one wishes to know what these theologians are saying, why not just read their writings themselves and be done with it? Of course, the book you are holding in your hand is not designed to replace these theologians' writings; on the contrary, it is intended to serve as a lure to peruse these primary texts themselves. It is no doubt possible to interpret these works without reference to the personal histories of their authors;

---

[1] In American census, the category "Asians and Pacific Islanders" designates a racially, ethnically, linguistically, and culturally disparate group of persons having origin in any of the indigenous peoples of the Far East, Southeast Asia, the Indian Subcontinent, or Pacific Islands. Included in this category are people from China, Japan, Korea, the Philippine Islands, American Samoa, India, and Vietnam. In the 1990 census, the population of Asians and Pacific Islanders in the United States was counted to be about 7.3 million, and 2.9 percent of the 250 million total U.S. population.

In this book "Asian-American" refers only to people from China, Japan, Korea, Taiwan, and Vietnam. One common element linking these people together is the "Confucian culture." For a brief history of these people in the United States see Jung Young Lee, *Marginality: The Key to Multicultural Theology* (Minneapolis: Fortress Press, 1995) 7–27, and Peter C. Phan, "Vietnamese Catholics in America," *The Encyclopedia of American Catholic History,* ed. Michael Glazier and Thomas J. Shelley (Collegeville: The Liturgical Press, 1998) 1434–5.

nonetheless a knowledge of the context in which they were composed would contribute greatly to understanding them. It is with a view to enhance the comprehension of these Asian-American theologians' works as well as to encourage further development of an Asian-American theology that this book is being offered to readers.

## An Asian Christian Theology: Method and Resources

In comparison with African-American and Hispanic-American theologians, Asian-American theologians are, professionally speaking, much younger siblings.[2] There are many reasons for the tardy development of a distinctive Asian-American theology, chief among which are the short time the Asians have been in the United States, their general lack of interest in academic disciplines other than the empirical and the scientific, and the still relatively small number of Asian Christians in this country. Not only the theological production of Asian-American theologians but also their number remain small. Unlike their African-American and Hispanic-American colleagues, presently they are not organized into a separate professional association. Nor do they possess an official journal or a center for theological training of their own.[3]

---

Religiously, statistics on Asian Americans are highly unreliable. On the basis of the annual General Social Survey from 1972 to 1991, it is estimated that among Chinese, 19 percent are Catholic, 30 percent are Protestant, and 14 percent belong to other religions. Among Japanese, 8 percent are Catholic, 38 percent Protestant, and 28 percent other. The majority of Filipinos are Catholics: 74 percent versus 20 percent Protestant. Among Indians, 9 percent are Catholic, 33 percent Protestant, and 44 percent other. Among the Vietnamese, some 35 percent are Catholic. Some 70 percent of Korean Americans declare themselves to be Christian. The percentage of Christians among Asian Americans is vastly higher than in their native countries (except the Philippines), suggesting a high rate of "conversions" of Asians to Christianity in the United States. See Peter C. Phan, "Asian Identity, Theology and Theological Education," *L'Universalité catholique face à la diversité humaine* (Montreal: Médiapaul, 1998).

[2] For a comparison of black, Hispanic, and Asian theologies, see Peter C. Phan, "Contemporary Theology and Inculturation in the United States," *The Multicultural Church: A New Landscape in U.S. Church,* ed. William Cenkner (New York: Paulist Press, 1996) 109–30, 176–92.

[3] I am speaking of specifically *Christian* Asian theology. There are, of course, numerous associations of Asian-American studies or studies of Asian religions as well as journals dedicated to Asian-American issues such as *Amerasia Journal.* There is a center for Asian-American theology called Pacific & Asian-American Center for Theology & Strategies, associated with Graduate Theological Union in Berkeley, California, as well as a Council for Pacific Asian Theology (for-

But this numerical minority does not lessen the fact that Asian-American theologians want to do theology in a different key. In the last two decades, like their counterparts in South America and Africa, Asian theologians, in North America and especially in Asia, have been voicing a trenchant critique of the theology of the First World. Tissa Balasuriya from Sri Lanka decries Western theology as largely irrelevant to Asians, ethnocentric, Church-centered, clerical, patriarchal, pro-capitalistic, devoid of socioeconomic analysis, and lacking orientation toward praxis.[4] Aloysius Pieris, another Sri Lankan, regards Western theology as unfit for the Asian situation of crushing poverty and deep religiousness.[5] Choan-Seng Song, a Presbyterian Taiwanese, faults Western theology for being overly rationalistic and lacking imagination.[6] Jung Young Lee, a Korean Methodist, criticized Western theology for its exclusivism based on the Aristotelian logic of excluded middle.[7] Many Asian women theologians reject Western theology for its patriarchy and androcentrism.[8]

To some these criticisms may sound too harsh and unjustified. The point here, however, is not whether they are accurate or historically wrong; rather, it is that there is a widespread perception that Euro-American theology is at least not meaningful or relevant to Asian peoples, and, as a result, a significant group of Asian and Asian-American

---

merly Morikawa Pacific Rim Ecumenical Conference), founded in 1989 and incorporated in 1990. There is also a recent journal named *Journal of Asian and Asian American Theology,* published by the Center for Asian Studies, 1325 North College Avenue, Claremont, CA 91711.

[4] See Tissa Balasuriya, "Toward the Liberation of Theology in Asia," *Asia's Struggle for Full Humanity: Toward a Relevant Theology,* ed. Virginia Fabella (Maryknoll, N.Y.: Orbis Books, 1980) 26, and Tissa Balasuriya, *Planetary Theology* (Maryknoll, N.Y.: Orbis Books, 1984) 2–10.

[5] See Aloysius Pieris, *An Asian Theology of Liberation* (Maryknoll, N.Y.: Orbis Books, 1988) 81–3.

[6] See Choan-Seng Song, *Third-Eye Theology,* rev. ed. (Maryknoll, N.Y.: Orbis Books, 1990) 19–23; Choan-Seng Song, *Tell Us Our Names* (Maryknoll, N.Y.: Orbis Books, 1984) 3–24; and Choan-Seng Song, *Theology from the Womb of Asia* (Maryknoll, N.Y.: Orbis Books, 1986).

[7] See Jung Young Lee, *Marginality: The Key to Multicultural Theology* (Minneapolis: Fortress Press, 1995) 64–70.

[8] See, for example, *We Dare to Dream: Doing Theology as Asian Women,* ed. Virginia Fabella and Sun Ai Lee Park (Hong Kong: Asian Women's Resource Centre for Culture and Theology, 1989); Chung Hyun Kyung, *Struggle to Be the Sun Again: Introducing Asian Women's Theology* (Maryknoll, N.Y.: Orbis Books, 1990); and Kwok Pui-lan, *Discovering the Bible in the Non-Biblical World* (Maryknoll, N.Y.: Orbis Books, 1995).

theologians have recently attempted to construct an alternative theology based on Asian methods and resources.[9]

Of course, this is not the first time that an effort has been made to construct an Asian theology. Prior to the theologians cited above there have been others, mostly Indian, who undertook the task of formulating a Christian theology on the basis of their own cultures. For example, attempts have been made to understand the Trinity in terms of the "trimurti" of Brahman, Vishnu, and Shiva. Other theologians sought to present Christ in terms of Hindu theology, e.g., Jesus as "Prajapati" (Lord of creatures), as "Cit" (consciousness), as "Avatara" (incarnation), as "Isvara" (the Cosmic Christ), as "Guru" (teacher), as "Adi Purasha" (the first person), as "Shakti" (power), as eternal "Om" *(logos),* as "Bodhisattva" (the Buddha who postpones enlightenment to help others achieve nirvana).[10]

In the last two decades, a younger generation of Asian theologians, under the influence of Latin American liberation theology, have applied new methods and brought new insights to enrich the older, more culture-based approaches. The result is not only a new theology but also a new way of doing theology. Of course, no Christian theology can be entirely new, but there are undeniably novel features in this emerging Asian theology. Like their Latin American colleagues, Asian theologians insist that theology is only a second act critically reflecting on the first act which is commitment to and solidarity with those who are victims of poverty and oppression. Theology is not "God-talk" based on some canonical texts in search of a practical application. Rather, it originates from Christian praxis (which may be called a "theopraxis," since it is inspired by God's preferential love for the poor and the oppressed realized in and by Jesus Christ), moves to critical reflection, returns to praxis, and the spiraling movement of praxis—critical theory—praxis repeats itself again and again in ever new contexts.

These contexts are discerned by a double method: social analysis and what Aloysius Pieris calls "introspection."[11] The former, popularized by Latin American liberation theologians, is used to identify the structural causes of the situation of poverty and oppression of the teeming millions of Asians such as colonialism, neocolonialism, economic

---

[9] See *Frontiers in Asian Christian Theology: Emerging Trends,* ed. R. S. Sugirtharajah (Maryknoll, N.Y.: Orbis Books, 1994) and *Asian Faces of Jesus,* ed. R. S. Sugirtharajah (Maryknoll, N.Y.: Orbis Books, 1993).

[10] In this field, perhaps best known to Western scholars are the numerous works of Raimon Panikkar.

[11] Pieris, *An Asian Theology of Liberation,* 80.

exploitation by multinational corporations, institutionalized violence, and military dictatorship. The latter, perfected by Asian sages, must also be pressed into service because Asia is characterized not only by crushing poverty but also by a deep and pervasive religiousness (which Pieris calls "cosmic religiousness"). After all, Asia is the birthplace of all world religions, including Christianity (what Pieris calls the "meta-cosmic" religions). Without the second approach, no theology can be authentically Asian. In a genuinely Asian theology, both social analysis and introspection are employed, so that both the "agape" of Christianity and the "gnosis" of non-Christian religions are brought together to produce a truly liberative theology for Asians.[12]

To interpret what the Christian faith means for Asians, Scripture and tradition will of course serve as a resource for Asian theologians. But they generally reject the hegemony of the historical-critical method as the only or predominant way of interpreting the Scripture, though they recognize its usefulness to discover the original meaning of a biblical text. For them the primary task of biblical hermeneutics is to concretize the Word of God, the incarnate *logos,* in the contemporary context for the people of today to help them regain their human dignity, and not merely to unfold the literal meaning of the text. In other words, the interpreter must not only *explain* the world *behind* the text but also *understand* the world *of* the text and *appropriate* the world *in front of* the text for the purpose of transforming oneself and the society. It is this personal and communal transformation that is the culmination of the hermeneutical enterprise as a whole.[13]

To achieve this goal, Asian theologians insist that all biblical interpretation be contextual. Interpreters must be cognizant not only of the context of the text but also of their own contexts, that is, their social locations as well as gender, class, and race biases and the sociopolitical, economic, and religio-cultural context of the people to whom the Bible is being proclaimed. The text is written by the "historical winners" who do not simply tell the story but *their* story, and the interpreter must be aware of the interplay among knowledge, power, and interests to identify the distortions and dysfunctions in the text and the possibilities of transformation it offers. In light of God's preferential love for the poor and given the presence of teeming masses of the poor in their continent, Asian theologians

---

[12] See Aloysius Pieris, *Love Meets Wisdom: A Christian Experience of Buddhism* (Maryknoll, N.Y.: Orbis Books, 1988), and Aloysius Pieris, *Fire & Water: Basic Issues in Asian Buddhism and Christianity* (Maryknoll, N.Y.: Orbis Books, 1996).

[13] See *Voices from the Margin: Interpreting the Bible in the Third World,* ed. R. S. Sugirtharajah (Maryknoll, N.Y.: Orbis Books, 1991).

adopt the perspective of the poor as the lens or focus in reading the Bible. The uppermost question in their minds is: How can the message of the Bible, especially as it is incarnated in Jesus, become the good news for those who are poor, oppressed, and marginalized?

Furthermore, because of the overwhelming presence of non-Christian soteriologies in Asia, Asian theologians also require the practice of inter-faith or multifaith hermeneutics. They reject the earlier apologetic ap-proach of using the Bible as a yardstick to judge the sacred texts of other religions. Rather, they read the Bible in light of other sacred texts and vice versa for mutual cross-fertilization.[14]

But the Bible and tradition are far from being the only resources for Asian theologians. An Asian theology must dig deep in the humus of Asian cultures to find therein the resources for its development. As Choan-Seng Song points out, "Resources in Asia for doing theology are unlimited. What is limited is our theological imagination. Powerful is the voice crying out of the abyss of the Asian heart, but powerless is the power of our theological imagining."[15]

The first resource is the billions of Asian people themselves with their daily stories of joy and suffering, hope and despair, love and ha-tred, freedom and oppression, stories not recorded in official books written by victors but kept alive in the "dangerous memory" (Johann Baptist Metz) of the "underside of history" (Gustavo Gutiérrez). In re-cent years, people as subjects doing theology, and not only as objects about whom theologians speak, have assumed a special role in Asian theology.[16] Korean theologians have developed a distinctive theology

---

[14] For examples of interfaith hermeneutics, see the brilliant essays of Samuel Rayan, "Reconceiving Theology in the Asian Context," *Doing Theology in a Di-vided World,* ed. Virginia Fabella and Sergio Torres (Maryknoll, N.Y.: Orbis Books, 1985) 134–9; "Wrestling in the Night," *The Future of Liberation Theol-ogy: Essays in Honor of Gustavo Gutiérrez,* ed. Marc H. Ellis and Otto Maduro (Maryknoll, N.Y.: Orbis Books, 1989) 450–69. See also Peter K. H. Lee, "Re-reading Ecclesiastes in the Light of Su Tung-p'o's Poetry," *Ching Feng,* vol. 30, no. 4 (1987) 214–36; Peter K. H. Lee, "Ta-T'ung and the Kingdom of God," *Ching Feng,* vol. 32, no. 4 (1988) 225–44; Peter K. H. Lee, "Two Stories of Loy-alty," *Ching Feng,* vol. 32, no. 1 (1989) 24–40; and Choan-Seng Song, *Tell Us Our Names: Story from an Asian Perspective* (Maryknoll, N.Y.: Orbis Books, 1984).

[15] Song, *Theology from the Womb of Asia,* 16.

[16] For reflections on "theology by the people," see *Theology by the People,* ed. S. Amirtham and John S. Pobee (Geneva: WCC, 1986); F. Castillo, *Theologie aus der Praxis des Volkes* (Munich: Kaiser, 1978); and Ernesto Cardenal, *The Gospel in Solentiname* (Maryknoll, N.Y.: Orbis Books, 1976).

called *"minjung* theology" as a faith reflection of, by, and for the mass in their struggle against oppression.[17]

The second resource is a subset of the first, namely, the stories of Asian women. Given the pervasive patriarchalism of Asian societies, the stories of oppression and poverty of Asian women occupy a special place in Asian theology. As Chung Hyun Kyung has said, "women's truth was generated by their epistemology from the broken body."[18] The women's stories (Korean *minjung* theologian Kim Young Bok calls them "socio-biography") are carefully listened to; then a critical analysis is carried out to discern the complex interconnections among the evil structures that produce women's oppression. Finally, theological reflection is done on them from the relevant teachings of the Bible.[19]

The third resource is the sacred texts and ethical and spiritual practices of Asian religions that have nourished and shaped the spirituality of Asian people for thousands of years before the coming of Christianity to their lands and continue to do so ever since. The sacred texts, together with innumerable commentaries upon them, serve as an inexhaustible fountain of wisdom for Christian theology. In addition, the ethical and spiritual practices prescribed by these religions can enrich the moral teachings as well as the spiritual practices of Christianity.[20] Consequently, an authentic Asian theology must enter into dialogue, with openness of mind and humility of heart, with Asian religions, to be enriched by them as well as to enrich them.

Intimately connected with these religious texts and spiritual practices is the fourth resource known as philosophy, since in Asia religion and philosophy are inextricably joined. Philosophy is a way of life and

[17] *Minjung,* a Korean word, is often left untranslated. By *minjung* are meant "the oppressed, exploited, dominated, discriminated against, alienated and suppressed politically, economically, socially, culturally, and intellectually, like women, ethnic groups, the poor, workers and farmers, including intellectuals themselves." See Chung Hyun Kyung, "Han-pu-ri: Doing Theology from Korean Women's Perspective," *We Dare to Dream,* 138–9. For a discussion of *minjung* theology see *An Emerging Theology in World Perspective: Commentary on Korean Minjung Theology* (Mystic, Conn.: Twenty-Third Publications, 1989), and David Kwang-sun Suh, *The Korean Minjung in Christ* (Hong Kong: Christian Conference of Asia, 1991).

[18] Chung Hyun Kyung, *Struggle to Be the Sun Again,* 104.

[19] See ibid., 103–9.

[20] For an example of how one of the most widespread and sacred practices in Asia, namely, the cult of ancestors, can be used to formulate a christology, see Peter C. Phan, "The Christ of Asia: An Essay on Jesus as the Eldest Son and Ancestor," *Studia Missionalia* 45 (1996) 25–55.

religion is a worldview, each being both *darsana* (view of life) and *prati-pada* (way of life). This philosophy, e.g., the metaphysics of *yin* and *yang*, should be pressed into service in order to explicate Christian beliefs such as christology and the Trinity.[21]

The fifth resource is Asian monastic traditions with their rituals, ascetic practices, and social commitment. Whereas these rituals and ascetic practices have been popularized and at times commercialized in the West, the last element, namely, social commitment, is less known and needs emphasizing. Pieris has consistently argued that the most appropriate form of inculturation of Christianity into Asia is not the Greek model of assimilation of a non-Christian philosophy or the Latin model of incarnation in a non-Christian culture or the North European model of accommodation to a non-Christian religiousness. Rather, what is required of Asian Christians is the monastic model of participation in a non-Christian spirituality. However, this monastic spirituality is not to be understood as a withdrawal from the world into leisurely prayer centers or "ashrams." Asian monks have always been involved in socio-political struggles through their voluntary poverty and their participation in social and cultural activities.[22]

The sixth resource is Asian cultures in general with their immense treasures of myths, folklore, symbols, poetry, stories, songs, visual art, and dance. The use of these cultural artifacts adds a very distinctive voice to Christian theology coming from the deepest yearning of the peoples of Asia. For example, *minjung* theology has made a creative use of real-life stories and folktale. These stories are narrated and sung at Korean mask dances *(talch'um)*, operas *(pansori)*, and shamanistic rituals *(kut)*.

## An Asian-American Theology:
## Similarities and Diversities

So far we have spoken of, albeit very cursorily, recent Asian theology in general and not Asian-American theology specifically. Of course, Asian-American theologians, in various degrees, do make use of the methods and resources expounded above. However, living in North America (the United States and Canada) and not in their respective na-

---

[21] See, for instance, Jung Young Lee, *A Theology of Change: A Christian Concept of God in Eastern Perspective* (Maryknoll, N.Y.: Orbis Books, 1979) and Jung Young Lee, *The Trinity in Asian Perspective* (Nashville: Abingdon Press, 1996).

[22] See Pieris, *An Asian Theology of Liberation,* 51–8, and Pieris, *Love Meets Wisdom,* 61–72, 89–96.

tive countries has made a difference in the way they do their theologies. Indeed, the burden of the essays in this book is precisely to show how residence in North America has shaped their theologies. For one thing, most if not all Asian-American theologians received their education and graduate training in Europe and/or the United States and were exposed, especially through their dissertations, to the ideas of influential Western philosophers and theologians. In their academic careers they have practiced their craft and achieved professional prominence according to the Western canons of scholarly excellence.

Beyond educational and professional training, however, the most influential factor on the theologies of Asian-American theologians is the fact they live in North America as members of a minority group. Whether they were born in this hemisphere or sought residence here or were forced by political circumstances to seek refuge in this part of the world, they are regarded, because of the color of their skin and ethnic origin, as immigrants. As Jung Young Lee argued, being immigrant means first of all being "in-between" two worlds, and as such being at the margins of the two worlds, i.e., the host country and the native country. Politically, economically, socially, and culturally, immigrants live where the two worlds intersect. They are thus marginalized, that is, distanced from the two centers of power, and are often characterized by the dominant groups as lacking in self-identity.

Like Mexican-American *mestizos* (persons of mixed race) who are rejected by Americans for not being American enough and by Mexicans for not being Mexican enough,[23] Asian Americans are estranged by Americans who think they have remained too Asian, not fully assimilated into the melting pot, and estranged by Asians who think they have been too Americanized, cut off from their cultural roots. This was true especially of Japanese Americans during World War II, as Paul Nagano's and 120,000 other Japanese Americans' imprisonment in concentration camps makes it clear, and of Korean-Americans, as Jung Young Lee's being denied full membership in the Ohio Methodist Conference testifies. On the other hand, many Asian Americans have found out upon visits to their native countries that they can no longer call them home. Julia Ching speaks for many Asian Americans when she writes:

> Again and again, I visited China. I saw the new hotels rise up, together with the skyscrapers. I saw the citizens change from blue and green to beige, from home-made cottons to brand-name trench coats. I still could

---

[23] On this theme, see the works of Virgilio Elizondo, especially his *Christianity and Culture* (Huntington, Ind.: Our Sunday Visitor, 1975) and *Galilean Journey: The Mexican-American Promise* (Maryknoll, N.Y.: Orbis Books, 1983).

not feel at home in this country of many paradoxes. I now belong to Canada, which has become my home. Revisiting China has helped me to accept my new identity, my sense of self and belonging.

However, being "in-between" and at the margins, as Lee further argues, is not altogether negative. Being "in-between" the two societies immigrants are also "in-both" of them. Paradoxically, being neither exclusively American nor exclusively Asian, Asian Americans are *both*. More importantly, belonging to both worlds and cultures, marginalized immigrants have the opportunity to fuse them both and, out of their respective resources, fashion a new, different world. In this way, being "in-*beyond*" the two worlds, they help reconcile the two worlds and centers of power by creating a new world with its own center. But this new center does not marginalize anyone because of race, ethnicity, gender, or class. Rather, the circle of the new world is all-inclusive, enabling both natives to be immigrants and immigrants to be natives. And if immigrants take Jesus as the model of their lives *(imitatio Christi),* they can contribute to the building up of a society according to the ideals of the reign of God in which freedom, justice, peace, and love dominate. Indeed, Jesus himself may be regarded as the immigrant or the marginal(ized) person *par excellence,* standing on the boundary between divinity and humanity, because he is both fully God and fully human, and reconciling them both in his person, and thus is the reign of God in the flesh *(autobasileia tou theou).*

Thus, Asian-American as well as other similarly hyphenated theologians can look upon their historical situation of marginalization as both a gift and a task. A gift because it enables them to draw from the rich and variegated treasures of the cultures of their native and host countries, treasures which they live and experience existentially and on a daily basis and which others may know only theoretically and occasionally (David Ng, following Tu Wei-ming, spoke of Chinese having a "Confucian DNA"). And a task because it is incumbent upon them to build bridges between these diverse cultures and to formulate a new, albeit necessarily incomplete and ongoing, synthesis of the Christian faith on the basis of the new culture they help bring about. Their destiny then is to "journey at the margins" and their theological task is to think on the boundaries, betwixt and between, with memory and imagination.

The essays in this book are not autobiographies but theological reflections on personal experiences. More precisely, they are attempts at autobiographical theology. Of course, not all autobiographies are theology: tell-all bestsellers and candid self-revelations on talk shows are rather indecent exposures than theological ruminations! In a narcissistic age such as ours which believes that public self-disclosure is an

intrinsically virtuous, psychologically therapeutic, and socially trans-
formative act, theologians must guard against polluting the cultural
pond further by publishing each and every of their thoughts and experiences, however ennobling and religious these are deemed to be.
Nevertheless, all theologies are unavoidably autobiographical because
theology is a critical and systematic reflection on faith and praxis,
one's own and one's community's. Faith, though not individual, is the
most personal and intimate act there is, and hence talking about it is
intimate and personal.

Among the various and legitimate ways of doing theology, there is
storytelling from the perspective of faith by which, as David Ng put it,
"one's life story becomes a lifestory, a way of relating the events to
providence." Storytelling is, of course, not the only nor necessarily the
best way of doing theology for everyone and everywhere. But it is Asia's
favorite way of conveying wisdom. It is highly appropriate then that
this book opens with Taiwanese Presbyterian Choan-Seng Song's essay
on how storytelling has functioned in his theology and in particular in
his christological trilogy. For Song method is not something to be devised beforehand which is subsequently implemented in the doing of
theology, otherwise it would be a constricting straightjacket; rather it is,
as he puts it, an "afterthought." "The method of storytelling," says he,
"is in the telling of stories." Reviewing his three-volume work on Jesus,
the purpose of which is to tell the Christian story of the Cross in the
Buddhist story of the Lotus, Song realizes that his method consists of
five stages. In essence, these stages lead him to discover the stories of
the reign of God which Jesus told in the stories of contemporary suffering, oppressed, poor Asians:

> Here is my conclusion: to know Jesus, to understand what he said and did,
> to experience his suffering, to fathom the redemptive meaning of his death,
> we also need to listen to those stories, lived, experienced and told by our
> fellow Asians, those men, women and children in Asia who remain outside
> the Christian church.

Jung Young Lee's visit to his motherland, North Korea, from which
he and his family were forced to flee, evoked memories of a happy
childhood as well as of war and Japanese occupation. His experiences
in the United States, first as a student and then as a minister and professor (including his being refused appointment as a Methodist pastor
despite his full qualifications) suggest to him that an immigrant is
someone living "in-between" and "in-both": "Wherever I went, however, people have asked me 'When are you going home?' I did not belong to America, but I could not return to my country, North Korea,
which had become a Communist nation. I was a man without a country,

seeking to find a new home." Elsewhere Lee finds in the dandelion a symbol of his condition as an Asian immigrant: a yellow weed on a green lawn which the owner repeatedly pulls up but which refuses to die and insists on growing back and blooms every spring.[24] These experiences, painful and bitter as they were, allowed Lee to see his life as "more or less a microcosm of Israel's sacred history" and offered him the resources to construct a multicultural theology, the key theme of his reflections and writings.

Julia Ching, a Chinese Catholic from Shanghai who has lived in Australia and the United States and is now settled in Canada, has also visited her native country from which she fled after the Communist takeover some thirty years earlier. As we have seen above, her repeated visits made her realize that she no longer feels at home in China and that she belongs more to Canada. And yet, during her meditation practices following her severe illness, her instructor told her that she is "more Oriental than Western." Appraising her life Ching acknowledges the truth of her instructor's observation: "I have always regarded life as a quest. I know myself to have been consumed by a quest for meaning, for giving myself to a greater cause. So mine has been very much a spiritual quest. It has been a quest that started in the East and led to the West, only to take me back to the East, culturally speaking."

Paul Nagano, a Baptist, describes himself as "a typical Japanese American" and yet claims that he has understood "what it means to journey at the margins of the American society." This is of course an understatement of gigantic proportions! During World War II, along with hundreds of thousands of other Japanese Americans, he was stripped of possessions, interned in concentration camps, and treated as "enemy alien" despite his American citizenship. Reflecting on this painful experience Nagano says without bitterness:

> With passing years, I am glad that I experienced marginalization, for this, to me, is the meaning of the Incarnation. Actually, I became aware of the connection between marginalization and the Incarnation during my search for identity. I became better able to identify with the oppressed, the marginalized, and the dehumanized, and at the same time I came to see myself as a person, made in God's image and likeness, and loved by the Creator. Marginality has led me to discover my humanity.

Like most third-generation immigrants, Nagano traveled back to his country to search for his roots and became aware of the need to be proud of his Japanese heritage. To younger Japanese who try to fit as

---

[24] See Lee, *Marginality*, 10–13.

much as possible into the American society, he offers three counsels: affirm their Japanese-American identity while frankly acknowledging their marginality, develop strategies of solidarity and common action with other marginalized ethnic groups, and work for the coming of the reign of God on the global level.

David Ng, a second-generation Chinese American Presbyterian, developed the theme of community out of his Confucian background. For him Church was community, even in the midst of the large bureaucracy such as the Presbyterian Board of Christian Education: "Within the life of this community within a large bureaucracy, my own sense of Christian mission, ministry, and community were nurtured." Later on, working for the National Council of the Churches of Christ, Ng continued to foster a vision of a global community. Professionally, the best place where Ng was able to put into practice his vision of community was at his alma mater, San Francisco Theological Seminary, where through a multicultural program and courses he attempted to build "a multicultural church in a multicultural society." Influenced by Dietrich Bonhoeffer's *Life Together,* Ng was convinced that there is no "cheap grace" and "cheap community":

> The community enabled by Christ is not based on human, sentimental notions of how people can learn how to get along and come to like each other, overcoming personal differences. The only thing Andre, Teresa, and Wah-mun have in common in the new community is their common experience of the saving grace of Christ. That is what ties them together. The community they have is not what they have created on their own. Community is a gift of Christ.

A true Chinese, Ng turned to his Confucian background to find the equivalent of the New Testament notion of community *(koinonia),* and to his great joy he discovered that it is a combination of two words, *tuen* and *kai,* meaning solidarity and responsibility respectively.

Jung Ha Kim describes herself as "a churched Korean American woman." She prefers the term "churched" to "Christianized" because it connotes fewer institutional ties. Indeed, already as a young child living in Japan she practiced her devotion in the Buddhist temple, the Shinto shrine, and the Christian Church at the same time:

> At times, I had to stop by the Zen Buddhist temple on the way back from the church, just to insure that God/the Lord/the Spirit/the Master/the Buddha had seen and heard my devotional sincerity. Neither did I feel anything inherently contradictory about performing religious rituals at all three places, nor do I remember anyone making an issue of my multireligious practices.

Coming to the United States at the age of thirteen, Kim found that her "keen sense of the helplessness of constantly being uprooted" was relieved by the Christian Church:

> Once I walked into the church, however, a whole different world of all-Korean and of all-too-familiar aura of kim-chee was waiting for me. I felt comforted and reassured that a community outside my own family was going through what I've been going through. People at the church seemed strangely very "Korean" in America. I was no longer alone.

As a result she brought all her immediate family to Christianity. But the most influential figure in Kim's understanding of multiculturalism and multireligiousness was her grandmother, who, a devout Buddhist, also became a Christian but continued her Buddhist practices. One day, Kim heard her grandmother chant the Lord's Prayer to a Buddhist tune! From her Kim learned that "a self-understanding is not so much how or what to name one's self, but how one experiences life." Hence, for Kim, the important theological questions become:

> What concepts and categories enable us to faithfully articulate our lived experiences and spiritual journeys? Which of the so-called main- and male-line Christian doctrines, which interpretations of the Bible and of rituals need to be dismantled and/or reconstructed in efforts to take seriously our own communal struggles and issues? What makes a person or people Christian? What "dangerous memories" are worth remembering in doing theology?

Unlike most of his colleagues, Peter C. Phan, a Roman Catholic, did not choose to come to the United States; rather he was part of the exodus of Vietnamese refugees who somehow were brought to America after the fall of South Vietnam to the Communists in 1975. Again, unlike them, he did not deliberately choose teaching theology as a career, being more "an accidental theologian," as he puts it. In "fits of piety," however, he would admit that his life as a theologian "betwixt and between," at the boundaries, has been foreshadowed by a series of events, from his French education to his philosophical studies in Hong Kong and at the University of London to his theological training in Rome and, finally, to his life as an immigrant in the United States. From all these experiences, he learned that "very few momentous and decisive things which shape one's destiny are within one's planning and control":

> Like most unimportant lives, mine is like a story without plot, a poem without rime, a quilt without a pattern. Only in the light of faith can my coming to the United States, which was totally beyond my wildest dream and yet radically changed the direction of my life, appear, in retrospect, as an event of the mysterious design that Divine Providence has conceived for me.

His own theological development—between memory and imagination—has been shaped by Orthodox iconography, Tillich's on-the-boundary theology, patristic social thought and anthropology, Rahnerian transcendental theology, Latin American and Asian liberation theology, and missiology. For him, an authentic Asian theology must be built upon three pillars: inculturation, liberation, and interreligious dialogue.

A Korean Roman Catholic, Anselm Kyongsuk Min has been extensively exposed both to Western philosophers (in particular, Hegel and Marx) and Western theologians (in particular, Karl Rahner and liberation theologians) during his graduate studies in the United States. While he is no longer "wholly committed to the Hegelian vision of totality or the Marxian vision of praxis and liberation," Min has by no means given up on "totality and liberation." On the contrary he is more and more convinced of "the necessity of a positively maintained tension between competing, total visions of life as well as between contemplation and praxis." Within this perspective he has tried to discern the contours of an ethnic Asian and, more specifically, Korean theology. Perhaps this concern had been sparked by the remark of one of his Jesuit college professors to the effect that Western civilization is superior to Asian and his challenge to refute his assertion, which the youthful Min gamely took on. Far from rejecting Western tradition wholesale as colonialist, imperialist, patriarchal, and ethnocentric, Min believes that "the theological challenge for Korean Christianity is precisely to retrieve and incorporate the best of the Western tradition into its own theological reconstruction." The other challenge, Min goes on, "is to retrieve the best of the Korean tradition of religions and cultures not only as passive objects of critical theological reflection but, more importantly, as active sources or loci of theological insights for an authentically Korean Christianity." Min, however, is conscious that he is not only a Korean but also a Korean-American theologian. Hence, he sees the necessity of retrieving both the Western and the Korean traditions for the needs of the Korean community in America that are different from those in the native country. The Korean-American community, as Min sees it, is characterized by separation, ambiguity, diversity, and love of the stranger. To respond to these needs, Min calls for "a political theology appropriate to Korean Americans as citizens of the United States who have both domestic responsibilities towards the common good and international responsibilities as the sole surviving superpower in an increasingly globalizing world." Central to this theology is Min's notion of "solidarity of others."

Andrew Sung Park, a Korean United Methodist, conceives theology as a form of Church ministry. For him, theology must be rooted in the faith of the community and serve the needs of the Church. On the other hand, the Church must welcome the contribution of theologians whose work is indispensable for the Church's task of making the gospel relevant to the contemporary world. On the basis of the sociopolitical situation of Korean Americans, especially their *han,* and using a theological method that includes "theopraxis," Park attempts to develop a theology that is "theo-concentric," "Christo-concentric," and "Spirit-concentric." As challenges for Asian-American theologians, Park urges his colleagues to fight against racism from the society and sexism within the Church, as well as against ecological exploitation.

From a cursory review of these theologians' works, it is clear that Asian-American theology is by no means monolithic. Of course, there are certain common themes and similar approaches, but there are also distinctive accents and emphases resulting from the theologians' different national, cultural, and religious backgrounds. It is useful to remember that Asia is a vast continent with immensely different cultures and languages. There is no such thing as a generic "Asian" or "Oriental," just as there is no such thing as a nondescript "Westerner" or "European." We must guard against the tendency to regard people different from ourselves as "all the same" and homogenize them with superficial stereotypes.

Postmodernist epistemology has drawn our attention to the importance of the social location as well as of interests of various kinds in the process of gathering information and formulating knowledge. It unmasks epistemological claims to universal validity as forms of domination and marginalization. Asian-American theologians acknowledge the particularity of every point of view, that is, the unavoidable relationship of every knowing subject to his or her situation, and hence they tend to be wary of premature or exaggerated claims to universality.

However, postmodernist epistemology can go too far in insisting on the particularity of the social location of the knower and falls into self-contradictory relativism. Thus there is talk of the "incommensurability" among different points of view. Asian-American theologians reject such a thesis, first of all because they themselves embody, not only in their thinking but also in their daily lives, the "hyphenization" or dialogue between and among cultures and worldviews. Furthermore, in the incommensurability thesis there is the hidden danger that people belonging to the dominant system can safely refuse to enter in dialogue with minority groups. Allow minority groups to "do their own thing" and "have their own space," they may say, as long as there will be no change in our ways of thinking and behaving, because we too can "do our own thing" and "have our own space." The trouble with this arrangement is that the dominant group's way of doing its own thing and having its own space leaves precious little room for others. The little space in which minorities live and move and have their being is tolerated, con-descendingly, as long as they do not disturb the status quo and challenge the privileges enjoyed by the dominant group.

Asian-American theologians have no wish to develop a theology so ethnic and contextual that so-called "main-line" theologians and Church authorities can look upon it at best as an interesting but harmless exercise and at worst as an entertaining curiosity at a freak show. Rather, their goal is to produce a theology that is the fruit of a dialogue among all cultures and systems of thought in which no one can claim and is granted a superior status, and in which particularity and universality are not related to each other in mutual contradiction but in dialectical tension, because it is only by starting from particular points of view that a universal theology can be constructed. The voices of minority groups and those of the dominant group will make up a new chorus in which all the distinct and various notes and lyrics are harmonized together into a new symphony. In short, what Asian-American theologians are attempting to do is to construct an "intercultural theology" for a new context characterized by the phenomenon of globalization.[25] It is with this aim in mind that this modest book is presented to the academy, Church, and society.

---

[25] On globalization as a new context for doing theology, see Robert Schreiter, *The New Catholicity: Theology Between the Global and the Local* (Maryknoll, N.Y.: Orbis Books, 1997).

# Five Stages Toward Christian Theology in the Multicultural World

*Choan-Seng Song*

In November 1990 the first volume of my trilogy on Jesus was published under the title *Jesus, the Crucified People*.[1] A little more than two years later, the second volume entitled *Jesus and the Reign of God* was off the press.[2] *Jesus in the Power of the Spirit,* the third volume in the series, came out in February 1994.[3] It has been a long theological journey for me. The completion of the trilogy gives me an opportunity to reflect on how I have gone about doing Christian theology all these years. The reflection is at once an after-thought and a forward thought, for it is an attempt to understand what I have done and how I have done it in order to set the stage for my continuing theological journey.

This is to say that completing this trilogy on Jesus has not brought my theological enterprise to completion. How could it? Theology is always on the way—*theologia viatorum*. When we think we have reached a terminus, a goal, or an objective in our theological effort, we at once realize that we are at the beginning of another journey, at the start of another pilgrimage, at the threshold of another adventure. This awareness makes us humble and expectant at one and the same time: humble because what we have done may only touch the tip of the iceberg, as it were, and expectant because there is always the mystery of God yet to be disclosed to us. We are urged to move on in pursuit of that mystery.

---

[1] *Jesus, the Crucified People* (New York: Crossroad, 1990).
[2] *Jesus and the Reign of God* (Minneapolis: Fortress Press, 1993).
[3] *Jesus in the Power of the Spirit* (Minneapolis: Fortress Press, 1994).

I think no one knows this better than Paul, a totally dedicated servant of Jesus and a matchless theologian. This is what he said, among other things, in his letter to the Philippians, probably from his prison in Ephesus around 56 C.E.: "Not that I have already obtained this or have already reached the goal; but I press on to make it my own, because Christ Jesus has made me his own" (Phil 3:12). He confides in us that the risen Jesus "appeared also to me, to one untimely born" (1 Cor 15:8), that he "was caught up to the third heaven, caught up into Paradise and heard things that are not to be told, that no mortal is permitted to repeat" (2 Cor 12:2-4). But it is this same Paul who also tells us in utter humility and joyful expectation: "For now we see in a mirror, dimly, but then we will see face to face" (1 Cor 13:12). These words of Paul's show us what theology must be and how there must be always in our theological chamber space for new insights and fresh thoughts despite all the theological wisdom from the history of the Christian Church put together.

## The Cross in the Lotus World

In the reflection that follows, I will focus in particular on *Jesus, the Crucified People,* the first volume in my trilogy. As I begin to undertake this theological exercise, I realize that I am doing something I seldom have done before: reflecting on the ways, or methods if you like, which I adopted in writing *Jesus, the Crucified People.* I have always maintained, and still do, that theological method is something of an after-thought. It is a pause you take after you have done the work, an exercise you do to recharge your theological engine, an effort you make to chart again your theological course. Method will not come at the beginning of your doing theology. You do not define and restrict— is not to define to restrict?—what you have to do even before you get started.

For me theology is like storytelling. The story unfolds itself as you tell it. It moves in all directions. It may even stray into byways. But this is the excitement of telling stories. A story grows and expands. It leads to new terrains and depicts new scenes. If this is what our storytelling is like, how much more so is God's storytelling! The story of creation— who are we to define it and restrict it? God's activity in the world—how are we to predict it and dictate it? God's ultimate goal for humanity and for the entire creation—how on earth are we to set a time-frame to it? From all this I have learned one important thing: the method of storytelling is in the telling of stories. Is this not tautological? Yes, it is. But this seems the way God goes about telling God's stories and unfolding God's visions and activities in human stories. If our doing of theology is a humble effort on our part to grapple with God's storytelling, can we do it in any other way than telling stories?

In telling stories one of the things that makes a lot of difference is the time and the place in which a story is told. Thus I should explain why I gave my trilogy the general title *The Cross in the Lotus World,* drawing particular attention to the expression "the lotus world." Let me quote part of the preface to *Jesus, the Crucified People:*

> The word "lotus" is of course symbolic of Buddhism. Although a great part of Asia has been under Buddhist influence for centuries, Asia as a home to other religions and cultures cannot be described entirely as a "lotus world." Still, this general title expresses in a symbolic way a theological effort to understand Christian faith in the part of the world not dominated by Christianity.[4]

The word "lotus" is used here in a symbolic sense. It is supremely a Buddhist symbol, a symbol different from other religious symbols including the Christian Cross. It stands for the heart of Buddhist faith, the faith that the Buddha, in his infinite compassion, seeks to rescue humanity from this world of suffering. It thus represents Buddhist spirituality that enables believers to cling to the Buddha for deliverance from the pain and suffering of this world and for attainment of eternal bliss in the next world. This lotus symbol reminds us, in other words, of the world of Asia shaped not by Christianity but by religions such as Buddhism. It also draws our attention to the people who are not members of the Christian Church but belong to other religious communities such as Buddhism.

By the expression "the lotus world" I meant the vast world of Asia into which Christianity entered as a relative late comer, and the majority of the people of Asia who have remained outside the Christian influence. Buddhism commands a large following of men and women in Asia, but it is not the only significant religion with which Christianity has to deal. There are equally great numbers of Hindus, Muslims, Confucianists, and those who practice ancestor worship. All in all, the lotus world is the world of Asia, the world shaped largely by religions other than Christianity, the world of people mostly adhering to the faiths and religions unrelated to the Christian faith.

If the lotus is used in this wider sense of the religions of Asia independent of Christianity, the Cross symbolizes Christianity and what it stands for. Then what does the Cross have to do with the lotus? How do the alien symbol of the Cross and the indigenous symbol of the lotus interact? Can the history of the Cross and the history of the lotus find

---

[4] *Jesus, the Crucified People,* xi.

themselves each in the other? How do the spiritual world of the Cross and the spiritual world of the lotus affect each other? These are important questions.

In recent years channels of communication are being opened and attempts made to build bridges of goodwill and understanding between the world of the Cross and the world of the lotus. These efforts and attempts, at both practical and theological levels, are to be encouraged and commended. But this is not what I tried to do in *Jesus, the Crucified People*. My effort has more to do with the self-understanding of the Cross in the world of the lotus. Mine is a theological exercise that begins with the awareness that in Asia the Cross neither finds itself in the world of Europe and America it left behind nor in an empty world, a *tabula rasa* world, in which it can do whatever it pleases. No! In Asia the Cross has come to stay in the lotus world. Not only this, Asian Christians themselves are in fact part of this world. How can such awareness not make a difference to the understanding of the Cross, that is, what Christian faith stands for? If the world of Europe and America has affected not only the outward forms of Christian faith but the understanding of its contents, how is it possible for Christian faith not to be affected by the world of Asia in which it has come to stay?

*The Cross in the Lotus World* is a theological exercise in Christian self-understanding in the world not defined by Christianity. It begins with the self-understanding of the Cross, the very symbol of Christian faith, in *Jesus, the Crucified People* (the first volume). It goes on to explore the meaning of God's reign, the very heart of Jesus' message, in *Jesus and the Reign of God* (the second volume). These theological efforts lead to a critical question of how we Christians in Asia are to deal with our own Asian cultures and religions in light of how Jesus was moved to do with his. This is the main theme of *Jesus in the Power of the Spirit* (the third volume). What is attempted in this work on Jesus is a drama, a *theological* drama if you like, of how the life and mission of Jesus are played on the stage or in the setting of Asia, the stage not set by Christianity but by other religions, the setting not shaped by the Christian cultural ethos but by the cultural ethos of other religions. And, of course, the central players in this drama are not doctrines, teachings, and institutions, but Jesus with women, men, and children of Asia today, just as Jesus played the drama of his life and mission with the men, women, and children of his day.

## Five Stages Toward a Theological Reconstruction

From Jerusalem two thousand years ago to Asia today is a long journey. On the way many difficulties have to be overcome and many fresh starts must be made. Many errors have been committed and many adjustments had to be made. But most of us Christians and theologians in Asia have not planned our own journey of faith and charted our own theological pilgrimage with Jesus of Nazareth who lived and toiled in his own day and time. Our Jesus and most of what we believe about him, think about him, and preach about him is believed, thought, and preached by the churches and their teachers in the West. We have, in other words, taken a shortcut in our faith in Jesus and in everything that has to do with him, including ways of worshiping him and church buildings in which we worship him.

But as more and more of us Christians and theologians in Asia have come to realize that though a shortcut in faith and theology may be handy and convenient, it deprives us of a direct and authentic experience of Jesus. "Jesus," it is true, is "the same yesterday and today and forever" (Heb 13:8), but the Jesus brought to us by the churches in the West may not be quite the same as that Jesus who is "the same yesterday and today and forever." How are we then to encounter for ourselves in Asia that Jesus who is yesterday, today, and forever? Surely this must be our main theological agenda.

To prepare ourselves for this theological agenda of ours, however, we have at least a few things to do. We need to settle our theological account with what we have inherited from the past. We must look for resources in Asia that may broaden and deepen our faith in Jesus. And we have to resort to villages and cities in Asian countries, to those habitats of ours where Jesus must be continuing his ministry of God's reign in ways not specified in our theological textbooks and in those guides for Sunday school teachers. Reflections such as these bring me to "the five stages" I have taken to reconstruct my theological reflection on faith in Jesus in *The Cross in the Lotus World,* particularly in *Jesus, the Crucified People.*

### Stage One: Asking a Fundamental Question

In the tradition of faith and theology in which we are nurtured, we are told that there is a consistent movement in God's purpose for the world. That movement works its way through Israel, comes to focus on Jesus, and takes form in the Christian Church. This seems beyond doubt and dispute. Is not our Bible itself structured in that way? There is the Old Testament (the *Hebrew* Scriptures, to be correct). Apart from the first few chapters of Genesis talking about creation, the entire Old Testament consists of stories of the people of Israel from the Exodus, to the rise and fall of the kingdoms of Israel and Judah, to the Exile in Assyria and Babylon, to the return to Jerusalem from the Exile.

Then comes the New Testament. Again, apart from the few chapters at the end of that strange book called Revelation that talks about a new creation, the New Testament consists of the stories of Jesus, and the stories of the apostles and the early Christian community. The most prominent personality among the apostles and the early followers of Jesus is, of course, Paul. A number of letters he wrote to the churches he associated with have survived to tell us much about those churches and especially about Paul's own faith and his theological reflection on it.

This forward movement from Israel to the Christian Church with Jesus at its center is said to represent God's saving purpose for humanity. In this divine scheme of things the people of Israel came to believe themselves to be the *chosen* people of God. But with Jesus the divine scheme of salvation took a decisively new turn. By rejecting Jesus, Israel was disqualified to be the chosen people of God. That mantel of election now falls on the Christian Church that received Jesus as the Messiah. Christians are now the chosen people of God destined for eternal salvation. To be a Christian is to believe in this divine scheme of salvation.

But this divine scheme of salvation is not as straightforward as it seems once it is tested in the waters of Asia. According to it, then, the great majority of the people of Asia remains outside it. In other words, they have no part in God's salvation; Christians alone are entitled to it. Is this not why Christian mission becomes a divine imperative for Christians? Do we not have to make all efforts to evangelize those who are not Christian? Is it not our responsibility to bring to them the gospel of salvation? Is it not our mission as churches and Christians to make known to them the name of Jesus? Is it not our "great commission" to "Christianize" the world in our generation? But, as we know, we Christians have not Christianized the world, not to say Asia. And there is no evidence that we can do so in the foreseeable future. To complicate the matter further, the West that has been "Christianized" has once again become "secularized."

But this is not all. More and more churches today have themselves become "secularized," not only in the West but also in the rest of the world such as Asia, the fruits of the mission efforts of the churches in the West during the past two hundred years. They allow themselves to be corrupted by self-interests, greed, and power. They have often become counter-signs and counter-witnesses of Jesus. Here the logic of salvation the Christian Church has used on Israel can be applied to itself: if God rejected Israel as the chosen instrument of God's purpose, are there reasons why God would not do the same with the Christian Church? If God's judgment began with Israel, could it not also begin with the Christian Church?

Related to what has just been said, there is another thing that became clear to me. The Christian assertion about God's salvation in fact begins neither with the history of Israel nor even with Jesus himself. That is to say, it is not a historical assertion but a dogmatic assertion. It is a very much Church-centered assertion that the Christian Church and it alone is the community of the saved. With this assertion at the center of its faith, the Church takes a look at Israel that preceded it and says that Israel was rejected by God. As to Jesus, he is understood, taught, and preached almost solely in terms of the salvation Christians have assured for themselves. In this way Jesus is Christianized. Faith in him is not so much faith in his prophetic mission as a means to assure one's own salvation in heaven.

How the Christian Church has come to consider itself as the center of the divine scheme of salvation is evident when it calls the Hebrew Scripture it inherited from the Jewish religion the *Old* Testament and its own Scripture the *New* Testament. Obviously, "old" and "new" are value-words and judgment-concepts. What is old is not as valuable as what is new. The old is something to be superseded by the new and replaced by it. This is precisely the way in which Christians view "the Old Testament" in relation to "the New Testament." Contained in "the Old Testament" is the old covenant, the covenant no longer valid and effective. God is no longer bound by it. In contrast, what one finds in "the New Testament" is the new covenant God has made with the Christian Church. It replaces the old covenant as the sign of the salvation God has bestowed on the Church and its members.

For the Jewish people, however, their Scripture is anything but old. Hebrew Scripture has been their Scripture for centuries, since the day their ancestors received the Torah from God through Moses on Mount Sinai. It will never grow old, for it is going to be their Scripture for generations to come. God's covenant with them too will remain valid and true forever. They may have committed sins against God and disobeyed God from time to time in the course of their history. They have been punished severely for it. But God has not abandoned them. God is still their God and they are still the people of God. It is this tenacity of faith that enabled them to survive horrendous tragedies such as the Holocaust in which several millions of them perished in Nazi Germany.

The Christian Church presses its logic of the old and the new even further. What is given in "the Old Testament" is the promise of God. But that promise of God is fulfilled only in "the New Testament." This theological scheme of promise and fulfillment has dominated the Christian faith and theology throughout the history of Christianity. Such a scheme deprives the ancient people of Israel of their direct relationship with God's salvation. In fact, most Christians think that God broke that direct relationship with the Jewish people. That relationship is now theirs. It is their privilege and not the Jews'. For Jews to regain that privilege, they must be converted to the Christian faith. Hence, the Christian mission to the Jews!

The Christian Church applies essentially the same theological logic in its mission to the people outside the Church. God may have made covenant with all humanity through creation, but that covenant does not lead those outside the Christian Church to salvation. They have some knowledge of God and God's salvation, but that knowledge is useless because it has nothing to do with Jesus. In making assertions such as this, Christians do not stop to ask whether they have understood what God did in and through Jesus. They refuse even to consider the possibility that God may be working also outside the church. They are insensitive to the spiritual depths demonstrated by people of other faiths, the depths they cannot even begin to fathom and comprehend.

These are some of the theological questions that I had to ask as I began to explore the meaning of "the Cross in the lotus world." Christians and theologians in Asia have to face them and respond to them. This is our theological agenda, although it is not the theological agenda for our counterparts in the West. It is our effort to respond to such questions that should shape our reflection on our faith and not the effort of Christians and theologians in other parts of the world, notably in the West, that should shape our faith and theology. I cannot emphasize this strongly enough; this is our theological homework and we cannot let others do it for us as in days past. I am not saying that whatever theological answer we may come up with has to be different from that of Christians and theologians in the West. Yes, some of the answers we give will be fundamentally different from theirs and some will be similar. Whether different or similar, my contention is that answers must not be the retail of what has been produced elsewhere. Having said this, I have to add that most likely we will come up with more different answers than similar ones. This is at once the excitement and the agony of doing Christian theology in the part of the world in which religions and cultures other than those of Christianity prevail.

### Stage Two: The Story of God's Reign

If the Church-centered faith and theology have relegated everything outside the Church, including the history and religion of Israel, to a secondary place, what should take their place in our practice of the Christian faith and our reflection on it? With this question I have taken the second step toward the theology of *Jesus, the Crucified People*. By asking this question, I do not mean to deny the importance of Church as a community of Christian believers in which faith is handed down from one generation to the next. But the Church has erred, and often erred badly and miserably. And the fact is that the Church continues to err and err badly and miserably. But not even this is what led me to ask that question.

The Church as we know it and experience it, the Church that has grown into its own history, and the Church that developed into many confessions and traditions, is after all not what prompted me to ask the question. What started it all for me is Jesus. I have come to think that our faith and theology should not be Church-centered, but Jesus-centered. I have just said that the Church has erred and continues to err. This is because Church has replaced Jesus as the center and has made itself the center. The Church-centered faith and theology are a wrong faith and a bad theology. When the Church makes itself the center, it preaches itself and not Jesus. Then the Church's own teachings, vested interests, survival, and ambitions become the paramount concern, not Jesus.

In our faith and theology Jesus must be restored to his place of honor. Jesus must be brought back to the center not just to be paid a lip service but to let him tell us what our faith, theology, and Church must be. But this does not yet solve our problem. As a matter of fact, there is so much of Jesus in the worship of the Church. So much of Jesus is constantly on the lips of those Christians who consider themselves "spiritual." But, is this Jesus in fact Jesus himself or the Jesus projected by individual Christians? Does this Jesus reflect Jesus himself or the interests and needs of particular Christian communities? Is this Jesus actually the Jesus who lived, toiled, suffered, and died on the cross, or the Jesus of Jesus-cult, Jesus as a cultic object, Jesus as an icon that inspires our piety but not our discipleship?

Jesus-centered faith and theology, in other words, do not solve our problem like the waving of a magic wand. Jesus by himself, Jesus disarmed, Jesus stripped of his message does not help at all. I can understand those theologians who now say it is more important to be theocentric than christocentric. They even want to replace christocentrism with theocentrism. They rightly point out that for many Christians Jesus divides people instead of uniting them and excludes men and women of other faiths from God's salvation. Such absolutist faith does justice neither to Jesus himself nor to God. I agree. But the problem is that for me as a Christian I do not know God apart from Jesus and Jesus apart from God. I cannot replace God with Jesus, nor can I replace Jesus with God. To be theocentric rather than christocentric is to me a false alternative. The problem is that Jesus for those "christocentric" Christians and theologians is "Jesus apart from God," while for those "theocentric" theologians God can be experienced as "God apart from Jesus."

Over against these two opposing views I must say that my faith as a Christian is faith in "Jesus-God" and in "God-Jesus." Note the hyphen in both expressions. The hyphen is not the equal sign. If it does not equate Jesus with God, it does not separate Jesus from God either. If it does not equate God with Jesus, it does not separate God from Jesus either. As a Christian, I came to know God in what Jesus said and did. And then there is this most important point: this God I have come to know through Jesus opens my eyes to see and understand what God is doing outside the Christian Church as well as inside it. In this way my experience of God through Jesus broadens and my experience of Jesus through God deepens.

At this point my hyphen sign changes into the preposition "in." I must now say "Jesus *in* God" and "God *in* Jesus." Jesus was able to say what he said and do what he did because he was "in" God and God was "in" him. Perhaps it would be more accurate to say, Jesus was in God *through the power of the Spirit* and God was in Jesus also *through the power of the Spirit* (recall that the third volume of my trilogy is called *Jesus in the Power of the Spirit*). And as we know all too well, what makes the Spirit Spirit is freedom. The Spirit cannot be controlled by anybody, not even by Christians. And the Spirit is the power not subjected to any other power, even the power of the Christian Church. If this "Jesus in God" and "God in Jesus" in the power of the Spirit occupy the central place in our theology, we no longer have to choose between being christocentric and theocentric. As a matter of fact, the Jesus both advocated by christocentric Christians and estranged by theocentric theologians is the Jesus *of the Christian Church* which makes an absolute and exclusive claim of salvation for itself.

What is the main concern, or main agenda if you will, of this "Jesus in God" and "God in Jesus" in the power of the Spirit? It is *the reign of God*. It is in the reign of God that God's saving purpose is brought to an intense focus in the life, ministry, and death of Jesus. That is why Jesus was almost totally preoccupied with it. He was "obsessed" with it. It was the central theme of his parable after parable. His extraordinary ministry, the ministry that offended the religious authorities and brought him close to the suffering people, was the ministry of God's reign. What he meant by it is summarized in what is known as the Sermon on the Mount in the Gospels of Matthew and Luke. "Blessed are you who are poor," Jesus is reported to have said, "for yours is the kingdom of God." And further: "Blessed are you who are hungry now, for you will be filled." How different was Jesus' message of God's reign from the teaching of the religious teachers of his day *and* from the sermonizing of preachers and evangelists today!

The story of Jesus, it became evident to me, is the story of the reign of God, that is, the reign *of God*. The "reign" and what it stands for in the message and ministry of Jesus is what relates God and Jesus.

Through the reign of God the story of Jesus is told as the story of God. Through it the story of God is told in the story of Jesus. The reign of God plays a crucial part in knowing Jesus and experiencing God. It is the key to unlock the mystery surrounding God. It is the key that opens to the nature of Jesus' ministry and even to the secret of what he is and who he is.

Note the word "story" here. From this point on that word takes on an increasingly important place in my theological effort. The reign of God is essentially stories. It consists of stories of God and stories of Jesus. It is not a concept that exists in a theological textbook but not in reality. Nor is it a projection of Christian piety in the world to come, a projection unrelated to the world here and now. The reign of God is a story that unfolds and expands, not a concept that abstracts and defines. It does not set boundaries around itself. In fact it seeks to break the barriers that separate it from the world around it.

There is another thing we should know about stories. As we know, a story took place once upon a time. But the same story can take place again here and now. And it will also take place in the days to come. That is to say, a story lives in the life and history of people and their community. The story of God's reign shares this common characteristic of story. It is not a self-contained story. It unfolds itself in history. It multiplies in the lives of people. That is why it often takes us Christians by surprise. It works in ways not anticipated in our Christian imagination. But as we listen more deeply to the story of Jesus as the story of God's reign, and not only as the story of the Christian Church, not only as the story of the salvation of Christians, we begin to know why the reign of God is always a story that surprises us because it even occurs in places we least expect it. We also begin to understand why the story of God's reign that we came to know in the story of Jesus has to multiply into many, many stories, countless stories as a matter of fact, of women, men, and children outside the Christian Church. The story of God's reign that does not multiply outside the Christian Church may be the story of the Christian Church, but not the story *of God*. And if it is not the story of God, how can it be the story *of Jesus?*

Here is an important point of departure for my theology. With this story of God's reign that I read in the story of Jesus, I turned to the Hebrew Scripture once again. What I found there are stories of God's reign developing, unfolding, and struggling to be born in the life and history of the people of Israel. Moses leading the Israelites out of bondage in Egypt—was this not a story of God's reign? The stories of the prophets such as Isaiah, Hosea, Amos, or Jeremiah, exposing the crimes of those in power and proclaiming God's love and justice—are these not the stories of God's reign? And the story of that servant of God who "was

wounded for our transgressions, crushed for our iniquities" (Isa 53:5)—
is this story not the story of God's reign?

What, then, relates the Hebrew Scripture and the New Testament?
It is not the scheme of promise and fulfillment but the stories of God's
reign. And where a story of God's reign is lived and told, there is God's
salvation. If this is the case, how can Hebrew Scripture grow old for
Jewish believers? And if it does not grow old for them, how can it become the "Old" Testament for us Christians? For Christians as well as
for Jewish believers, Hebrew Scripture is the "new" testament that contains story after story of God's reign in the history of ancient Israel.
These stories of God's reign are not replaced by the story of Jesus as the
story of God's reign. On the contrary, they, identified with the story of
Jesus, tell us how God was doing God's saving work in Israel in times
before Jesus.

If it is the reign of God that provides the link between stories of Hebrew Scripture and the story of Jesus, does it not also serve as a link between stories outside the Christian Church and the story of Jesus? This
is the question to which I turned next. The question can be asked in another way: Can one find stories of God's reign outside the Christian
Church? To answer the question, we must keep clearly in mind what we
said about the reign of God, or rather what Jesus meant by it in his life
and through his ministry. The reign of God in this case is not a Christian idea, not a theological concept. It is the life and ministry of Jesus
dedicated to the realization of God's will on earth as in heaven. It is the
lives and efforts of those men and women who suffer and die for love,
justice, and truth—love, justice, and truth not unrelated to Jesus' life
and ministry.

The question can, then, be further reformulated in a number of
ways that test the Church-centered faith and theology. Are there, for example, stories of people striving for peace and justice in their society?
Of course. Do these stories, then, have anything to do with the story of
God's reign that we witness in Jesus? They must have. Have there been
women and men who, for the sake of love and truth, rather die than
live? Yes, there have been. Do they reflect something of the story of
God's reign Jesus lived and died to tell? They do. How opening ourselves to stories enables us to ask questions very different from doctri-
nal questions we asked before! And how different are the answers to
which stories lead us from those traditional presuppositions of Christian
faith and theology!

The world of stories! This is the world of the reign of God. We are
forever indebted to the writers of the Gospels of the New Testament who
chose to tell stories of Jesus rather than to wrap Jesus up in theological
concepts and formulas. They wrote their accounts of Jesus after their ex-

perience of the risen Jesus. But it is for us a stroke of luck that they decided to give account of the risen Jesus in a story-fashion. This must have enabled them to remember experiences they had with Jesus as they lived with him, heard him, saw him go about his work. They also remembered how panic-stricken they were when Jesus was executed and died on the cross. That is why we have their Gospels mostly in stories. And these stories of Jesus, these stories of God's reign, now enable us to hear in the stories of many men and women in Asia, both in the past and today, that echo God's Reign for which Jesus came and died.

### Stage Three: Stories of God's Reign in Asia

In the second stage we have crossed the theological boundary set up by the Christian Church, and removed the barriers constructed by its faith and theology. Asia has to be different now for us Christians. Yes, Asia as a geographical name has not changed. Asia with the vastness of the area it covers on earth and Asia that is a home to more people on earth than any other continent remains the same. And in Asia we still find a great variety of races, cultures, languages—many more, as a matter of fact, than anywhere else in the world. Asia in this way will be always Asia.

But the Asia in which stories of God's reign can also be told change our image of Asia fundamentally. We have been taught to consider Asia as entirely "pagan," that is, the part of the world that does not know the true God and outside God's salvation in Jesus. But can Asia, in which stories of God's reign can also take place, be entirely "pagan"? We have been told that Asia with so many religions and superstitions is a continent of idolatry. True, there are many religions in Asia: Buddhism, Confucianism, Islam, shamanism, ancestor veneration, primal religions, and many more. Asia is abundant in superstitions too. If Paul were to come to Asia today, I am sure he would say the same thing he said to the people of Athens two thousand years ago. "Asians," Paul would probably say, "I see how extremely religious you are in every way. For as I went through country after country and looked carefully at the objects of your worship, I found among them altars dedicated to every conceivable deity" (cf. Acts 17:22-23).

Paul, who said Athenians were "extremely religious" and not "extremely superstitious" according to the more correct rendering of that particular Greek word, would, I am sure, unlike some single-minded missionaries and over-jealous evangelists, say Asians are "extremely religious," and not "extremely superstitious." For there is a fundamental difference of attitude and mind-set when you say someone is "religious" versus "superstitious." You may not agree with the way in which other people are religious, but you may be able to affirm their religiosity. You recognize sincerity in their religious way. But being "superstitious" is quite a different matter. When you say some people are superstitious, you imply your disapproval of their "superstitious" way. You may not just be disapproving of it; you may be in fact condemning it.

But the situation is in fact much more complicated. Most Christians and particularly preachers and evangelists are not used to making a fine distinction between "being religious" and "being superstitious." With a sweeping stroke they dismiss all other religions—Buddhism, Taoism, or ancestor rites, as not any better than superstitions. What is worse, these religions for them are idolatrous religions. And, of course, to believe in idols and worship them is the height of superstition. The Christian Church in Asia, whether through missionaries from the West or through indigenous Christians who inherited missionary Christianity, have not been able to see Asia other than through the lens of idolatry. Asia is a huge continent of idols and superstitions. It has to be saved from the sin of idolatry.

Asia has never been presented to the Christian Church as a space and time of God in which stories of God's reign can also be found. How much we Christians in Asia have missed! Surely we have heard stories of how the poor and the oppressed rose up in revolt against the tyrannical emperors and rulers. But it never occurs to us that these stories have anything to do with the reign of God. We have from time to time come across stories of Buddhist monks and believers who devote their lives and even give them up so that others may live, but we never take time to think whether these stories tell us something about the reign of God for which Jesus lived and died. And, of course, there are men and women suffering for the cause of justice and freedom, so that even we Christians may enjoy justice and freedom in our society, but we seldom stop to think whether they are closer to Jesus than we Christians are.

It is stories such as these, abundant in Asia, that set me on my theological journey of *Jesus, the Crucified People*. In the prologue of this book, I began with a play called "The Gold-Crowned Jesus" written by Kim Chi Ha, a Korean Christian poet and writer. When he wrote that play he must have wrestled with questions similar to those I raised above. The play is about Beggar and Leper, two men representing the men, women, and children at the bottom of society, poor, despised, and oppressed. They are not Christian. In contrast to them there is a cement statue of Jesus with a gold crown on his head. The play consists of the dialogue between these two poor men, and between them and the gold-crowned Jesus. It is also a dialogue between the underprivileged people in our society and the privileged Christians who worship power and money in the Church. The dialogue reaches its climax when the gold-crowned Jesus, imprisoned in a cement statue, asks these two men alienated from society and abandoned by the Church to rescue him from his imprisonment in rigid traditions and rituals, in power and gold.

The plea of Jesus—with a gold crown and imprisoned in a cement statue—to these two poor and sick men outside the Church is worth reproducing here:

> I have been closed up in this stone for a long, long time . . . entombed in this dark, lonely, suffocating prison. I have longed to talk to you, the kind and poor people like yourself, and share your suffering, I can't begin to tell you how long I have waited for this day . . . this day when I would be freed from my prison, this day of liberation when I would live and burn again as a flame inside you, inside the very depths of your misery. But now you have finally come. And because you have come close to me I can speak now. You are my rescuer.[5]

When Kim Chi Ha wrote this play he was serving a life sentence in prison because of his struggle for freedom, democracy, and human rights in Korea. The plea he put on the lips of the gold-crowned Jesus reflected his own longing to be free to be with his own people and to struggle with them.

But these words, whether or not the author intended, are much more than autobiographical. They tell us something not contained in our catechism and in our theological textbooks: those people estranged by society and Church, these women, men, and children who are not Christian, can be much closer to the Jesus who toiled and suffered like they did. The stories of these people have much more to tell us about Jesus than the stories we Christians tell at our Sunday worship service, at our celebration of the Lord's Supper, at our evangelical rallies. Their stories are part of Jesus' story. There is much more "Jesus" in them than in our Christian stories. At least the stories of Jesus with a gold crown on his head venerated in the Church are *no part* of Jesus' story.

If this is the case, there is nothing to prevent us Christians from looking for stories from our indigenous soil of Asia, stories told outside the Christian Church, stories unrelated to Christianity. These stories have a message for us Christians, just as the stories of Leper and Beggar in the play "The Gold-Crowned Jesus." We Christians have always insisted that we have the message of salvation for those who are not Christian. Yes, we do have a message for them. The question is what that message is. Is it the message of Jesus? Is it the message of God's reign for which Jesus lived, suffered, and died? Those people outside the Christian Church have a message for us Christians too—the message that the

---

[5] Quoted in ibid., 11.

world in which power and money are worshiped not only by those who rule over us but also by those "pious" Christians in Church is a wrong world, an upside-down world. They also have another message for us— the message that Jesus of Nazareth, Jesus who lived very closely with the poor and the oppressed, Jesus who died the death of a religious here- tic and a political criminal, is much closer to them than to us Christians.

Here is my conclusion: to know Jesus, to understand what he said and did, to experience his suffering, to fathom the redemptive meaning of his death, we also need to listen to those stories lived, experienced, and told by our fellow Asians, those men, women, and children in Asia who remain outside the Christian Church. We do not just listen to them. We must hear in them how God is speaking to us Christians. We must perceive in them the footsteps of Jesus. We must see in them what the reign of God meant to Jesus. Just as Leper and Beggar in "The Gold- Crowned Jesus" are asked by Jesus to rescue him from imprisonment in the power and riches of the Church, these stories from our native Asia will rescue us from our aloofness from our own cultures, from our igno- rance and arrogance toward the religions around us, and from our aliena- tion from our sisters and brothers in Asia who do not share our form of Christian faith with us. These stories can help make our faith "become indigenous" and our theological efforts in Asia take root in Asian soil.

### Stage Four: Identifying a Theological Problem

We have gone outside the Christian Church to listen to the stories of God's reign. This was an important step we had taken. It enables us to be liberated from our ignorance about the life and history of our own peoples, from our arrogance toward the world of cultures and religions from which the faith and theology inherited from the West has alien- ated us. With the story of Jesus as the story of God's reign and with the stories of people in Asia that reflect the story of God's reign we now must return to the Christian Church, to its faith and theology and look at it with a new eye. This is the fourth stage in our theological journey.

As I took this step, I noted one problem in particular in the tradi- tional faith and theology. It turned out to be a long story—a story that began almost as soon as Jesus' life and career on earth was over and has continued ever since until this day. The story, in other words, spans the entire history of Christianity and its faith and theology. But here I have to make this long story short, only pointing out some turns of events that contributed to what I consider to be a root cause of the Church-centered faith and theology.

It began with the apostles, particularly with Paul. Their experience of the risen Jesus was, no doubt, traumatic. In the case of Paul that ex- perience turned Saul the persecutor of the new faith in Jesus into Paul the pioneer missionary of that faith. For Paul it must be this experience in particular that gave rise to his faith in Jesus as the Christ, the messiah, the savior. It has also to be noted that his persecution of Jesus' followers before his conversion must have been very much a part of his consciousness of sin. Is it not natural that Paul thought of salvation more in relation to that sin of disobedience and rebellion than in relation to Jesus' message of God's reign? As to Peter and his fellow disciples, the fact that they had deserted Jesus to die on the cross must have played an important part in their experience of sin and in their emphasis on salvation from sin. It is not difficult to understand that their "theology" of sin and salvation also became the overriding concern of the early Church. It is this faith and theology that has become the central preoccupation of the Church and Christians. But, is this how Jesus understood sin and salvation? We seldom ask ourselves.

In a nutshell Jesus' message was: "The time is fulfilled, and the kingdom of God has come; repent, and believe in the good news" (Mark 1:15). "The reign [kingdom] of God" and "the good news" make up the heart of Jesus' proclamation. The good news in this instance is the good news *of the reign of God*. The reign of God has come in the person of Jesus. Jesus has identified it in the poor, the hungry, and the oppressed. This reign of God is the good news. Then there is Jesus' call for repentance. If we consider what Jesus said and did throughout his ministry, we have to say that Jesus was calling the rich and the powerful to repent. They must repent of the way they live, the way they exploit the powerless people, the way they make religion as a matter of the privilege only they can enjoy. Is this not why Jesus told a parable, for example, of the rich man and the poor Lazarus (Luke 16)? Was he not reported to have exclaimed: "How hard it will be for those who have wealth to enter the kingdom of God!" (Mark 10:23)?

The concern of the early Church did not seem quite the same as that of Jesus. Peter in his sermon on the day of Pentecost urged his listeners who asked him what to do, saying: "Repent and be baptized every one of you in the name of Jesus Christ so that your sins may be forgiven; and you will receive the gift of the Holy Spirit" (Acts 2:38). Peter, in his sermon handed down to us by Luke, related repentance and forgiveness of sins, particularly the sin of "crucifying Jesus" (2:36). There is no reference to the reign of God. Already in the apostles' minds Jesus as the risen Lord, Jesus as the Messiah, even Jesus as the Son of God, becomes separated from Jesus as the proclaimer of God's reign, or Jesus as what he stood for in relation to the reign of God during his life and ministry.

Salvation is also the central theme of Paul's faith and theology. In his letters he refers to "the kingdom of God" a few times, but it does not seem to be the heart of his message. Nor does he mean by it what Jesus meant by it. The fact that salvation is his central concern is most clearly shown in his wrestling with the relation of the salvation of Gentiles and that of Jews in Romans 9–11. He has rejected the election of Israel as the norm for the scheme of God's saving purpose. But he has to tell himself and Gentile Christians that salvation of Gentiles does not mean condemnation of Jews for eternity. "I ask, then," he writes, "has God rejected his people?" His answer is an emphatic no: "By no means!" (Rom 11:1). In this theological debate on salvation we have the beginning of theological debates on salvation in later times—debates that divide the Christian Church and vitiate our relationship with people of other religions even to this day.

Whether Jews or Gentiles, for Paul it comes down to this: "If you confess with your lips that Jesus is Lord and believe in your heart that God raised him from the dead, you will be saved" (Rom 10:9). For Paul Jesus replaced the law as the way of salvation—salvation from idolatry, from immorality, from division, from selfishness, and salvation into God's love, righteousness and eternal life. In Paul as well as in Peter, one seems also to hear echoes of John the Baptist who preached repentance of sin in the wilderness of Jordan. The reign of God that occupied the central place in Jesus' message and mission, if not entirely absent, is at least muted in the message of the apostles and the early Church. They now understand themselves as the new people of God who possess God's salvation in ways no other people do, not even Jews.

Salvation has replaced what Jesus meant by "the reign of God" as the principal concern of the early Church. It is this concern for salvation that the Christian Church has taken over and developed out of proportion with other concerns of faith and life. And the self-understanding of the Christian Church and Christians as the new people of God in a special relation with God's salvation has not only distorted our perception of Jews as people of God, but also our attitudes toward people of other religions as lost to God. To be saved or not becomes the overriding theme of Christian preaching and Christian mission. As to the reign of God that preoccupied Jesus' life and ministry, it is relegated to a secondary place. It is not the reign of God understood and lived by Jesus that defines what salvation means, but salvation as gaining a special privilege as Christians both on earth and in heaven that defines what the reign (kingdom) of God means.

### Stage Five: Jesus and Stories of People

From our discussion on salvation we have learned one important lesson: theological ideas delimit our theological imagination and theological norms restrict our theological development. Not only do we ourselves as Christians become restricted and limited in our views on life and world, we also in our faith and theology turn God into a very limited and restricted God. The space of our faith shrinks and the room of our theology narrows.

But in stories I find my theological space expands. To read stories of people outside the Christian Church—their myths, legends, and real life stories—is a liberating experience. Of course, I have read Christian stories—stories of the development of the Christian Church, stories of missionary outreach and endeavor, stories of heroes of Christian faith, great missionaries, and dedicated Christians. But these stories confined me to the world envisioned by the Christian Church. It is a "Christian" world that I encountered in those stories, the only world that, according to most of us Christians, is important in God's eye, the world of the people saved from their sins and granted God's salvation.

But there are stories outside the Christian Church—stories of people around me, stories of the society in which I was born, and stories of Asia of which I am a part. What a big world these stories represent! It is infinitely larger than the "Christian" world. What a variety of stories this wider world of Asia contains! There are myths of creation and destruction, myths of how human beings and other living beings came to be. There are legends of how nations in Asia were founded and legends of gods and heroes who came and went. And aside the world of myths and legends there are stories that tell real history—history of the rise and fall of dynasties. There are, of course, stories of faiths and religions. Above all, stories of how women, men, and children in various countries of Asia and at various times in the history of their nations struggle against evil powers, how they suffer and die, and how they persist in their hope for a better world in which to live.

The space these stories open up for me is as immense as Asia. It is a world full of surprises to us Christians. To be able to go out of the space defined by the Christian Church and venture into the space as vast as Asia is also a great challenge. That vast space must be my theological space—the space that is inhabited by people of Asia, that houses many religions and cultures, that tells countless stories of hopes and despairs, of lives and deaths. This world of stories is the world of the real people of flesh and blood and not the world of theological ideas and concepts. It is the world of tears and laugher, and not the world constructed by Christian theological minds and missionary enthusiasm. It is also the world in which men, women, and children commit sins and crimes one against another and in which they strive, often in vain but sometimes successfully, to reveal the divine light shining in the darkness of human hearts and human community.

When I read stories in Asia in this way, stories to which I am not an outsider but an insider, stories that tell as much about myself as about my fellow Asians, I begin to realize how much the story of Jesus, that is, the story of his reign of God, is reflected in them, and how much they reflect the story of Jesus, that is, the story of his reign of God. I do not need to construct a theological framework to fit these two sets of stories together. I do not have to work out in advance theological norms and categories that legitimize whatever relationship that may exist between them. Nor do I need to set up criteria that may enable me to make a "correct" selection of stories from both sets of stories in order to theologize about them.

What I need most is a theological mind not prejudiced toward those stories indigenous to Asia but alien to the Christian Church. What I have to equip myself with is a theological imagination that can help me image God and God's activity in them. And what I have to do is to apply the same theological imagination to the stories in the Christian Bible, especially stories of the reign of God that Jesus told not only in words and parables, but with the life he lived with the poor and oppressed of his time. And, of course, his life of suffering and death—is it not related to the lives of millions upon millions of people in Asia in the past, the present, and the future?

Jesus and stories of people! *Jesus, the Crucified People* is a conversation between the story of Jesus and stories of people of Asia. It is not a leisurely conversation over a cup of tea. It is not a theological debate over imaginary theological issues. And it is not an exercise to prove who is more right than others. Yes, it is a *theological* conversation, but the conversation is theological because it has to do with God as well as humanity, because God is called upon to bear witness to what has been going on in the world in which human beings struggle for hope in face of hopelessness and for the meaning of life always overshadowed by death.

Conversation is in fact no longer adequate for a theological exercise such as this. The conversation is so intense that the conversation partners find themselves crossing each into another. They interact with each other in the stories. They enter into the lives, worlds, histories, represented by what they tell one another. I find myself in your story and you find yourself in my story. My story is your story and your story is my story. I now believe that this would be the way Jesus would listen to the stories told by people of Asia, for that was the way he listened to the story of the poor and the disinherited of his day. And that is the way he identified himself with those despaired in body and in spirit. An invisible bond was thus formed between him and the people. Even if many of these people, including his own disciples, were to betray him, even to denounce him before the authorities, and to desert him, they were soon to regain that spiritual bond forged between them and Jesus.

It is the same bond that I am sure would be forged between Jesus and the people of Asia in the story of Jesus and stories from Asia. As the story of Jesus and stories from Asia interpenetrate each other, a theological space is also opened for the stories of Hebrew Scripture. Stories from other parts of the world also come into play. What takes place is a theological feast of stories—the story of Jesus, stories from Asia, stories in Hebrew Scripture, and stories from the rest of the world, told as stories of God's reign. What we encounter here is a theological world of stories, or better, the divine-human world of stories. If our theology is to be *theo*-logy, do we not have to go about it in this *divine*-human world of stories? And if our christology is to be *christo*-logy, that is, an effort to encounter Jesus of Nazareth, that human being in which "the Word of God become flesh," then is there any other world in which to engage ourselves in christology than in this divine-*human* world of stories?

The theological journey I have undertaken in *The Cross in the Lotus World* is a long one. It has reached a station on the way. The journey must continue. But we must take a pause to give ourselves a rest and to get ourselves ready for the next stretch of our road. During this brief pause let me remind ourselves of those words with which I concluded the prologue of *Jesus, the Crucified People:*

> The messianic contour of Jesus becomes increasingly sharpened as he absorbs more and more into himself the struggle of the people to live in faith, hope and love. *God is the story of Jesus. And Jesus is the story of the people. . . .* The real Jesus is the love of God that creates miracles of life in the world. He is the pain of God mingled with the pain of humanity. He is the hope of God that people manifest in the midst if despair. He is the eternal life of God that people live in spite of death. Jesus is, lives, and becomes real when people, with unflagging faith in God, engage each other to bring about a new world out of the ruins of the old world. The real Jesus is the light of God's salvation that men, women and children kindle in the darkness of hell. The real Jesus is that power of God's truth that people manifest in the face of the power of lies wielded by the powers and principalities of this world. Jesus is the story of such people. And being the story of such people, Jesus is the story of God.[6]

In the company of this Jesus Christian theology in Asia can go a long way. With him we Christians and theologians in Asia can continue our theological journey with confidence in God who makes all things new (Rev 21:5).

---

[6] Ibid., 14.

# A Life In-Between:
# A Korean-American Journey

*Jung Young Lee*

In the summer of 1991 I had a chance to visit my motherland, North Korea, with a group of United Methodist and United Presbyterian ministers. I had a few important items on my agenda for my visit: I wanted to meet my youngest brother Jung-yul, the last of my surviving brothers; I wanted to visit the place where I was born and raised; and I wanted to learn more about the life of Christians in North Korea. Visiting my motherland more than forty years after leaving it was such an overwhelming experience that I will never forget it. When I arrived in the Pyongyang airport, everything was so radically changed that I did not recognize it at all. I felt that I was in a strange place, somewhere I had never been before. Yet I felt a deep and abiding affection for the land which welcomed me and touched my heart. I felt like a total stranger, wholly isolated from my motherland; yet, paradoxically, I also felt that I belonged there and was a part of it. I experienced simultaneously a sense of separation and unity, repulsion and attraction, alienation and belonging, rejection and acceptance.

When I returned from a brief trip to the Diamond mountains, Jung-yul, my youngest brother, was waiting for me in the hotel lounge. He had been only seven or eight years old in 1950 when I left him in North Korea during the Korean war. I did not recognize him at first, but I was deeply attracted to his presence. Suddenly, our eyes met, and we intuitively recognized that we were brothers. We hugged each other and cried with the joy of reunion after more than forty years' separation. He was so skinny that his cheek bones stuck out, his eyes were sunken, and his face was as dark as charcoal. However, our joy soon changed to sorrow.

There was a long moment of silence. It felt like an eternity. There were no words to help us communicate. The gap between us was too wide for us to connect. I felt as if I were standing on the other side of the Grand Canyon, unable to understand how he felt. I knew that something bothered him, something deeply buried in the past. Past memories of tragedy and suffering were too much for him to account. How fully we two understood the tragedy of the separation between North and South Korea! The innocent suffering of the Korean people in the past was crystallized in my encounter with my brother.

## My Life in North Korea

Despite the oppression and suffering of the Korean people under Japanese rule, our family was not divided. The oldest and most powerful member of our family was my great grandmother, who lived more than ninety years. She was a towering figure, the matriarch of our family. She was the first Christian in our town, and dedicated our land to build the small church that she, my mother, and her children attended. My grandmother lived under the shadow of her powerful mother-in-law. She was never free to do what she wanted. She seldom spoke, and quietly served my great grandmother. My mother, however, suffered the most. She served everyone in our family. She obeyed and served my great grandmother, my grandmother, and my father, as well as taking care of us. I was the third child, the second son, and had two younger brothers who stayed in North Korea with my mother.

My oldest sister went to South Korea with her husband, who was a renowned scholar and journalist. He was later kidnapped by a secret agent under Syungman Rhee's government and killed. His body was never found. My sister tried to live by herself in South Korea, but she could not make a living. She died in 1962, leaving her two children in an orphanage. My older brother, Jung-ho, graduated from Kwangsung, a Christian Mission school in Pyungyang, North Korea. He also went to South Korea before the Korean war and joined the South Korean Army to support himself. He was wounded at the Rakdong river battle and imprisoned by the enemy for several months before he was assigned to work for the Department of National Defense. After retirement from the army, he became a successful businessman. He died a few years ago in Seoul, leaving behind his wife and four children.

Born into an aristocratic family, my father had enjoyed all the privileges and luxuries that were available. He went to Seoul and studied at Baejae Hakdang, which was founded by Reverend Henry Appenzeller, the first American Methodist missionary. Although he was baptized while in school, my father never considered himself a Christian. He continued to be a Confucian until his death. He and I went to South Korea during the Korean war. Although he had obtained the best education available at that time, he did not succeed in his career. He was a failure in the new society; honest in his dealing with people, he was unable to compete with less scrupulous men. He also was too idealistic. He was terminally ill with cancer when I stopped by Seoul on my way to visit North Korea in 1991.

In North Korea I told Jung-yul about our father's terminal illness. I said, "I am afraid that our father might have already passed away." He heard me, but he was emotionless. After a long pause, he said bitterly, "I really don't know who our father is. All I know of him, I was told by our mother. She blamed him for abandoning us, leaving behind young, helpless ones in the ocean of fire. I am sorry to say this." I had nothing to say. I also was guilty of leaving my mother and younger brothers in Pyungyang, which was later almost completely destroyed by American air bombardments. I paused a moment and recalled the circumstances under which we had left the city. "I am glad you have survived," I said. He only nodded a few times. "What happened to our mother?" I asked. "She died several years after you left," he said with tears in his eyes. "What happened to your brother?" I asked. "He died later, because he drank too much." There was an infinite emotional gap between us which could not be bridged by our short encounter.

My younger brother, who is now deceased, was only a few years younger than I. He was a genius. He had planned to go to the south with us, but he was scared of the air bombings and never crossed the Han River.

"You are the only one of us surviving in North Korea, and I am the only one of us who came to South Korea who has survived. I hope our reunion may be a sign of the reunification of our motherland." He said, "Yes, I certainly hope so. Our mother said again and again that I must work toward the re-unification of our country. 'That is the only way,' she said, 'the only way for the reunion of your brothers.'" Our mother died without seeing the reunification of her children; our brothers and sister died without seeing the reunification of our country; and our father died without returning to his family in the north. All, except Jung-Yul and I, had died without seeing those from whom they had been separated. "I hope we shall live to see the reunification of our motherland," I said. We held hands tightly as a sign of our promise to work toward the reunion of separated families and the reunification of our motherland.

A few days later, I was finally granted permission to visit the village where I was born and grew up. The village was once known as Hyang-bong-ri, the Fragrant Peak, because of the beautiful hills and mountains that surrounded it. It was also known as Saemkol, the Place of the

Spring, because of the famous spring of water that came from there. Although I got permission to visit, I had difficulty finding the village. It had changed and its name had been changed as well. Finally, we found a U-shaped town nestled among hills in the west, north, and south. "That must be the town I am looking for. Let's go!" The driver wanted to drive the car to the village, but I insisted on walking because I felt that I must walk on the same dusty road I had walked on more than forty years ago. Although the village had changed so much that I could not recognize it, it was waiting for my return. The sun was already in the western sky when we walked toward the village. As I walked from the northern end westward on the rouged and dusty road, I had mixed feelings. "Is this the place which I dreamed about and wept over for so many nights because I missed it so much?" It was not even a desirable place to live, although I was deeply attached to it. Every step I took was sacred, for I was stepping into a sacred place.

When I had gone about thirty yards, I saw to the right a large building. It was the town council meeting house. I knew instantly that it used to be the old town house. I recalled the activities that had taken place there. When Korea was liberated from Japan on August 15, 1945, right after World War II, I joined other young people in town at the old town house. We made Korean national flags and distributed them to everyone in town. When the South Korean army occupied the village in the autumn of 1950, I left the basement of our home and joined other youth in this house to welcome the South Korean soldiers. We showed our allegiance to South Korea by holding up the South Korean flags and by wearing the white arm bands of the YMCA. The house had been the center of our activities since Korea's liberation from Japanese rule. I found that it was still used as a public hall where town meetings were held and where the office of the Communist party cell was located.

There were many old trees on the left side of the road, across from the town council house. The oldest of them had been regarded as the guardian of the village when I lived there. I used to be afraid of passing it in the evening because a spirit was supposed to reside in it. I still felt the presence of that spirit as I stood there, even though the tree no longer existed. However, a couple of trees were still there. They had been huge trees even when I was young. The trees did not seem as big as I once had thought them to be, but they were the only things that still remained. I remembered a small pond under the trees, where I used to come to fish, but I did not see the pond anymore. I asked an old farmer passing by whether he knew of the pond under the trees. He said, "Yes, I heard that there was a pond, but it is no longer there." I could almost spot the exact place where the pond had been, but it had become a page of fiction.

I walked a few more yards and then stopped abruptly in the road. I suddenly recalled that my mother had come with me to that very spot, in order to send me off to Russia in the summer of 1950. She did not want me to go to Russia, even though I had to go there to get advanced training for a brief period for my factory work in Kangsu, near Pyungyang city. She knew that she could not stop my going away, however much she wanted me to stay with her. I felt again her unbearable pain. I remembered her weeping over my departure. She gave me a small bundle of money she had saved for me to use in the foreign land. It was early in the morning on July 25, 1950, the day Korean civil war began. Once again I recalled vividly her waving hands, facing to the east. I had turned back again and again to capture the last minutes of her appearance. However, I never made it to Russia because of the Korean War. Now, I felt that she was still standing there, and, this time, she was welcoming me home.

We came to the center of the village where the famous spring was located. The village was known as Saemkol or the Place of the Spring because of this spring. Fresh spring water was still flowing over the well as before. It was the same water that I drank and that all villagers shared. It was the womb of the village. This was where women spent their social hours and men stopped by to quench their thirst. I wanted to drink the spring water, but I was stopped by the driver. He said, "You should know that you must not drink or eat anything that is not prepared for you. If you become ill, I am responsible. Please restrain yourself." I recalled instantly that I was a guest, and knew that I could never return to my past. I wet my hands with the spring water. The water was cold and fresh, just as I recalled. Everything seemed changed, but the spring was the same. The ever-flowing spring symbolized the living memories coming out of the buried past.

Beside the well I met an old man who looked somewhat familiar to me. I asked him about the village. He said, "I am the only one left who has been here for more than forty years. All those who used to live here were transferred to another place." I asked him whether there was still the house of Saemkol, which was our house before we left. Our home was known as the home of "saemkol" because my family was the patriarch of our tribe. He pointed and said, "Of course, I know it. People wanted to preserve it, but it was too old. We have rebuilt a new house on the same spot." Suddenly I recognized him; he had been the chairman of the Communist party cell in our village.

He was the son of our servant and did not even have a third-grade education. He was about thirty years old when the Korean War broke out. Because of his loyalty to the Communist party, he was made the chairman of the Communist cell in our village. I could not forget him.

He once gathered the young people of the village, including me, into a school house, where we were given physical examinations and ideological tests with the view to draft us into the North Korean army. Because I told the examiner that my elder brother had joined the South Korean army, I was taken into a separate room, where I, along with several youths from other towns, was tortured. When Korea was liberated from Japan and the Communist party took over, the landlords' properties were divided and given to the peasants. This man received a good portion of the land we used to own, and had demanded that my father confess his past sins of oppression. In my mind, I saw my father kneeling before him and asking for his forgiveness. He hit my father to humiliate him before the public. Remembering these chilling memories, I became afraid that he might recognize me. I left him and hurried toward the house to which he pointed.

The house was rather new. It was covered with fresh tiles and had a small courtyard, but it was smaller than our house. A middle-aged man came out of the house and explained to me that the former house had been too old and had been replaced. When I lived there, the house was even then a few hundred years old and was the largest one in the village. I did not believe the building had needed to be replaced, for it could have survived another two hundred years. Rather, I think they put up a new building so the townspeople did not have to remember the old Confucian landowner who used to live there. The man explained to me that the present structure was not only an exact replica of the old one, but also had been built in exactly the same place. He showed me the old walls which were preserved in the present structure. When I told him that this had been my house, he was greatly surprised and said, "You must, then, remember this wall," and pointed to the northern side. I did not remember it at all. I asked the caretaker if I might sit inside the house, but my request was denied. It was my house but I was not even allowed to stay in it for a while. I was a stranger in my own house. Moreover, what I remembered of my home was its splendid beauty. My memories were so different from the present reality that there was an infinite gap between them, once again. With great disappointment, I left.

After I left the house, things seemed more familiar to me than before. I recalled the road leading toward the southern hill, which had also been a part of our property. I spent many of my childhood hours on that hill. But the south hill too had changed. The huge pines and chestnut trees were replaced by only a few small fruit trees. As I walked east on the U-shaped road, I came to the tip of the hill, where once there had been a small church building. There was no building there now. As I looked for the spot where the church had been, an elderly man, who seemed to be a member of the Communist party, came along. I asked him what had happened to the church. He said, "I heard a church had been here." He pointed to almost the exact location where I stood. He continued, "None of us believe in God any more. We do not need the church." For him, and for most of the people in the village, the church meant nothing. But it had meant a great deal to us when I lived there. My great grandmother had not only donated the land for the church but had also built the church. I stood there for some time, because it was the most sacred place in the village to me. As I stood there, I recalled the life of the small church in that village.

My mother had been a faithful Christian and used to take me to church. The young pastor who served the church came on bicycle from Chasan or the city of Mount Mercy, and conducted Sunday morning and Sunday evening services. He also came for Wednesday evening services whenever possible. However, the early morning prayer services were led by one of the elders in the church. My mother never missed the early morning prayer services. She would get up at four o'clock in the morning to go to the prayer service. After returning from the service, she prepared breakfast for the whole family. Occasionally, I attended those services with my mother. All I could remember was a dozen people who would come to spend most of their time singing, praying, and reading the Bible. What I enjoyed most was seeing the beautiful dawn break in the eastern sky when the service was over. I also liked to breathe the fresh air and to slide on the icy road in the winter.

I attended many of the Wednesday evening services which lasted almost two hours. By the time we left the service, it was dark. On many occasions, my mother carried a lamp to guide the people. Because the road was narrow, a line formed behind my mother. I was always right behind her so as to see the road better. I was often afraid that the wind would blow out the oil lamp. The villagers were always afraid of ghosts appearing at the old guardian tree, so when we passed by this tree, we usually sang a hymn aloud. One of our favorite hymns was "Onward Christian Soldiers." We sang so loudly that everyone in the village could hear us. The church gave much joy and excitement to many children, especially during the Christmas season, which was the most exciting time of the year for both believing and non-believing children. Most children, whether they believed in Christ or not, came to the church to receive candies at the Christmas Eve service. Many non-believing children called Christmas the "day of burning shoes," because Christmas in Korean is "kuju-tansang" ("kuju" means shoes, and "tanda" means burning). A huge wood-burning stove was located at the center of the church. On Christmas Eve, wood burned in the stove throughout the day. Many children stayed up late on Christmas Eve to go caroling to all church members. Everyone wanted to go caroling, because this was an occasion to be together. It was fun to wake people up. When we arrived to our home for caroling, my mother and my great grandmother would come out and stand outside the door until we finished singing. Then they brought out candies for all of us.

Countless memories flashed through my mind as I stood on that sacred ground. "Without the church, what kind of fun do the village people have?" I wondered. Learning of the loss of the church was the greatest disappointment of my visit to the village. Nothing but stones remained to remind me of the sacred place. I picked up a couple of the crystal stones from the ground and put them in my pocket.

When I came to the edge of the village, the sun was already behind the western hill and darkness had begun to spread across the village. I hated to leave, but the driver was impatient. I wanted to stay there as long as I could. A golden sun-beam lingered on the eastern meadow. As I watched the evening sun reflecting from the endless rice fields, I remembered the exodus of our people from the village. On December 7, 1950, Chinese soldiers pushed toward the south and the United Nation army was retreating. The night was cold and the road was snow-covered and treacherous.

As we drove, I saw the path along the rice fields that eventually led to the city of Mount Mercy, the county seat, about three miles away. I was reminded that Mount Mercy was the city where I went to public school during the Japanese rule. We were forbidden to speak Korean and our names had been changed to Japanese, depriving us both our language and our names. Our identity was completely erased; we were nobody. We became marginalized. I had walked and run on that path thousands of times to attend school. I wished there had been time to visit the school in Mount Mercy. As we drove away, I watched the fading sunlight in the east.

We arrived in Pyungyang, the capital of North Korea, the city where I had made a final farewell to my mother and younger brothers. More than forty years ago, we walked all night and all day, and finally arrived in Pyungyang. We stayed overnight in a relative's home. The next morning, my mother decided to stay there with Jung-yul, my youngest brother, who had broken his leg during our journey to Pyungyang. My younger brother, my father, and I decided to go farther south, intending to return within a few weeks. My mother came out to the gate and said farewell to us by waving her hands as we left. "We will be back soon. Take care of yourself," we said, believing we would return soon. None of us knew that it was our last farewell.

We could not cross the Han river, because the bridge had been destroyed by the American air bombing. No sooner had we left than we saw Pyungyang become an ocean of fire, as American planes flew over the city and bombed everywhere. I cried out, "Oh, our mother and youngest brother must be dead. How could anyone survive!" My father responded, "We cannot return. We must go forward." We arrived to the north bank of the frozen Daedong River and crossed the ice. However, as we began crossing the icy river, American jets appeared and shot at us. Many of those with us were killed, including my younger brother, Jung-hong. No matter how much we looked for him when the jets left, we could not find him. My father and I decided to continue our journey south. It took almost a month for us to come to the thirty-eighth parallel, which divided North and South Korea. Although we had never intended to come all the way to South Korea, we crossed the dividing line on January 1, 1951.

By crossing the thirty-eighth parallel, I could not return to my motherland, North Korea. We became permanent refugees who were accepted by neither North nor South Korea. As a refugee, I began my life of struggles. In South Korea, I became a homeless beggar, a servant of a wealthy old man, and a laborer in the Pusan harbor.

These memories flashed back to me during the few days I remained in Pyongyang. When I left with the other Methodist and Presbyterian ministers, Jung-yul, his wife, Jung-hong's wife, and my cousin came to the airport to see me off. They begged me to come back to see them again. I promised them I would, but, in the back of my mind, I knew my promise was conditional. I had promised my mother I would return soon, but had been unable to keep that promise. Now, seeing my family waving their hands at the airport, I was reminded of my mother who had waved her hands in farewell. "Will this be another final farewell, like that which took place more than forty years ago?" I thought to myself.

When the airplane safely took off from the rough concrete runway, I relaxed, but my heart was heavy. "Why do I have to go through Beijing and Tokyo to go to Seoul? It would take me only a couple of hours to drive from Seoul to Pyungyang. Why can't I see my brother as often as I want?" I thought about the tragic division of my motherland. "Who divided it?" Recalling that the United States was one of the four nations responsible for the division of my motherland, I was deeply troubled by my identity as an American. "How can I be proud to be an American?"

Soon the airplane landed in Beijing. We stayed there for a couple of days and then left for Tokyo, intending to fly from Tokyo to Seoul, and then to Kennedy Airport in New York. However, there was a layover at Kimpo Airport in Seoul before our flight to New York. I decided to call my father, who I knew was terminally ill. My brother-in-law answered the phone and told me that my father was still alive, so I decided to stay with him for a few days before returning to America. My father was very glad to see me again. He understood me, but had difficulty speaking to me. I told him about my visit to North Korea, informing him about my mother, brother, and our native land. He was saddened, and tears fell from his eyes. He said softly and slowly, "I still have two sons, one in the north and one in the south. I am glad that you are alive. Do you remember how we came to the south?" "Yes, I remember," I said. These were the last words we spoke to each other. He soon lapsed into a coma and was never conscious again. He died several days later.

## Life in the United States of America

On July 20, 1955, I took a Pan American Airline flight to San Francisco. Coming to America was a shocking experience. I had never expected America to be so radically different from Korea. Everything was different. Even the land and the sky seemed to be different. People were tall, and white or black. I could not understand their language, even though I had learned English in Korea. Had there not been a couple of other Koreans with me on the flight, I would have felt completely lost. We had four hours to wait in the San Francisco Airport before our flight to Chicago. The other Korean students and I decided to eat at the airport restaurant, but we could not read the menu. We wanted a good but inexpensive meal. In fact, we were looking for a meal that cost less than a dollar. We all ordered the same meal, one for thirty-nine cents. It turned out to be a dessert, a frosted cake. After finishing the cake, we waited for the rest of the meal, for we had heard in Korea that American meals had many different courses. As we waited for the main dish, the waitress came and gave us the checks and left. We called her back by waving our hands. She returned and spoke to us, but we could not understand her. We demanded more food. She brought us the same menu. We pointed to the same thing we had ordered before. She brought us each another slice of the cake. We ate it and waited for more food. She returned and added 39 cents more to each check. We called her again. This time she was exasperated, and said angrily, "What do you want?" We were scared and said to each other in Korean, "Let's get out of here." This was our first experience of America.

It must have been very difficult for the first Koreans who came to this country. They were students, like us, and political refugees. They arrived in 1883, a year after the signing of the Shufeldt Treaty, which opened Korea to the West. A few years later there were about sixty-four in all. Large-scale Korean emigration to Hawaii began in 1903, and by 1905, fifty years before I came to this country, more than seven thousand Korean immigrants had come to Hawaii. Some of them came to the west coast and settled in the San Francisco area. But there were no

Koreans to help us at the airport. We were like pioneers in this country, for we did not have anyone to rely on.

I took a domestic airline from San Francisco to Chicago, where, a few hours later, I transferred to yet another airline. When I finally arrived at the Toledo airport, one of my two American sponsors was waiting. He and his wife asked me a lot of questions, but I did not understand them. All I could say was "Yes, Yes," and I nodded my head many times. They shook their heads and looked at me curiously. They knew that I did not understand them. I was taken into their car. Because I was used to the small Jeeps in Korea, I was quite impressed with their big passenger car. A couple of hours later, we arrived at a small city where I was supposed to attend college. They stopped the car at an ice cream stand and asked me to order something to eat. I was really hungry, for I had not eaten anything for almost twelve hours. All I could say was "Big." They ordered me a banana split. It was really tasty.

Soon, we arrived at a pink wooden house. As soon as we got out of the car, a ten-year-old boy came toward the car and said, "Tom." I was shocked to hear a boy call an older person by his first name. The driver of the car introduced to me, "This is my son." When I heard this, I was again shocked. How can a son call his father by his first name! It is the most disgraceful and barbarian thing I have ever heard of. I almost grabbed the boy's head to discipline him, but I remembered that I was only a guest. I felt sorry for his father. I recalled that when my father was imprisoned because the Communist party accused him of belonging to the bourgeoisie, I went to the jail to deliver him some food. An officer asked me who it was for. I replied, "For my father." He asked, "What is your father's name." I could not tell him my father's name, because to call one's father's name in public was a disgrace. He knew why I could not say it. He gave me a piece of paper and a pen, and I wrote my father's name on the paper. Thus, it was unbelievable for me to hear a son say his father's first name in public. This was the first cultural shock I had when I arrived in this country.

The house had several rooms, including a huge living room. I was given a room attached to the living room. Owning a grocery store in the city, my sponsor was a wealthy person. He showed me every room and the furniture in it. Although he was proud of his wealth, I was unable then to appreciate his hospitality. I was deeply preoccupied with something that he could never have understood. However much he wished to entertain me, it was useless. The gap between my world and his was too great to bridge. Soon he realized that I needed rest after my long journey from Korea, and the family allowed me to go to my room to rest. However, as soon as I got into my room I shut the door tight and sobbed bitterly. The loneliness of being in a totally strange country was unbearable.

I could not help but cry, and I cried hard for a long time. Then I heard someone knocking at the door. When I opened the door, the owner of the house stood there. He asked, "What did I do to hurt you? Please tell me." He repeated it again and again. I was unable to explain myself to him. I shook my head many times and pointed my finger to myself, meaning that it had nothing to do with him but with me. I did not know whether he understood me or not. He left and went back to his room. I cried all night, because I was so lonely. When I came out the next morning, everyone looked at me strangely. No one even said "good morning" to me. I saw that they were unhappy with me. In fact, they were mad at me. They did not even try to understand me. This cultural misunderstanding cut us apart forever. I was sent to the other family which cosponsored my coming to America, the father of whom was a Methodist minister. I stayed there for a few weeks before school started.

As a Methodist minister, he understood me better than did most Americans. His wife was a warm person, although she was very talkative. They had three children who were enrolled in public school. They greatly helped me to adjust to American life. I helped the children with their math homework. I cleaned the rooms, washed dishes after dinner, mowed the yard, and planted gardens. It was like my second home. During school days, I worked twenty hours a week to support myself. I cleaned toilets at school during school days, washed and waxed cars at a gas station on weekends, and cleaned a barber shop in the evening.

During the summer vacation, I worked day and night at an RCA branch company on the outskirts of the city. I went to work early in the morning and returned at midnight. My job was to sweep the floors and clean desks and toilets. Because I did not have a car, I rode a bicycle nearly fifteen miles to work, although riding a bicycle on the highway at midnight was dangerous. My friends at the factory used to warn me, "Someday you will be run over by a car." I had to take risks to travel the highway by bicycle at night, but I knew that God was my protector.

Several months before graduation from college, I became restless for many days and nights. I found myself more and more inclined to spirituality, and began to question my life's purpose. I decided to go to seminary to become a minister.

I wrote letters to my father in South Korea to let him know of my decision to enter a theological seminary to become a Christian minister. He was very disappointed. He believed many ministers were dishonest, and did not want his son to become one of them. As a Confucian father does, he demanded that I continue my major in chemistry. I had to choose between honoring my father's wish and honoring God by heeding the call to ministry. It was one of the most difficult questions that I had ever had to settle. I finally decided to follow my own conscience and accept God's call to the ministry. The last letter I received from my father stated, "You have disgraced your father by disobeying him. I do not regard you as my son any longer." I heard nothing more from my father for many years, although my brother wrote me a few times and urged me to please my father by reversing my decision. However, I was certain my decision was right, and I would not change it. Thus, I was cut off not only from my people but also from my family. My journey was marked with loneliness, alienation, and suffering.

When I came to the seminary, I began to notice that education was more than classroom or laboratory work. It had to do with other areas of life as well. When I became actively involved in social life, I became aware of my place in this country. Unfortunately, it was in the seminary that I also became vividly aware of racism. Later I was made keenly aware of racism in the Church. When I finished my theological education, I was supposed to be ordained as an elder at the Ohio Conference of the Methodist Church in June 1961. The annual conference was held at Lakeside, Ohio, about twenty miles west of Cleveland. Although I had attended annual conferences for a few years (since I was active in the United Methodist Church), this conference was special to me. I was to be admitted to full conference membership and ordained an elder. Before the admission of candidates to full membership, there would be a final review of candidates by the Board of Ministerial Qualifications at the conference. When I met with them in a small cottage at the Lakeside campground, they asked me many questions that I had to answer as a candidate. At the end of the examination, the chairman of the board asked me to wait for a few minutes so they could confer and let me know of their decision on my qualifications. I knew that I had met all of their requirements, so I did not expect anything but good news. When they returned to the conference table, the chairman of the board said:

> We definitely think that you have met all the requirements for ordination and full membership in our conference. You have attended a Methodist seminary and done quite well. You were ordained a deacon a year ago and served the Methodist church as an associate minister for two years. You also answered all the questions we asked you. As far as we are concerned, you meet all the qualifications for full membership in our conference. However, you must know that, once you have been admitted to our conference, the bishop is responsible for appointing you to a local church, and unfortunately, no congregation in our conference wants you as their pastor. You know what we mean.

Indeed, I knew what they meant. I was unappointable because I was of a different race. I walked away, thinking that a conference that discriminates because of racial origin was not a place for me.

I came to the shore of a huge lake and stood alone, watching the waves coming in. It was nearly sundown. The sound of the waves reminded me of my old friends and my family in my homeland. I thought of my mother, left behind the iron curtain, and of my father, who had advised me not to go into the ministry.

"He was right, he was right. I wish I had obeyed him when he pleaded with me to change my mind," I said to myself. But, on the other hand, I knew that my commitment to the ministry was unchanged in spite of my having been denied admission to the conference. I knew that God loves all kinds of people.

As I was meditating at the water edge, I heard a familiar voice calling me, "Jung, Jung." It was our bishop, just coming from his cabinet meeting. He asked me to join him for dinner at the Lakeside Hotel. I was delighted to see him again. Although many ministers did not like him because of his authoritarian leadership style, I happened to know him well.

On the first floor of the hotel there was a nice restaurant where many well-known ministers and committee members came to dine. A nice table was reserved for the bishop and his guests. The wife of my bishop and a bishop from Washington joined us for dinner. My bishop introduced me to the bishop of Washington, saying, "This is Jung. We are so proud to have him. This year's ordination service will be special for us, for he is the first Asian coming to our conference." While I did not want to tell him in front of his friend, I felt that I had to correct his belief that I had been accepted. So I told him, "I am sorry. I will not become a member of the Ohio Conference." My bishop was almost shocked at my words.

"Jung, what is the matter with you?" His voice shook a bit.

"The chairman of the Board of Ministerial Qualifications thinks that you will not be able to appoint me to a local church because he feels that no congregation would like to have me as their pastor. That is why the Board denied me."

"No, that is unfair," he said, "Tell him that I want you to come into our conference." He was upset, and the bishop of Washington was also uncomfortable to hear what had happened to me. Although the food was delicious, we did not have a pleasant dinner. By the grace of my bishop, however, I was ultimately admitted as a full member of that conference. God works in strange ways!

Since no local church was in fact interested in me, I was asked if I wanted a janitorial job in a huge university church. I was told that it was the only job available for me at that time. "It pays a good salary and many people want to have it. We will be happy to appoint you as a janitor if you are willing." My instant reaction was "No." I was ordained to preach the Gospel, not to clean the church, I said to myself. However, I have since regretted that I did not accept that special appointment. I would have learned to be a humble servant had I taken that job. However, I went back to school to maintain my conference membership on a special appointment status. I became a student again and found a part-time job at the Inner City Council of Churches. Although it was a part-time job, I devoted full time to my service to the people in the inner city. Soon a small church in the inner city lost a pastor and I was asked to replace him. I was glad that I was finally given a church to serve. I became a supply pastor to this church, although I was a fully ordained elder in the conference. The wage I received from the church was only one-third of the minimum salary of an ordained minister. I basically volunteered my service to the church, and the congregation knew it when they accepted me as their pastor.

The church was located in a neighborhood consisting of factories, especially breweries, and lower income houses. Most of the people in this area worked in the factories, and there was much alcoholism. People gradually accepted me as their minister. My three years of ministry in that inner city church is an unforgettable part of my life.

Three years later, however, I left the church and went to Washington, D.C. While it was painful for me to leave the congregation, whom I loved, I had an experience in Washington that is among the most memorable moments of my life. I participated in the Washington march and witnessed solidarity among all kinds of people. I heard Martin Luther King Jr.'s famous speech on the American dream, which gave me hope for my life in America.

Later I moved to Boston and continued my education. My new job was to teach theology and world religions in a small liberal arts college. Later, I moved to a state university and then to a theological school, moving from the Midwest to the East coast. Wherever I went, however, people have asked me, "When are you going home?" I did not belong to America, but I could not return to my country, North Korea, which had become a Communist nation. I was a man without a country, seeking to find a new home.

Born into an aristocratic family, my journey began in a small village in North Korea. I went to public school under the Japanese occupation and learned to speak and write Japanese. I was given a Japanese name, "Koizumi Ohnobu," which may never be erased from my memory. When Korea was liberated, the north became a Communist country where I experienced rapid social and political changes. I became a victim of the civil war, leaving my homeland, my mother, and brothers. In South Korea, I was a penniless refugee, seeking food and shelter for survival. Finally, I came to America to study science. Against the will of my father and brother, I became a minister, pursuing the meaning of my marginal existence in the new world. As a man without a country, my journey continues in exile, heeding the advice of Jeremiah:

> Build houses and live in them; plant gardens and eat their produce. Take wives and have sons and daughters; take wives for your sons, and give your daughters in marriage, that they may bear sons and daughters; multiply there, and do not decrease. But seek the welfare of the city where I have sent you into exile, and pray to the Lord on its behalf, for in its welfare you will find your welfare (Jer 29:5-7, RSV).

## Postscript: Emerging Theological Themes

Perhaps the greatest gifts in my life are the sacred memories of my past. Every step I have taken, every direction in which I have moved, and every event in which I have participated is part of the memories which are the source of my theological reflection. As I approach my sixtieth birthday (which, according to Asian tradition, completes the full cycle of human life), I realize that my life has been more or less a microcosm of Israel's sacred history. I began with the memory of a lost paradise and now seek a new paradise on earth.

A small farming village in North Korea was my symbol of paradise. Since coming to North America, I have wept many nights because I missed that village. My beautiful memory of the small village where I was born and grew up is still sacred, even though my recent visit revealed my birth place to be a tiny, insignificant town at the end of a dusty and stony road. The garden of Eden in my sacred memory is the town of Nazareth in reality. Nevertheless, my homeland, the mother of my existence, has had, and continues to have, a profound and lasting impact on my theological thinking.

I remember the regimented life and forced labor during the Japanese occupation, and later the Communist regime in North Korea. I lost my identity when my Korean name was changed to a Japanese name and I was forced to learn and to speak the Japanese language. During the Communist regime, our lands were taken away and we were forced to work the stony farm land to pay for our "oppression." This experience was similar to that of the Jews in Egypt.

The exodus of my people began on December 7, 1950. Thousands and thousands of people left their homes in North Korea and fled south when the Chinese counterattacked the South Korean and United Nations forces. Every road was filled with refugees. Most of them were Christians, fleeing systematic oppression in North Korea. Crossing the thirty-eighth parallel, which divides North and South Korea, was like crossing the Red Sea. We had no one like Moses to guide us. Neither a pillar of cloud nor a pillar of fire led us; rather, flying jets and the sound of gunfire hastened our journey.

Like the Hebrews, I too experienced the wilderness, not for forty years but for four, during which I roamed from one place to another without shelter and sustenance. It was a miracle, or by the grace of God, that I survived starvation and physical torture.

My coming to the United States is like the Israelites' arrival in the Promised Land. After years of poverty, starvation, fear, and suffering during the tragic war of 1950, the opportunity to study in a rich and peaceful land was the highest aspiration of my life. My friends envied me, for very few students were selected to come to study in the United States. When I came to America, I thought, "This is it; everything is solved in my life." America represented the land of promise, the land of milk and honey.

After years of residence in this country, I began to realize that for me the United States was no longer a land of promise. It had become a land of exile, and I was a stranger in the land where I now hold my citizenship. The color of my skin, the shape of my face, and the peculiar character of my culture alienated me. People still ask, "When will you go back to your homeland?" I have no answer, because I have no homeland to return to. I must find a way to make my dream a reality, and to help make this nation a promised land, where all kinds of people, small or tall, black or white, yellow or brown, male or female, can live in harmony. I hope that someday this beautiful mosaic will be realized in America.

# The House of Self

*Julia Ching*

> There is a beginning. There is a not yet beginning to be a beginning. There is a not yet beginning to be a not yet beginning to be a beginning. . . . Now I have said something. But I don't know whether what I have said has really said something or whether it hasn't said something (Chuang Tzu).

"What are your earliest memories?" I remember my husband, Willard G. Oxtoby, asking me. "I remember as a kid growing up in California eating at an American Chinese restaurant every Tuesday night. We had chow mein and chop suey; I never knew there was so much more to the cuisine. And I remember being told that if I dug down far enough in our backyard sandbox, I'd reach China."

"I also remember being told that if I dug hard enough in our front yard in Shanghai, I'd reach America," I replied, laughing. "But instead of sandboxes, we had a few bamboos, and some begonias."

I looked out at our back yard, where the white hydrangeas were in full bloom, with their petals clustering together as flowerballs. I hated to see them wither, but planned to harvest them in the fall and keep them in the dry form; I might even spray gold paint on them, I mused. I did not work so much outdoors. That was Will's task. He loved digging around, pulling out a small, dead bush after the winter took its toll and replacing it with something new.

Fortunately I have Will, as well as my own parents, brothers, and sisters. Their existence reminds me of the rootedness and reality of my existence. And they helped me define myself. I have a kind of community as well with my work at the university and with my scattered friends, a precious network of relationships.

A man with a sunshine temperament, Will has limitless intellectual curiosity. His patrimony is the Bible. It is interesting, he said, to pause over the fact that the Hebrews have believed in a God whose name was Yahweh ("He who causes to be") and who says, "I am who am" *(ehyeh)*. This God is telling us his or her identity, without depending on others, in this case impossible peers, to tell us anything. But for us, he continued, *not being God,* we cannot tell ourselves who we are without the help of others.

When I ask myself, "Who am I?" I should also ask myself a more fundamental question: "Am I qualified to answer this question?" Because in a sense the question cannot be answered by myself, but only by somebody else. For our memories are the thread that keeps our lives together. But our memories may also perplex us and arouse mixed emotions. And the thread is not always so strong or so straight.

## Between East and West

When I returned from Australia to the United States, I taught first at Yale University. Students came to my office to see me, big fellows whose families could afford the fees. They sometimes told me things like:

"I feel so alienated. My parents divorced when I was four. I've been commuting between parents since. I hardly know where I belong or who I am."

"I really need to discover myself. One way I'm trying is by having staring sessions with my girlfriend. I stare at her and she stares at me. We're trying to help each other find ourselves."

"I find the pressures very hard. Here I'm expected to do well in my studies, to be good at parties as well as student politics, and also be an all-around athlete. Besides baseball and basketball, there's winter skiing."

Ironically, I was visibly Asian and had come from faraway Australia. And I was no sports coach. Their feelings of loss in the country of their birth helped me somewhat overcome my own feelings of estrangement. I got used to not seeing the Australian gum tree or hearing the kookaburra laugh, or whatever the metaphorical equivalents are for a jackass (which the kookaburra is) resting on a log and making strange sounds. I got used to missing people who speak my native tongue. But sometimes I also asked myself the question: "Who am I?" I sensed that I have lived different lives, all in one life span. In fact, I had spent most of my life seeking an answer to this question. Yet the more I sought, the more the answer eluded me.

I believe it was the psychoanalyst Carl Jung who once quoted someone as having said that the Westerner cannot tolerate the meaninglessness of a merely static universe: he or she must assume that it has meaning. But the Oriental, according to him, does not need to make this assumption, because he or she embodies it. Jung's own comment is that both positions are right: "The Westerner seems predominantly extroverted, the Easterner predominantly introverted. The former projects the meaning and considers that it exists in objects; the latter feels the meaning in himself or herself. But the meaning is both within and without."[1]

Poised between East and West, I have become increasingly puzzled by the contrast often made of West and East, that somehow the Western mind is marked by a greater rationality than the Eastern. Certainly, in things religious, the Easterner finds the believer in the West affirming so much that goes against reason, for example theological doctrines such as the Trinity, the incarnation, the resurrection—even if the language of theology tends to be a rational one. In the Orient, spirituality is valued more than religion because it is closer to experience and more relevant to life.

The Psalmist has twice pronounced that "the fool has said in his heart: there is no God" (Pss 14:1; 53:1). But the Easterner asserts that it is foolhardy to be so sure that there is a God, for how can you tell? And it is conceit to presume that one tradition has been told of it while the others have not. In the fourteenth century Nicolas of Cusa, a German cardinal and scholar, said that God is like a circle whose center is everywhere but whose circumference is nowhere. Now that is no geometric circle. God, it appears, created time and space not for himself or herself but for the earthlings, for those placed "in the loop"—between the heavens and the earth. But God traverses in and out of the loop, always within the circle without a circumference.

And when we look for God, when we search everywhere, to and beyond the horizons, the circle's alleged limits, we may not find God. But when we look inside, within ourselves, in the profound recesses of our hearts and the hearts of others, we sometimes find a few traces.

## War Memories

Digging, but not outdoors. And a lot of it. That is what I have been doing lately. I did not get to meet Will through digging, but the meeting became occasion for some such work, as Will was very curious about me: my sense of self and my past. I refer here of course to the digging into my consciousness.

My earliest memories were of war. I remember hiding underneath a blanket-covered table. The windows were shaking, but the glass had paper cut designs pasted on it to keep it from shattering. On the other

---

[1] Carl Jung, *Memories, Dreams, Reflections* (New York: Pantheon Books, 1963) 317.

side of the Pacific, Will also remembers air-raid drills in his California elementary school, where they practiced crouching underneath their desks, spreading out pieces of newspaper on the oiled pinewood floor during the drills to keep the oil from their clothes. The curtains and roller blinds were drawn over the windows in case the glass should shatter.

*Windows and curtains. Windows are made for fresh air to come in, and for us to look out. But sometimes, we do not want to look out. And we do not want others to look in. So we pull curtains over them.*

My family moved from Shanghai to Hong Kong. From a big, urban sprawl to a budding island set in the lush tropics, rocks that gave shelter long ago to pirates rushing out of the ocean. *Hong Kong,* the "Fragrant Harbor," which allegedly once harbored the notorious band led by the Fragrant Lady, the nickname for a woman pirate leader.

Nineteen hundred forty-two was also a fateful year for Hong Kong. And December 8, the Feast of the Immaculate Conception, was a fateful day that year, when the Pacific War started in my part of the world. On that day, a Catholic school holiday, I accompanied my older sister to purchase food and returned home to find out the war that had been going on for years in China had extended to Hong Kong.

I remember huddling together with my family and the families of other tenants underneath a staircase during a bombing raid, as some adult woman from the same apartment building was yelling and screaming: "Oh, they've hit us, they've hit us!" On Christmas Day the bombing raids stopped, but house searches soon began. My family all lined up; my mother put ashes on her face to make herself look old. The Japanese soldiers searched the men's pockets. They did not touch the children, but I was scared.

Running away and hiding. That was what we had to do. That is what I still recall. And that is what still gives me compassion as I watch the news of the regional wars in our own days, whether in Bosnia or Chechnya or Lebanon.

It was a different Shanghai, now under Japanese occupation, to which we returned. I was attending a primary school. One day I went to school only to find Japanese soldiers stationed at the gate. The school's principal and all the male teachers had been taken in for questioning and would be absent for a week. But I had my history lessons. We had a Japanese-speaking teacher. He was from Japan, he spoke only Japanese in class, and he could not have enjoyed his work very much. The students were not cooperative. One girl always made irritating noises during his class. In winter we once played in the yard with the teacher instead of having class. Everyone threw snowballs at him, the poor fellow.

He appreciated Chinese poetry. From time to time he would write some lines on the blackboard, such as these lines from the famous Li Bo:

Moonlight in front of my bed
I took it for frost on the ground!
I lift my eyes to watch the mountain moon
And then look down as I dream of home.

Was he dreaming of Japan, he who had probably been a student of Chinese poetry in China?

Once, late at night, we received a strange visit at home from a young man. I remembered him whispering to my father behind closed doors. Some days later my sister Alice told me that our elder brother, my half-brother, had died. "Killed in action," she said, refusing to elaborate. I only knew that he was a student who had joined the Communist guerrillas. For me, he was a rather dour figure, a vegetarian. And he once threatened to burn my hair if I cried too loud during the air raids.

Why did he join the Communists? I often asked the question, and never got a clear answer. According to Alice, he was a patriot and wanted to fight the Japanese invaders. She told me, "I also heard he went to join his girlfriend behind enemy lines."

I also loved my Aunt Daisy, my mother's only sister, and her husband, a high school teacher, whom I call uncle. "In another ten years, our girl will be your age," he once said. I found out later he was an underground worker under Japanese occupation. "What is an underground worker?" I asked Alice, the fount of all wisdom. "Do they dig underneath the city streets?" In those days, Shanghai had no subways. "Hush, hush," was the reply. "You wouldn't want to lose your head over this." I was properly intimidated. I had nightmares. For years after these events of my early life I had bad dreams of Japanese soldiers and their bayonets. And then my family had to flee Shanghai once more because of the Communists who were overrunning China. I was about thirteen when we returned to Hong Kong.

Is China a country or a civilization? people sometimes ask me. My answer is quite simple: China is both. China is a country now under Communist government, where most of the people have been influenced by the same culture, with traditions like Confucianism, Taoism, Buddhism. But some of the people are Muslims, especially in Central Asia, and others in Tibet and Inner Mongolia are Tantric Buddhists. Their cultures are different from the mainstream. But China is also a civilization because there are many Chinese who live outside that country and yet share the age-old culture. I know Malaysian Chinese, even Australian Chinese or Canadian Chinese. Some of them no longer speak

Chinese, but they still share the same cultural feelings: for the family, for the food, for the old country.

What links all these people together ideologically? Is it Confucianism, Taoism, Buddhism, or all three and more? I would say it is the mysterious *more*. Even those who rebel against Confucianism, disdain Taoism and Buddhism, still feel themselves culturally Chinese, and not just for the food. Even the cultural rebels have never been able to leave their cultural Oedipal circle. And that is why they may still be rebelling. Perhaps this is true of some of the Communists. Perhaps not.

After all, there is a strand in Chinese culture and history that is dark and unattractive. It is also present in other cultures and histories. Its name is power at any cost. Some Communists became Communists for reasons of principle and patriotism, and later compromised their principle, perhaps even their patriotism. Others might have joined up just for the status of being a party member, for the connection with power and privilege.

I felt strangely that I could in some ways understand the Communists. I had close relatives who became Communists as students. They had influenced one another. They were idealistic to start with. And then, later on, they had to deal with a ruthless party machinery. Some were crushed by it.

For me the first big decision I made, which would somehow draw me apart from other countrymen, was receiving baptism while at a Catholic school. I was a good student, a bit too serious. I was searching for certitude and commitment, and felt that faith was the answer. In some ways that was not so different from regarding Communism as providing the answer to what a country needed.

This decision did not please my parents, while it made me feel different from so many people who are content with being human without adding to it any religious denominational distinction. But it shaped much of my life and identity, including the commitment, honored for twenty years, to serve the institutional Church in a religious order. A commitment that had given me the tension of multiple identities and conflicting loyalties to traditions, cultures, values.

## Zen Retreat in Japan

I remember visiting Japan several times as an adult. "Do you find many differences between Japan and China?" my friends asked me. "It's hard to say. You see, I haven't been back to China in ages," was my reply. And then, after some reflection: "I find many differences in practice. Such as their sitting so much on the floor, and showing so much respect to one another. I guess it depends on how much importance you give these small differences."

"And what about the big differences?"

"Well, the Japanese are islanders. They themselves admit that their national character is bound to this fact. They seem to have a basic insecurity. That's why they are always asking themselves whether they are unique. That's why they have to explain their differences from other countries and cultures." After a pause, I continued: "But the Chinese, on the other hand, are mostly mainlanders. They have a big population. But they can always sprawl out on the Asian continent. They are less insecure about themselves as people. Even if they've been recently quite insecure about themselves as a people, a nation, because of their political reverses of fortune."

While in Japan I decided to join a retreat run by the Christian-Zen center where Zen Buddhist techniques are used. These techniques include riddles *(koan)* that help the mind go beyond the discursive method of thinking and even empty itself of all thoughts and images. I stayed there for eight out of ten days.

As I recall, the group arose around 5 A.M. every morning and went to bed at sundown. In between, we made probably six fifty-minute sessions of *zazen* or "sitting in meditation." We sat on a *tatamis* facing a blank wall with our legs crossed and covered with an apron. The aim is to savor a kind of silent illumination as the mind is freed to reveal itself to be what it really is: the Buddha-nature, or, in Christian—Pauline— terms, the "Christ in me."

And what is "Buddha-nature"? According to Mahayana teaching, Buddha-nature is present universally, in every sentient being, human or animal; that is why everyone can be saved. Once upon a time in China a disciple had asked his master for confirmation of this truth:

*"Has the dog Buddha-nature?"*

And received the answer, *"No!"*

Superficially, "No" means the dog does not have Buddha-nature. But what does "No" mean for Mahayana Buddhists? We might say that the question was superfluous to begin with, since all sentient beings can be saved and the dog is a sentient being. So "No" can mean "Don't ask me such a stupid question."

Buddhists love to use negative language to point to the beyond. "No" points to a kind of mystical state of the mind, beyond concepts and images, which is sometimes called the "no-mind." And this "no-mind" is a reflection of the immanent but transcendent All, the world-soul, which the Buddha-nature may be interpreted to be. And so "No" means "Yes, of course," for those who have ears to hear.

In between the sessions of silence we walked briskly or did vigorous house-cleaning, which reminded me a little of the monastic experience. So too did our meals in common. Except that the group was mixed, the fare was vegetarian, and everyone also rinsed his or her bowl after the meal and drank its contents.

The director was an elderly and gentle-looking German Jesuit priest, a naturalized Japanese. I declined to go to see him, mainly because you had to crawl on your knees, in line, to his door, and then talk to him in the kneeling position.

I loved the silence of Zen meditation, and became accustomed to the task of emptying the mind, which I preferred to discursive, Ignatian meditation. However, I found the constant sitting on the floor very tiring, for we sat on the floor not only during meditation, but also whenever the director gave us an exhortation. The Japanese are accustomed to sitting on the *tatamis,* but not the Chinese. We Chinese started sitting on beds or chairs a thousand years ago. After a few days, I thought my legs were starting to atrophy.

I had gone to Japan with certain negative memories and found there a hospitable people, very courteous and exemplifying what they have valued in their culture. I wondered what I could expect in China, which I wanted so much to see again.

## Things Fall Apart

Things fall apart, the center cannot hold
Mere anarchy loosed upon the world,
The blood dimmed tide is loosed and everywhere
The ceremony of innocence is drowned
The best lose all conviction, while the worst
Are full of passionate intensity (William Butler Yeats).

I cannot forget my old roots, those from which I have been physically sundered but to which I am still culturally bound. The old country. The Middle Country. I grew up during the War with Japan and the civil war. I had heard of the Cultural Revolution, the Anti-Confucius Campaign. I am never unfazed when confronted by those who say that China is forever in turbulence, what with revolutions and famines.

If ever a country or people was in need of healing it was China after the Cultural Revolution. Things had indeed fallen apart. People had killed or wounded one another. The country still carries a huge collective scar.

*Is China beyond redemption?* I often wondered. Having spent much of my life on the periphery of the mainland, I longed to revisit its center. And yet I was afraid of what I might find there.

My memories of China are of both a native land and of a country revisited that I could hardly recognize, where I did not feel at home. I went back for a visit in 1979, the first of many such until I got very sick.

Henry Kissinger was in China. Richard Nixon was in China. And, of course, Pierre Trudeau was there long before them. These people prepared the way for many others. And now I too was on my way to mainland China. But, of course, this was not a first time for me.

And now on to mainland China, the country that calls itself the Middle Country. China had been in turmoil for a long time. War and revolution followed upon each other's heels, and Mao Zedong even wanted a permanent revolution.

At last I was to return to the country of my birth and youth and of my ancestors, after about thirty years' absence. I was penetrating the Bamboo Curtain, a curtain harder than the Iron Curtain because it hid from view by the outside world its own Communist system and isolated China from other countries, including other Communist countries. That first time when I went to China by myself I was very excited at getting a visa, and even more excited when I arrived in Beijing, the city of my dreams. More than other cities in today's China, Beijing represents the heritage of Chinese history and tradition. There used to be two walled sections, the northern inner city and the southern outer city. The inner city is laid out in the form of a square, with a fifteen-mile wall all around. Inside of this is the former imperial city, also in the form of a square, with over six miles of red plastered walls all around. Inside this is the "Forbidden City," with over two miles of walls all around. This is the heart of old Peking, the site of the imperial palaces.

I visited the former palace, which was originally built over a fourteen-year span about seven hundred years ago and is now a museum. It stands on a north-south axis, as the emperor always faced the south. It is supposed to be a little cosmos, reflecting the symmetry of the larger universe. It has glazed, golden tiles on its roofs and red lacquered pillars to support them. And it has 999 rooms, each no doubt with countless stories to tell.

Everywhere in China I saw huge mementos of the Great Helmsman Mao, who had recently passed away. I found portraits and statues, and reprints of poems and calligraphy from his hand. And the living multitudes who passed by these mementos were almost invisible, because as individuals each was much smaller in size and stature when compared with the deceased man they honored. *The blue ants*—how I hated this label.

I visited Mao's mausoleum and paid respect to the man's physical remains. I actually had an argument with the travel service guide, who had wanted my group to go on a Sunday morning. I wanted to go to church instead. Perhaps it was less out of piety than out of curiosity.

"You mean you won't go to pay your respects to the Chairman?"

I paid my respects to him *after* going to church, by just joining a line of locals outside the mausoleum and buying my own ticket. And I succeeded in going to Mass at the Catholic church, the church connected to Matteo Ricci, an early Italian Jesuit who went to China during the Ming dynasty about four hundred years ago. I met a Frenchman there who pointed out to me a stone cross hanging loose on top of a nearby building.

"That used to be where the priests lived. The Red Guards tried to pull the cross down, but they didn't quite get it down. How sad to see the cross so. Someone should just take it down."

"Yes. It may be dangerous to leave it that way."

A zealous Catholic who had been teaching in China for a year, he told me how religion was once more being tolerated by the Communists, but that the believers could hardly accept the news when it first came. They were told they could go to church on Sundays, but they did not dare. The Communist cadres eventually had to command the Christians to go to church on Sundays before they started going.

The Beijing Hotel had woven curtains with bamboo designs. I searched for them in the city and eventually found some at a roadside stall. I loved bamboos and wanted to surround myself with them, even in the frigid north. I wanted to have bamboo-design curtains and paintings of bamboos and real-life bamboos. "These bamboo-pattern curtains will cover the windows but allow light in," I mused. "I can use them back home."

Then I visited the ancient city of Xi'an, the capital of so many dynasties—the Qin, the Han, the Tang, to name a few. It was the favorite destination for Japanese visitors who know that their ancient city of Kyoto was modeled on the plan of the ancient Chinese city of Chang'an, now Xi'an. But today's Xi'an is not yesterday's Chang'an. A casual visitor can find no real city planning. Instead, I found ugly modern block buildings on streets full of donkey carts and pedestrians. In addition, Xi'an has its overcast skies and ubiquitous soot.

Karl Marx was right after all, I thought. *He never expected a Communist revolution in China. He found there only the Asiatic mode of production. And the donkey carts are still here.*

When I was greeted by my Aunt Daisy and her husband each was clothed in the same color as the great masses. Two professors, one active and one retired. Uncle was the underground worker during the Japanese occupation.

"I remember your urging me to return to serve the motherland," I told them. "You wrote those words on a book you gave me long, long ago." The response was slow.

"I don't remember having ever said such a thing," Aunt Daisy replied.

They urged me to stay with them in their two-room apartment, which shared a kitchen and bath with two other units. The rooms were coal-black from the soot of winter heating and the windows and walls were partly covered with newspapers. The bed was a board with a mat.

"Have you any books, reading materials?" Uncle asked, looking quite starved.

"I didn't dare bring any. But here are some pages from my airline magazine." I passed him those pages, and the English professor quickly devoured them.

It was foolish to ask where their own book collection had gone. The Cultural Revolution explained everything and I did not wish to reopen old wounds. *Communism wanted to do some material good to the people,* I thought to myself. *Instead, it has only stripped their souls.*

"We take to heart the words of the writer Lu Xun," Aunt Daisy said. "He said we should see the old water buffalo as a role model. It works so hard but never complains."

"But why should human beings use a water buffalo as a role model?" I could not help speaking out. "I thought Chinese culture is based on humanism." Auntie and Uncle were silent. I found out later that humanism had become a banned word under Communism.

*China is suffering because its own soul has been torn out of its body,* I thought.

Together we visited some famous sites, which I could not have found without them. The Pagoda of the Big Wild Goose, a beige-looking, square-shaped, seven-storied brick tower first built 1,300 years ago, where the monk Xuanzang worked on his Buddhist translations from the Sanskrit texts he brought home from India. He was a great translator, and before that he was a great traveler. Stealthily, he left the country out of zeal for religion. In two years he crossed mountains and deserts. He covered thousands of miles. He visited many sites in India and learned all he could of Buddhism there. After fifteen years he returned home to a hero's welcome with a treasury of texts.

I had many other things to see, including the museum with the terra cotta army of a ruthless emperor, the first unifier of the empire. The army consisted of horses and horsemen bearing real-life expressions, buried with him to serve him underground. The emperor himself was put to rest nearby in a huge underground mausoleum, complete with rivers of mercury to assure incorruptibility. But that place was not open to the public.

*The whole of China,* I reflected, *sat on layers of history waiting to be unearthed. This is not Greece or Rome, where only a few potsherds might await archaeological digging. This is a country whose historical dawn is only beginning to be revealed. This is an archaeologist's paradise.*

For example, it appears dolls originally came from man-made figures buried with the dead. These were later outfitted with moving arms and legs, the better to serve the dead in the nether world. Even the terracotta army of horsemen were early dolls, made for a despot who loved to wage war. That tyrant also took with him underground living beings, including all those who constructed his underground mausoleum and the childless women of his harem.

Confucius is reported to have been furious with the new dolls of his time, not because they had moving arms and legs, but because their use as burial figures reminded people of the custom of burying the living with the dead.

*O how much have the mountains and valleys and the pavilions that dotted them witnessed over a span of thousands of years.*

## Confucius and Sons

I also went to Qufu, the birthplace of Confucius or Master Kong, where guests were lodged in the ancient family's former mansion. For me this was the heart of Old China. The three-thousand-year-old city gate was still intact. People went around on donkey carts. The town has only two important sites: the Confucius temple and the Kong clan's mansion, one next to the other, but each occupying a huge acreage.

The Confucius temple was carefully designed with a north-south arrangement and lateral buildings directing attention and traffic to the main hall at the center of the compound, a reflection of the perfect moral order called Confucianism. It included various historic sites, like the place the Master used to give his lectures and the tree he had supposedly planted.

This is sacred ground, the symbolic middle in the Middle Country, where a man stood firm for 2,600 years.

And he said:

> Anyone can run to excesses,
> It is easy to shoot past the mark,
> It is hard to stand firm in the middle (Ezra Pound).

*Confucius was persecuted for standing in the middle. Even if his posterity prospered because of his name.*

The Confucius clan's cemetery, situated outside the town, was like a great park with overgrown grass. But the tomb of the Master was plain, with the stone marker in front of a mound. Next to it stood the tomb of his son, and next to that stood the tomb of his grandson.

"The Red Guards had actually dug up the mound, but found no human remains."

"So was he buried here or not?"

"Maybe they didn't dig deep enough."

Or maybe . . . Where would he be, anyway?

*Maybe Confucius and I are both dreaming. And you are dreaming too.*

*Who was Confucius?*

He was the teacher of old, over 2,500 years ago, who wanted to be in politics but found his real calling instructing disciples. He taught *jen* or human-heartedness. *Jen means loving others.* So he pointed the way to becoming a good man, a superior man, without being of the aristocracy.

*And that was a revolution in itself in those days.*

He was the semi-deified sage, venerated by later generations, whose name was invoked by one and all to justify every return to the old order and every reform measure. He could do nothing wrong. He was the uncrowned king, sitting in judgment over history.

*And that was why the Confucius mansion was allowed some of the architectural trappings of an imperial palace.*

He was this patriarch of old, hated by the young in the generation of our parents, who wanted to exercise their own judgment in the choice of career and marriage. They were the ones who cried: *"Down with the old curiosity shop of 'Confucius & Sons'!"* And their voices still have echoes today. . . .

He was this feudal figure maligned by the Communists in their own party purges, made into a murderer and worse than a murderer.

*Confucius, a murderer?*

And there is this icon of a kindly, bearded gentleman who represents Chinese civilization, past and present, whose inspiration has guided the economic prosperity of the Asia Pacific region.

*Confucius inspired the Chinese everywhere to work hard?*

Some pundits have even begun calling Chinese Communism Confucianism. And some Communist leaders have also begun to show respect to the ancient sage. What does all this mean? Is Communism really Confucianism—both for its friends and for its foes? No, it is not, I insisted. Confucianism had its contributions and its shortcomings. Communism had its inspirations and its repressions. They are not one and the same. Confucianism will endure longer than Communism, I predicted. It has more to do with the soul of the Chinese. Even if Confucianism needs to change, to transform.

*So many things have been done in the name of Confucius. Will the real Confucius please identify himself?*

I found the family mansion a bit ostentatious. Old Chinese mansions occupy a lot of ground, with rooms built around courtyards. This one had three times nine courtyards. And glazed tiles in gold color, permitted only to royalty. But Confucius was considered royalty posthumously.

Such enclosures, like those of Taoist or Buddhist temples, also indicate a depth of being more characteristic of the Chinese spirit than the grandeur of cathedrals and basilicas in Europe. The West seems to display everything it has. The East leads you gradually into its mysteries. The West points upward. The East points inward.

I went to Shanghai, the city of my birth. China's largest and busiest city, with a population exceeding ten million, Shanghai is situated on a delta plain barely above sea level. I did not know what to expect, but I was not pleased with what I saw. As I arrived at the hotel near the Bund, formerly a fashionable place on the river banks, I could smell raw sewage in the river waters. Most of the city's buildings, built before World War II, looked in need of repair and renovation, and the streets were full of potholes. A cousin pointed to a house we passed and said, "This is where you were born." When I looked back, it was gone.

I figured that it was not so important. I now have a different identity. I am from Shanghai and Hong Kong, and America and Taiwan, and Australia and Canada, with some time in between spent in Europe. That is the way my life has unfolded.

I found out that huge statues of Chairman Mao dominated even the entrances to university campuses because, during the Cultural Revolution, some groups sought to hide on campus behind the statue, using it as a shield. Apparently, they hoped that rival groups would not dare aim their gunfire at the statue. But their hopes were in vain. The shots still came.

During those terrible years China was in much greater chaos than the outside world knew. There was no real government. Things were being run by revolutionary committees, and their members knew nothing about how to run things.

I hopped on a truck with a cousin and visited another half-brother, George, in a prison camp. This was actually a "labor factory" where machine axles were made by the inmates' cheap labor. Many inmates had lived here for decades. George was about sixty years old. He had been a banker in Shanghai and got into trouble in the fifties, twenty years earlier. I did not know him that well, since he was much older.

"For what crime has he been placed here?" I asked the warden. The warden was astonished that someone from abroad had gotten there, and he was quite uncooperative.

"Ask him yourself. He knows."

"Maybe because I once said Mao Zedong should be hanged upside down, like Mussolini," George replied. "I was very angry when I couldn't get a job." His sentence of ten years had lapsed long ago. But the camp authorities had found one reason after another to keep him there.

Callously and falsely you have made me confess my crime on that piece of
    paper.
Here I cry to Heaven for redress,
But Heaven is too far above me!
Oh, how I yearn for an upright judge (Li Qianfu)!

*Twenty-five years in return for a few angry words, reported to the police
by his wife.*

I went to a shop to have my name carved on a stone chop. It would
make a good souvenir to have my Chinese identity engraved in stone. I
got it back, with the character written backwards.

"But . . ."

"It's not a word I recognized," the seal engraver, a young girl, started
to sob. "I never went beyond grade four. We had a Cultural Revolution."

*Homecoming,* I told myself. But I also asked myself: *Do I belong here,
or do I not?*

I returned to China looking for my old country and found an even
older, more decrepit one. It called itself new and belittled everything
old, such as courtesy, culture, civilization. No one under forty said
"please" or "thank you." They just pushed and shoved. I witnessed
people quarreling, such as in front of housing authorities, over pieces of
furniture and other things stolen from them during the Cultural Revolution. I realized emotions were still raw.

*Revolutionary class struggles do not lead to reciprocal love, that is for
sure.*

*Things have fallen apart. . . .*

Again and again I visited China. I saw the new hotels rise up, together with the skyscrapers. I saw the citizens change from blue and
green to beige, from home-made cottons to brand-name trench coats. I
still could not feel at home in this country of many paradoxes.

I now belong to Canada, which has become my home. Revisiting
China helped me accept my new identity, my sense of self and belonging.

## The House of Self

After getting very sick about six years ago, I was lucky to make
friends with Cy, a Japanese woman married to an American and living
in Toronto. Her son had married my niece, which brought us together
too, as Will became friends with her husband Jack. Cy was very sick two
years earlier, but managed to recover enough to help herself and others. She advised me to meditate twice a day for twenty minutes each
time. She herself had learned that from Transcendental Meditation, and
it had been a great support.

"Meditation frees the mind so that it can release healing power," she told me. "It slows down the heart rate and our metabolism. It increases *alpha* brain waves, which help us to relax."

I was very touched; I realized that I needed spiritual resources as well. I wanted to meditate. I had not done so seriously for many years. And I was a bit afraid to cross once more over the threshold, to the other side of consciousness. I contacted Don, a colleague who had been Will's longtime friend and was a known mystic who ran meditation classes. And he responded. He was allergic to animals, he explained, but willing to come provided we worked in a room off limits to the dog and cat.

"I can recommend that you visualize light in your meditation," he instructed.

I was at first troubled. I feared any wavelength of radiation. The doctor suggested that my previous massive radiation treatment over twenty years ago might be the remote cause for my recent ailment.

"I guess I should visualize spiritual light," I finally agreed.

Don seated himself on a chair facing me in our den. I sat on a cushion placed on the steps leading upstairs, with legs crossed, in a pseudo-lotus position as I had done during Zen practices in Japan. I closed my eyes, as he counted slowly from one to ten.

"Tell me what's happening," he inquired.

I was feeling instant peace, with a glow of light between my eyes absorbing me. Somewhat wary of the interruption, I replied, "I feel the divine, in the light between the eyes." I was surprised at what I said. I felt a hush, as he was also entering a special state. After all, "Revelation does not flow from the unconscious; it is master of the unconscious. It takes possession of the existent human element and recasts it: Revelation is encounter's pure form" (Martin Buber).

After about twenty minutes he started to talk again. He said I should ease my way out of meditation slowly. So he counted backward, from ten to one. And he told me after the session that things had happened much faster than he had expected. "You're on the right track," he said, obviously pleased that this pupil was sensitive to spiritual experiences.

"And you're more Oriental than Western," he conceded. "You don't quite meditate according to any Christian rules."

"But I orient my intention to God," I explained.

I felt that sickness and recuperation had made my nerves, and with my senses and spiritual faculties, more "attuned." I could feel the refrigerator's creak and the door bang much more than before. I was surprised at the speed with which meditation brought a sense of peace.

He gave me spiritual tips. "Feel the protective mantle of the Lord around you, or, if you like, you can visualize your guardian angel."

"I do feel I need a guardian angel right now," I replied to this Protestant friend.

"Close your eyes and you may find one," he counseled.

I closed my eyes, but found none.

"I guess I'll have to visualize the image of the big angel with wings helping a little boy walk across a bridge."

He did not exactly approve. It sounded too Catholic for his taste as a United Churchman, and appeared out of context for someone like me doing Zen-like meditation.

Another day he proposed that I meditate on the House of Self.

"Look inside yourself and see this House."

"Yes, I see it."

"Describe it for me."

"I see a garden path, lined with trees, leading to the House of Self."

"Yes?"

"I see myself walking on that path, toward the house, with my dog on the leash."

He was a bit annoyed. "No, no. No dog. Leave it behind."

"Well, too bad, if you won't allow the dog. I'm now in this house, and I want to decorate it. May I open its windows, and put plants and flowers around?"

"Yes, yes, if you wish." He found me a bit sassy. And preoccupied with the dog.

"Have you experienced disturbing signs in your unconscious, in or out of meditation?" he also asked afterward. Some people, he explained, could find their hands making involuntary motions during meditation. Others might see things, have visions that are pleasurable or terrifying.

"I've had nothing out of the ordinary. But I could say sometimes I get terrifying images arising out of nowhere, usually out of meditation. I often imagine someone is seeking to plunge a knife into my stomach."

"That certainly comes from the negative unconscious. What do you do about it?"

"I tell myself, No, no."

"Keep it up," he said. "You can convert negative energies into positive ones."

So I returned to meditating twice a day, which gave me support in my daily life. I told Don I did it strictly for my health. "I want to live," I said.

Slightly disconcerted, he replied that he thought it better to surrender yourself to God's will, as he was doing.

"I believe in fighting," I replied. "I believe that there's not necessarily a *God's will* in every circumstance. We can make our will God's will, provided what we do is good."

"That's also true," he admitted. "I sometimes find you so Oriental. I no longer know whether you're Buddhist, Taoist, Confucian, Christian, or all of the above. I guess it doesn't matter."

I was touched by his words.

"You're right. Thank you. My *beta* brain waves sometimes go the agnostic way, while my *alpha* waves are Zen and Taoist. But then, so often, my religious imagination remains very Christian, for better or for worse."

"Will you explain yourself further?"

"You see my conflicts. I want to believe in a loving God. My meditation is oriented in that direction, even if I follow various methods. But I often feel God's punishing me, or at least, he's taking it out on me."

I continued, in a louder voice: "And if I seem irreverent, God, I want to trust in your mercy. Otherwise you wouldn't be God."

"I sense anger in you," Don reported quietly.

"Yes, I know. I still have to learn to forgive. The hardest people to forgive are myself and God. I must yet learn how to forgive God."

I was angry at my condition. I was angry at God. But I also had no one to turn to, no higher power, except that same God. I felt trapped in my faith.

As I was discovering, physical healing involves total healing, going beyond coping with various medical conditions to the acceptance of one's life and those circumstances beyond one's control, with their positive as well as negative consequences. In fact, all healing depends on the cooperation of mind and body, often with the mind directing the body to fight against sickness, by reinforcing the will to live, and even by going beyond oneself to embrace others, while also letting oneself loose through relaxation and meditation.

I have always regarded life as a quest. I know myself to have been consumed by a quest for meaning, for giving myself to a greater cause. So mine has been very much a spiritual quest. It has been a quest that started in the East and led to the West, only to take me back to the East, culturally speaking.

## The Inner Smile

"For many cancer patients, the body has become the enemy. It has betrayed them by getting sick and threatening their lives" (O. Carl Simonton, M.D.).

I often thought of these lines from one of the books that I had read and found helpful. Mine was a ravaged body, all the more sensitive after its encounters with the scalpel. I had become allergic to everything: to acids and sweets that stung my lips, to dust and dust mites that made me sneeze, to bright light that troubled my eyes.

Taoism has always been concerned with the body as well as the spirit. In fact, it has been associated with immortality. As I was searching for healing, I decided to adopt a few Taoist methods recommended by a contemporary self-help manual. I began with the Inner Smile: "Taoist sages say that when you smile, your organs release a honey-like secretion which nourishes the whole body. When you're angry, fearful or under stress, they produce a poisonous secretion which blocks up the energy channels" (Mantak Chia). The question is, I told myself, how to make the body help itself. For just when you feel that the body is the problem, you may have some solution present in that problem.

Some medical study has suggested that the thymus gland, located somewhere above the heart, at the point where the second rib joins the breast bone, has a special role in controlling the healing energies of the body. Increasing the activity of the thymus gland supposedly will result in a greater ability for the body to ward off cancer because it can activate the T-cells that recognize and destroy abnormal cells.

The Inner Smile, I learned, can make an important difference. It is closely related to the thymus gland and can increase its activity and strengthen our immune system. And for Taoists, the thymus gland is the seat of love, of enlightenment, and of life energy. The Inner Smile begins with the eyes and extends to the other senses and to the glands. And I found it interesting that the Taoist manual combines moral instructions with the exercises. *"Smile to all the parts and organs of your body. Check out your whole system—your senses, your organs, your arms, your hands. Smile to them. Tell them you love them and want them to get involved in healing you."*

The Inner Smile prepares us for meditation and for living altruistically. It fosters love for one's self, as well as love for others. It leads to the meditation called the Microcosmic Orbit, which I have described earlier.

It is a form of Chinese yoga or *qigong,* and it reflects the Taoist understanding of body and spirit. For each of the three Cinnabar Fields into which the Taoists divide the human body has an important "spirit" or deity in residence. Sometimes, Taoists speak of innumerable spirits or deities resident in the body and in charge of its many vital organs. Of course, we can take all this symbolically to refer to the tremendous importance Taoists give to the human body.

This sounds a bit like Plato, who talks in the *Timaeus* about the three faculties of the soul: the rational located in the head, the spirited located in the chest, and the appetitive located in the abdomen. But we must comment that, for the Chinese, the human being is more of an animated body and not so much of a spirit incarnate. The emphases are different.

And the Inner Smile is not just Taoist, but also Buddhist. The Buddha-figure shows someone who radiates his inner, spiritual joy by a discreet smile on the face. In Chinese Buddhism, art and devotion transformed the Buddha of the Future, Maitreya, into the laughing Buddha, "Mi-lo," a figure we often find decorating restaurants because he is somehow in charge of monastic dining halls.

And Zen Buddhism, representing a spiritual revolution within the Buddhist religion, has favored laughing men known as "holy fools." Laughter represents inner liberation, the kind that comes with insight and mystical enlightenment. Indeed, legend said that Zen was started by the Buddha, in silence—while holding a flower in his hand—he smiled at a disciple.

It is just as well that I do not worry about religious boundary lines anymore as I learn to accept myself.

My attitude toward cancer is simple. *We all have to go one day. But one way to fight cancer, a sickness which arises so mysteriously and so suddenly, is to say No to it. No, if I have to succumb, it won't be to you, or to any one of your side effects.* I made this resolution, and then turned to relaxation.

Some time afterward I had a chance to exchange meditation insights with Cy, who told me: "When I meditate, I just feel the presence of my ancestors around, supporting me. And I include in this supportive presence all I love: my family, my relatives, my friends. . . . And you, Julia, you're very much there."

I recall what a relative back in mainland China had told me. He had suffered so much during the Cultural Revolution when he was exiled to Chinese Central Asia. He was not a particularly religious man, yet he related to me his experience with sickness and recovery:

"I thought I was dying," he told me, "when I was put on the back of a truck and taken to a hospital. But suddenly I felt the presence of my deceased mother-in-law, who had been so kind to me in life. She put her arm around me, and I felt well again."

A mother-in-law hardly counts as an ancestor. But the power of love may cross the boundaries of this life and the next. All those who have loved me and preceded me to the other world are not beckoning me to join them yet, I felt. *They are protecting me and helping me to get well.*

*So this is the meaning of life. To be happy about ordinary things, with family and friends. But then, the ordinary is really the extraordinary. I am so fortunate to have such family and friends. I just wish the same happiness to the whole world; I would like to leave it a better place than I found it.*

That was always Will's life goal as well. That was why he was always doing dishes, at home and when invited out.

"I don't mind you calling me the laughing Buddha, after Mi-lo," he likes to say. "As you know, I love a good meal, and this has left an impact on my shape."

And we laughed together.

*Laugh at yourself, and smile at the world. Smile at yourself, and laugh at the world.*

But especially, laugh together at each other's jokes and foibles. That is the best marriage therapy.

Smile, smile again, I told myself. Smile into the body, smile at the protective spirits, and especially smile at the people around you. Smile especially at Will, who smiled so much, and who was now often at a loss to help me.

"I knew you were getting better," he said, "when you started smiling at the dog again."

And so it was. I have much to learn also from my pets. *They* do not appear to have problems of split personalities. Their bodies are very important to them, even if they, presumably their souls also, are so well disciplined.

I have become like a wounded animal that no longer dares to roam, even after the healing. Or like a small bird preferring to remain under the watchful eye of a parent. For the future, I must overcome fear with hope and courage.

The candles in the churches are out,
The stars have gone out in the sky.
Blow on the coal of the heart
And we'll see by and by . . . (Archibald MacLeish).

# A Japanese-American Pilgrimage: Theological Reflections

*Paul M. Nagano*

Driving one night with my wife, Florence, on Nimitz Freeway in Oakland, California, I had a flashback to days gone by when I traveled the same freeway. I turned to my wife and said: "We are so blessed!" I was thinking of our Japanese-American identity and our countless Japanese-American friends up and down the West Coast and Hawaii. Here, in northern California, we have so many Japanese-American friends. We had been privileged to live in Seattle, Washington, where we served the Japanese Baptist Church and made many friends there. We have deep friendships with many Japanese Americans in Los Angeles, where I was born, educated, and served the Evergreen Baptist Church (formerly the Los Angeles Japanese Baptist Church), and in San Diego, where I served as summer supply pastor in the Ocean View United Church of Christ, a Japanese-American church. We also have wonderful Japanese-American friends in Hawaii, where we served the traditionally Japanese Makiki Christian Church, and where two of our children have made their home.

## Japanese-American Identity

However, what most identifies us with the Japanese-American community is the internment in the "concentration camps"[1] where 120,000

---

[1] "Concentration camps" is the term used by Eugene V. Rostov, *Japanese American Evacuation Claims*. Hearings before Subcommittee no. 5 of the Committee on the Judiciary, House of Representatives, San Francisco, August 30–31, 1954, pp. 95–6.

Japanese Americans were incarcerated during World War II. With such a web of connections and having been born of Japanese-American parents (my father being a "Nisei")[2] near "Little Tokyo," the Japanese town of Los Angeles, I am culturally and ethnically a typical Japanese American. Through writing a dissertation on the Japanese-American search for identity I have come to realize what an exciting privilege it is to be a Japanese American. At the same time I have understood what it means to journey at the margins of the American society! I became aware that reality, in a multiracial and multireligious society, is more than any one or the sum of all possible perspectives. The reign of God is a world made up of diverse identities and cultures coexisting in a genuine and interdependent community. And the goal and dream of America is to be a truly democratic nation made up of people of diverse cultures and religions living in unity, freedom, justice, and dignity.

Allow me to share with you my story as a Japanese American with the hope that it will contribute to the building up of the reign of God and the realization of that American dream.

## Loss of Identity and Dignity—Family No. 34391

While attending Boyd Street Grammar School in Los Angeles at the age of ten, I served on the "Safety Committee." It was quite an honor! With a badge strapped on my arm I had the privilege of raising the flag of the United States of America and leading the Pledge of Allegiance each morning to begin the school day.

But, at the age of twenty-two, I had an identification tag with number 34391 hanging from my coat lapel and was escorted by U.S. armed guards into Poston, Arizona, one of the ten concentration camps hastily constructed by the government to house more than 120,000 Japanese aliens and "non-aliens" (70 percent of these Japanese were U.S. citizens). I was forcibly placed behind barbed wire fences with military guards on watch towers to defend me from my enemies. The irony of it all was that guns were pointed inward at us in the camp, and the barbed wire fences were designed to keep us from escaping.

To avoid too subjective a description of my first impressions of my forced internment, let me use the description by Alexander H. Leighton, a sociologist who has conducted a study of the interned Japanese in Poston Relocation Center:

> They begin to file out of the bus, clutching tightly to children and bundles. Military Police escorts anxiously help, and guides direct them in English and

[2] "Nisei" means second-generation Japanese American.

Japanese. They are sent into the mess halls where girls hand them ice water, salt tablets and wet towels. In the back are cots where those who faint can be stretched out, and the cots are usually occupied. At long tables sit interviewers suggesting enlistment in the War Relocation Work Corps . . . . Men and women, still sweating, holding on to children and bundles, trying to think . . . . Interviewers ask some questions about former occupations so that cooks and other types of workers much needed in the camp can be quickly secured. Finally, fingerprints are made and the evacuees troop out across an open space and into another hall for housing allotment, registration and a cursory physical examination. . . . In the end, the evacuees are loaded onto trucks along with their hand baggage and driven to their new quarters.[3]

After a two-hour process of registration our family of four was shown to a room that was twenty by twenty-five feet, which we were to share with the Mizumoto family of three. We created a little privacy by hanging army blankets over a rope. We were given canvas bags and ordered to fill them with hay to be used as mattresses. The dusty room had several cots. Totally exhausted, I threw myself on the makeshift mattress and was rescued by sleep from the nightmare that was taking place in my real world. It was the most traumatic day of my life! What, I wondered, would tomorrow and the future bring?

My brother Jack was serving in the U.S. Army. Imagine, he was not permitted to visit his family before he was sent overseas because the camps were in military restricted areas! Among the many questions we were asked at the camp in Poston, two dealt with our political loyalty:

Question 27: Are you willing to serve in the armed forces of the United States on combat duty wherever ordered?

Question 28: Will you swear unqualified allegiance to the United States of America and faithfully defend the United States from any or all attack by foreign or domestic forces, and forswear any form of allegiance or obedience to the Japanese emperor, to any other foreign government, power or organization?

Although I answered "Yes" to both questions, it was for me the ultimate insult to question my loyalty when all I had worked for and all my rights as an American citizen had been stripped away from me. Here I was being detained in a concentration camp as an "enemy alien." These questions triggered three haunting thoughts in my mind: Am I an American or a Japanese? Where do I belong—to the United States or Japan? And, what would my future be? These questions eventually led me to search for my identity.

---

[3] Alexander H. Leighton, *The Governing of Men* (Princeton, N.J.: Princeton University Press, 1945) 64–6.

One of the hardest things that I had to face was volunteering for the U.S. Army. I remember fervently praying to know God's will. I recall walking across the fire break in the camp, making my way to the U.S. Army recruitment office. It was a truly lonely and traumatic walk. In my recruitment registration I specified that I was applying to be a chaplain, since there had been a call for Japanese-American chaplains. Later the War Department called me in and informed me that my application had been rejected on the ground that I did not have seminary training. I was twenty-three years old at the time and had just been ordained without a seminary education because of the internment emergency. I did graduate from college but curfew restrictions and internment prevented me from traveling to Chapman College for graduation. (Incidentally, after fifty-two years, through the kindness of Fumi Chida and Georgene Chida Uesugi, who had connections with Chapman College, I received my diploma!)

## Personal Marginalization

Although my journey had always been at the margin of the American society, the aftermaths of Japan's attack on Pearl Harbor and World War II deepened my marginality. To add insult to injury, I was reduced to a statistic—No. 34391. An American citizen, I was stripped of my rights; uprooted from my home, friends, and familiar surroundings with very short notice and incarcerated in the desolate wilderness; denied education and graduation; treated as an "enemy alien" despite my American citizenship; and watched over by the guards and guns of the U.S. Army. Marginality for me meant being a non-entity or a nonperson and loss of my being and identity.

With passing years I am glad that I experienced marginalization, for this, to me, is the meaning of the incarnation. Actually, I became aware of the connection between marginalization and the incarnation during my search for identity. I became better able to identify with the oppressed, the marginalized, and the dehumanized, and at the same time I came to see myself as a person, made in God's image and likeness, and loved by the Creator. Marginality has led me to discover my humanity.

## Search for Roots and the Japanese-American Identity

In the summer of 1992, as a family, we were able to visit my grandfather Manzo Nagano's grave in Kuchinotsu, Nagasaki, one of the cities where the U.S. dropped the atomic bomb on August 8, 1945. What a joy to travel together as a family, searching for our roots, and breathing in the richness of the culture and landscape of Japan!

Because of Mount Unzen's eruptions, trains were not going to the fishing village of Kuchinotsu where my grandfather was born and died. We hired a van and took a two-hour drive along the coast of Kyushu, the southernmost island of Japan. It was breathtaking and fascinating—harbors with fishing vessels, farms on the hillsides, quaint shops and elegant resorts, and Mount Unzen still belching out smoke. So this is where our roots on my father's side lie.

When we arrived at Kuchinotsu, we were met by the assistant mayor of the city and escorted into the city hall where we were welcomed by the city fathers. Much to our embarrassment, because of the hot and humid weather, we were dressed casually, in shorts and T-shirts, while the city fathers were attired in formal black suits. The welcome by the city dignitaries was a total surprise. After formal greetings and tea, we were escorted to the Nagano family grave site. It was on a hill right next to a Buddhist temple. The temple people cared for the graves, and everything was in perfect condition. As we made our way to the cemetery, our granddaughter insisted that we purchase flowers for the grave. We went to a flower shop; however, there was no one there. A relative of mine said, "It's all right to help yourself, I'll pay them later." I thought to myself, "What a trust!" At my grandfather's grave we all presented burning incense and bowed in reverence before the grave.

In visiting my grandfather's grave and paying my respects to him, I experienced what might be called a "belonging" or a "homecoming" experience. It was somehow related to my intuitive search for identity. For our children it was a very meaningful and awakening experience. I wondered what was going through their minds as they reverently participated in the Buddhist rites. After the visit to my grandfather's grave, I went to the Buddhist temple to visit the monk and make him an offering. The monk assured me that he would make special prayers on our behalf to my grandfather and care for the grave. While we were paying our respects, a television crew from the Nagasaki TV company arrived to take pictures of our family for their news program that evening and the following morning.

We were next escorted to the Kuchinotsu Marine museum where there was an exhibit honoring my grandfather, Manzo Nagano. The exhibit had a Canadian flag, pictures of Manzo Nagano, pictures of the family, a map of British Columbia, Canada, with an arrow pointing to Mount Manzo Nagano—a mountain dedicated and named in his honor at the centennial celebration of Manzo's entrance into Canada in May 1877, the first Japanese to settle in Canada.

Grandfather Manzo Nagano was born in 1853 in the fishing village of Kuchinotsu of the prefecture of Nagasaki. Manzo was the fourth of seven children. He gained considerable skills as an apprentice carpenter and worked on a British merchant ship that made trips to Shanghai, China, and Victoria, British Columbia, Canada. These ships sailed out of Nagasaki (possibly also out of Kuchinotsu), one of the few ports in Japan where foreign ships were allowed to anchor. The Meiji Restoration (1868–1912) was well under way by the late 1870s, and Japan was now open to countries that had been denied access during the Tokugawa era (1603–1868), a time characterized by cultural and economic isolation and political control by the Shoguns.

Not being the first-born son, Manzo was left on his own. The Japanese family traditions, unlike the American, accorded the first-born son rights and privileges that younger sons, not to mention daughters, could not expect. My grandfather developed his own sense of adventure, and in 1877, during one of his trips to Canada, decided to jump ship in Victoria. He first lived among the Native American Indians until he learned enough English and the local fishing methods. He worked at catching salmon, and later was introduced to gill-net fishing as an alternative technique. He also worked as a lumberjack and, later, alongside the Chinese immigrants on the construction of the Canadian railroad.

In 1886, at age thirty-three, Manzo returned to Japan and married Tsuya Ichi, a seventeen-year-old girl from a respectable farming family. They returned to Canada and four years later, on December 7, 1890, Tsuya gave birth to Manzo's first son, my father, George Tatsuo Nagano. Manzo named his son after King George of the United Kingdom. Within three years his wife, my father's mother, died at the age of twenty-three. Finding it difficult to raise my father alone, Manzo returned to Japan with his three-year-old son to seek a second wife.

After returning to Canada with my father and his second wife in 1896, Manzo began developing skills for business. During the gold rush of 1897 he opened a store selling equipment and supplies to prospectors headed for Klondike. Building on his successes, Manzo expanded his financial enterprises by purchasing a hotel and starting one of the earliest boarding houses for Japanese immigrant laborers. Manzo also opened three other stores, one of which was an oriental curio shop located in his hotel. He also contracted laborers to work on the Canadian railroad.

Manzo prospered in Victoria through the 1910s and 1920s. However, after a serious illness, Manzo returned to Kuchinotsu, Nagasaki, in 1923. Apparently he was rich enough to hire the best Japanese doctors to find a cure for his lung disease. He died in 1924 at the age of seventy-one and was buried just a few blocks from where he was born.

In searching for my roots I came to the realization that in Japan I would be accepted, honored, and treated with dignity. I feel I would not be accorded the same treatment in the United States where there will always be racial marginalization. To be marginalized means never being at the center—never being fully accepted, never being totally assimilated, never being treated on the same level as the dominant majority.

## Not Japanese and Not American

My father was a "Nisei" while my mother an "Issei."[4] Chronologically, my father would be more appropriately grouped with the Issei. In fact, however, he was one of the oldest Niseis in America. My father was educated at Central Elementary School and North High School in Victoria, Canada. Japanese was essentially his second language. Growing up we spoke English at home, but frequently attempted to communicate with our mother in Japanese. At home my father's behavior was in accord with Japanese customs, though his education and public life were typically Canadian-American.

At the time it was a common practice that marriage of Issei males was arranged by parents or friends. My grandfather arranged my father's marriage when my father was twenty years old. As a result, in April 1910 a twenty-one-year-old lovely lady named Seki Uchiki, who had lived in the prefecture of Tochigi but worked in Tokyo, arrived in Victoria to work for the Naganos. My father did not know that a bride had been chosen for him until Manzo announced the marriage to him. During the first meeting with his prospective bride, my father confessed to her that he was then more interested in playing baseball than in marriage. My father recalled that his stepmother (Tayoko) had arranged the entire affair and that she (according to my father's diary) "said do this and that and she's the boss, you know. O well, it kinda happened so."

My sister, Junko Nagano Morisaku, who was born and raised in Japan (because my mother wanted her to be educated and nurtured in the Japanese culture), described the marriage as follows:

> After two weeks from her arrival, Manzo announced the wedding. Tatsuo [my father] was so surprised. He didn't want to get married. But it was Manzo's decision. Nobody could change his decision. They got married on May 18, 1910, at the Fujin [Women's] Home in Victoria. After the ceremony, there was a party at the big hall of the Naganos. While the party was going on, Tatsuo's baseball friends came and asked Tatsuo to go to Vancouver for their baseball games. He left for Vancouver and didn't come home for three days.[5]

---

[4] "Issei" means first-generation Japanese American.

[5] Junko Nagano Morisaku's (my oldest sister) description of the marriage of my father and mother in Richard Chalfen, *Turning Leaves: The Photograph Collections of Two Japanese American Families* (Albuquerque: University of New Mexico Press, 1991) 34–7.

Evidently, my father's Western upbringing was in conflict with my grandparents' Japanese background. The Confucian heritage of the Japanese culture, with its insistence on strict obedience to the parents and respect for the elders, the subordinate role of women, and familial control, led to conflict. My father found it difficult adjusting to the Japanese culture; this may have led to his leaving home and his father's business and moving to the United States on July 20, 1917.

I have mentioned at some length my father's cultural conflict because, in my search for identity, I have come to realize that I need to cultivate a high regard for my Japanese background and cultural heritage. I have come to understand that my ethnic heritage and culture are foundational to my identity. To have a healthy pride in my Japanese-American identity I must discover and affirm my Japanese culture and roots. It was also important for our children to learn to respect our Japanese origin and culture as well as other cultures as part of their identities.

## Poverty and Oppression in the United States

My father's emigration from Canada to the United States, leaving his father and the family business, was out of character for the eldest son of a Japanese family. It bespoke not only the clash of cultures but also a sense of independence and individualism that my father had acquired as a result of his acculturation. My father was neither a Japanese nor a Canadian American. His move to the United States also took place in response to an increasing anti-Japanese agitation in Canada and the Japanese government's opposition to the immigration of Japanese laborers to Canada and the United States.

Poor and dogged by racial discrimination, my parents and my oldest brother Tyrus (named after Tyrus Cobb, the greatest ball-player of the day, a sign of my father's addiction to baseball) moved to Ocean Park in Los Angeles County. The first census of Los Angeles County in 1893 listed only 41 Japanese; by 1900 the number increased to 1,200. In 1910 the Japanese population was 8,461, and by 1920 (the year I was born) there were 19,911 Japanese residents in the county, almost four times as many as in any other Californian county.

The total Japanese population in the United States in 1910 was 72,157. In 1920, it was 111,010; in 1930, 138,834; and by 1940 it had decreased to 126,947 due to anti-Asian sentiments and increasing competition for jobs. The 1990 U.S. Population Census reported the Japanese population in the United States (including Hawaii) to be 847,562.

Between 1918 to 1942 my family lived in several places in Southern California. Dad worked in Sierra Madre and La Canada on labor camp farms. His diary records his jobs as "cleaning up dishes, cups and drinking glasses" at the Strand Cafe in Venice, California, picking lemons in La Canada, picking cantaloupes in Watsonville, and digging trenches in Imperial Valley. Many of these farm jobs paid one dollar a day. Later he became a foreman, wine-maker, produce man, and janitor. He worked wherever he was able to get a job. He finally was able to own a small fruit and vegetable market which eventually he had to close because he was unable to compete with the growing supermarkets. My mother worked as a housemaid, a laundress, a seamstress, a cook, and a kitchen-helper.

Marginality was evident not only in employment but also in different levels of society. The term "yellow," often used to refer to Asians, has come to mean "coward." The word, of course, did not imply that all Asians in America, especially the Japanese, were cowards, but Asians tended to accept the negative connotation in silent resignation because they believed that it was futile to protest. Yet Japanese history is full of stories of bravery and retaliation. It was even once thought to be virtuous to take revenge out of loyalty to one's lord, even at the cost of one's life. But instead of retaliating the Japanese in America adopted the posture of *shikataganai*—"you can't help it, accept it, it is your fate, your karma"—and *gaman*—"grin and bear it." Consequently, the dominant society believes that the Japanese are cowardly ("yellow") and can be oppressed with impunity. The forced evacuation and internment of Japanese Americans in concentration camps during World War II is a case in point. It was the dominant society's oppression and marginalization of Japanese Americans and the latter's lack of resistance as a people with a cultural and ethnic identity.

Beginning in 1856 laws were enacted against Asians, beginning with those curtailing the immigration and naturalization of the Chinese. As early as 1905 Japanese children in California were ordered to attend segregated schools. In 1906 a California law barred marriages between whites and "Mongolians" (Asians). In 1910 the U.S. Supreme Court upheld the 1870 Naturalization Act excluding Asians from citizenship. In 1913 and again in 1920 the California Alien Land Act preventing Asians from acquiring land was enforced. In 1924 the Exclusionary Immigration Act stopped all Asian immigration. In 1942 Executive Order 9066 evacuated all Japanese aliens and "non-aliens" (American citizens) from military zones on the West Coast and had them interned. In 1950 the McCarran-Walter Act conferred the right of naturalization on Asians not born in the United States and set a quota of one hundred immigrants per year from Asian countries; only in 1965 did the National Origins Act raise the Asian immigration quota to 20,000 per year per country, the same as for immigrants from European countries. In 1967 the segregation laws were ruled unconstitutional by the U.S. Supreme Court.

The Japanese were considered incapable of being assimilated into the dominant white population that controlled the United States. My Japanese-American immigrant family is a case study of the difficulties of cultural and racial integration. The white-preference culture of America and the political, economic, and social domination by the Euro-Americans made it impossible for Japanese Americans to be anything other than marginal people.

Both my father and mother were hard-working people. Although they possessed a deep appreciation for Japan and its culture, they wanted their children to have a good life as American citizens. They were willing to take on any job to hold their family together and gave us a good education in the hope that our generation would find a better life. For me, my parents and the Japanese immigrants (Isseis) are the real heroes in the building of America.

In my father's diary (which he kept in English almost everyday from 1919 until his death in 1979, a period of sixty years), my birth was recorded with the words: "Another boy is born." This happened on June 17, 1920, at 9th Place near San Pedro Street in Los Angeles, California. I was the fourth and youngest child. My sister, Junko, the eldest, was born in Japan and was educated there. My brother, Tyrus, five years older than I, was born in Victoria, Canada, and my brother, Jack, two years older, was born in the same house where I was born. In 1924 we moved to 444 East 4th Street (near Little Tokyo, Los Angeles) where my mother managed Mayfair Hotel, a boarding house for "all kinds for one night," as my father put it. I still remember helping my mother make beds, kill bed bugs, and fumigate the rooms.

Subsequently we moved into the house next door and experienced a more home-like atmosphere. The big treats came when our family went to Little Tokyo from time to time for dinner. My dad organized the neighborhood kids in various sports teams. We had our baseball competition in the small school yard of the Boyd Street Grammar School we attended.

In his study of the Japanese Americans sociologist William Peterson writes:

> Indeed, in many respects the Japanese Americans are now more American than Japanese—in loyalty, language, and way of life. Let us hope, however, that the subnation is not completely melted into the national pot, that it will continue to train its members in the courage, perseverance, and dignified self-esteem that have marked this people's history in the United States.[6]

---

[6] William Peterson, *Japanese Americans: Oppression and Success* (New York: Random House, 1971) 232.

I agree with Peterson that Japanese Americans as well as other racial minorities must not be melted into the national pot, but must teach their members to retain the courage, perseverance, and self-esteem of their parents.

## Seeds of Christian Faith

My parents were nominal Christians. My mother, with her strong Japanese upbringing, held on to her Buddhist heritage. Later she became a Christian, I suppose, due to the fact that she lived in America and I am a Christian minister. To Americanize us our parents sent all three of us boys to Christian Sunday School.

One of the great influences on our lives was the All Nations Boys' Club located about five blocks from our house in a multiethnic district of the city of Los Angeles. There we met "Tommy" Thompson, director of the Boys' Club, who made a deep impact on our lives. For one thing, we were prevented from developing racial prejudices as we were part of a community made up of various ethnic groups of the inner city. We mingled, played, fought, and kept company with boys of this cosmopolitan ghetto.

We learned later that Tommy and his wife, Esther, had planned to be missionaries to India. However, Tommy's eyes were so bad that he could not pass the medical exams required for overseas service. Instead, he served in this Methodist inner city mission to help the poor children of immigrants. In time, we attended the All Nations' Methodist Church, where we were introduced to Christianity. Here I learned the Lord's Prayer, the Twenty-Third Psalm, John 3:16, and other parts of the Bible. In reflection, what impressed me more than anything else was the genuine love of Tommy, Esther, and the Sunday school teachers. They really and genuinely cared. I remember Miss Tarr and Miss Hoge, who were our Sunday school teachers, visiting our home when we were absent or ill to see if there was anything they could do for us. For poor Japanese-American families, these gestures of love and care meant a lot! I am convinced that real evangelism is sharing the good news of God's love through personal love and care, and not merely by means of words. We were important to our Sunday school teachers and to the Thompsons— they treated us with respect and not as marginal people. It was Tommy and other Christians who led me to follow in the footsteps of their Lord who became my Lord.

When I was thirteen we moved to 2319 East 3rd Street in Boyle Heights. There I attended Hollenbeck Junior High School and later Roosevelt High School, a school that had twenty-one different ethnic players on the varsity football team. It was a great blessing for me to have friends that were Jewish, Italian, Russian, Mexican, Polish, Chinese, African American, Caucasian, Japanese, etc. With that kind of experience one does not feel suspicious of strangers with different skin colors and cultures.

After high school I went to Los Angeles Junior College on Vermont Avenue (later Los Angeles City College). During those college years I was restlessly searching for a major and a future profession. Determined to rise from poverty and oppression, I took a business course hoping to obtain employment that would bring me a steady income. As a Christian I now realize I was confused about the values of life. I did not take my Christian faith seriously, obsessed as I was with the desire to make money in later life.

Whether it was what Christians term God's "call to ministry" or my schizophrenic longing to please God and seek mammon at the same time, I do not know. However, I was very ambivalent during my freshman year. In a sense, I was a loner. Whereas my peers were taken up with dancing, sports, and other social activities, I was interested in the things of God. I sought out an off-campus Bible class during lunch break and reached out to people who had the same interests. Some of my friends must have thought that I was strange, perhaps a little too religious. I remember attending a dance with my friends and not enjoying it. On the way home, I had a chat with Ernie, my buddy, who was going through a similar struggle. We both prayed, seeking God's will for our lives

Subsequently two decisions were made: I changed college and switched my major from business to psychology. With my new-found passion to serve God and others, I volunteered my services wherever needed. I combined classes with extracurricular activities and athletics. I was on the varsity basketball team of the Los Angeles Pacific College (later merged with Azusa College). The college granted me a scholarship, for which I assisted with physical education courses and taught a course in art. Those years in this small college were most enjoyable. Athletically, I was wholly accepted. Socially, however, I was marginalized. When I was dating a young Caucasian lady, the daughter of the president of the Board of Trustees of the college, I was brought before the board and asked to discontinue my relationship with her.

Not long afterward I was invited to help develop two American Baptist Christian missions, one in Torrance, the other in Wilmington, California. During my service as student pastor, my call to Christian ministry was confirmed by the baptism of eighty-five young people in both of these missions. But all of this came to a traumatic and sudden end. On December 7, 1941, with the bombing of Pearl Harbor by Japan, the Western Army Command closed down these areas and my work at the missions came to a halt.

# December 7, 1941, Pearl Harbor and the War with Japan

"Damn you, Jap!" The words were hurled at me as I was sitting at a late lunch at Daniel's Cafe in Gardena, California, on December 7, 1941. My immediate response was, "Nobody can call me a 'Jap' and get away with it!" I got up to face the insulter, ready for a fight. It was a strange reaction on my part. I was on my way to minister at a Japanese American Baptist mission located on the waterfront at Wilmington in the San Pedro harbor. How unbecoming for a minister to get into a fist-fight! We scuffled a bit. Then the proprietor intervened and shouted, "We are at war with Japan! Japan has just bombed Pearl Harbor!" He turned up his radio and I was stunned to learn that we were actually at war. I could not believe what was happening—the United States at war with Japan! What was going to happen? What will this mean for me and for all the Americans of Japanese descent?

Curfew was imposed from 8 p.m. to 6 a.m. One would be jailed if found on the street during that time. The curfew prohibited all evening activities. One night my father did not come home by 8 p.m. We were all worried. My dad returned the following day and told us that he had been picked up by the police for being out after 8:00 p.m. He was locked up with others at the Los Angeles Police Station. He tried to evade jail by claiming that he was a Chinese and used what little Chinese he knew to prove that he was not a Japanese. However, his ruse failed because at his arrest he had given his name as Nagano. Incidentally, the name of the Japanese admiral commanding the fleet headed for Pearl Harbor on that dreadful day was Osamu Nagano. Fortunately, however, there was something positive in this sad incident. While in jail my father met many of his Japanese-American friends. Though anxious, he had good company and spent the night talking with them about the good old days.

Dad was radically changed after the bombing of Pearl Harbor and his one-night stint in jail. He became noticeably quiet and withdrawn. I remember he was very subdued when we went to complete our compulsory registration. He found it difficult to answer the questions asked of him. The war with Japan was too much for him. Having succeeded in finally reaching a certain economic security, we were devastated by this war. All that our parents had worked for came to nought. Our bank accounts were frozen. Anything related to Japan was destroyed. Cameras, radios, recorders, pictures, records, and books were confiscated by the government or destroyed, never to be recovered again. Bargain hunters and junk dealers descended in hordes. Frightened and confused, we became easy preys to swindlers. A postwar survey reveals that

80 percent of goods privately stored were rifled, stolen, or sold during their owners' absence.

## Executive Order 9066—Evacuation and Internment

The marginalization of Japanese Americans in the United States was singularly evidenced by their evacuation and internment in concentration camps during World War II. The cause of their marginality was simply their Japanese ancestry. This was explicitly stated by General John L. DeWitt, commander of the Western Defense, before a congressional committee: "A Jap's a Jap. They are a dangerous element. . . . There is no way to determine their loyalty. . . . It makes no difference whether he is an American citizen; theoretically he is still a Japanese, and you can't change him. . . . You can't change him by giving him a piece of paper. . . ." (The first sentence—"A Jap's a Jap"—did not appear in the official edited record of his testimony. However, it was played up in stories written by newspaper and wire service reporters who covered the hearing.) Grodzins observes:

> This extraordinary statement followed not only the essential racial doctrine of the Third Reich, but almost the same figure and almost the same words as Adolf Hitler himself. In *Mein Kampf* Hitler mocked at the idea of giving German citizenship to a Pole, a Jew, an African, or an Asiatic.[7]

Thus, the rights of citizenship and justice were denied on the mere ground of ancestry.

Attorney General Biddle wrote President Franklin Delano Roosevelt two days before the latter signed Executive Order 9066, which stated: "A great many West Coast people distrust the Japanese and various special interests would welcome their removal from good farmlands and elimination of their competition." Biddle asserted for the record what he plainly believed was racist and economic motivations behind all the public pre-evacuation hysterics.

In recounting what happened to the Japanese Americans during World War II, the 1982 report of the Commission on Wartime Relocation and Internment of Civilians of the United States Government concludes:

> The promulgation of Executive Order 9066 was not justified by military necessity and the decisions which followed from it—detention, ending detention and ending exclusion—were not driven by analysis of military con-

---

[7] Bill Hosokawa, *Nisei: The Quiet American* (New York: William Morrow, 1969) 260–1.

ditions. The broad historical causes which shaped these decisions were race prejudice, war hysteria and a failure of political leadership. Widespread ignorance of Japanese Americans contributed to a policy conceived in haste and executed in an atmosphere of fear and anger at Japan. A grave injustice was done to American citizens and resident aliens of Japanese ancestry who, without individual review or any probative evidence against them, were excluded, removed and detained by the United States during World War II.[8]

## Biblical and Theological Interpretations of Marginality

The evacuation and internment of Japanese Americans resemble the Hebrews' exodus out of Egypt. One of the theological themes of our experience of marginalization in forced evacuation and internment is God's identification with the oppressed and marginalized people. We read in the book of Exodus: "I will take you for my people, and I will be your God; and you shall know that I am the Lord your God, who has brought you out from under the burdens of the Egyptians" (6:7). The Hebrew people, I believe, were chosen by God for two reasons: They were oppressed and marginalized, and God wanted to bring justice, mercy, righteousness, and communion to all peoples through the love and suffering of the chosen people. The temptation for human power is to control and rule, while God's redemptive purpose is for "justice, kindness, and humility" (Mic 6:8). God's identification with the oppressed and marginalized is also at the heart of the Christian Gospel. In Christ God has identified himself with the poor, powerless, and marginalized people.

It is my conviction that genuine community develops as the result of God's Spirit being manifested in various instruments and made personal in, though not exclusively, Jesus of Nazareth. Moreover, the communion and harmony among humans is essentially religious. The goal of humankind is not to achieve uniform philosophical interpretations of the universe. Nor is it to arrive at common scientific, political, or aesthetic principles. God's ultimate end may include all these various instruments and approaches, but the essential unity of humanity is religious. Christian faith calls for a universal reconciliation and unity mediated through God's truth and love as incarnated in Jesus. This unity is manifested in the fellowship of humans united with God and with one another. The communion that God wills is a fellowship of love

---

[8] Report of the Commission on Wartime Relocation and Internment of Civilians, *Personal Justice Denied* (Washington, D.C., 1982) 18.

and justice constituted not by historical evolution but by God's working in history through the Holy Spirit and the transforming work of the Logos. The ultimate of history, the supreme goal of humanity is a fellowship of love—an order of life in which God reigns supreme in each human heart, in every human relationship, and in all creation.

Such a community of love and truth may possibly be developed through philosophical reflections and other perspectives. However, according to Christian faith, it can only be achieved by a change of the human heart as the result of faith in God's love and grace revealed in Jesus Christ—in his life, teachings, death, and resurrection. This faith brings a change from a self-centered life to a God-centered life. Community is the result of God's love for us and our love for God and for one another. God's love at work in our human community is the creative and preservative force behind the cosmic and historical movement toward spiritual unity.

The Christian community is essentially composed of people who have become a part of the new humanity, the "new creation." Any kind of human association whose members are not bound together by a common faith in Christ and a common experience of renewal by Christ cannot justifiably be called church. The Church seeks to give corporate witness to Christ and comes together in Christ's name to consider issues relative to God's purpose for the world and expresses by its actions the one Body of Christ.

The *logos* is universal and not limited to Jesus. The *logos* is found also in religious communities other than the Christian Church, hence the need for ethnic as well as theological and religious pluralism. This demands the elimination of every form of marginalization in every aspect of life. To achieve this goal, as far as the Church is concerned, three things are required. First, renewal of the Church to become the Body of Christ and an ecumenical community of reconciliation and love; second, abandonment of the imperialistic conception of the Church by recognizing the presence of God's revelation and grace in every nation, culture, and history; and third, respect for and appreciation of the contributions of all ethnic groups to the fulfillment of God's purpose in the world.

## My Journey at the Margin

My journey at the margin of the American society and my search for identity as a Japanese American have led me to conclude that my marginality is a permanent predicament, no matter what changes may take place in the attitude of the majority whites toward non-whites. Human nature tends to seek power over and control of others; and people at the center do not willingly give up their dominant position in favor of those who are on the margin. This is true in the Unites States as well as in Japan, where the indigenous Japanese dominate other non-Japanese Asians.

Japanese Americans in the United States have been striving to be accepted by the dominant whites. But no matter how hard they try to achieve acceptance by conforming to the social and cultural norms of the majority, they will always exist at the margin. In spite of social contacts that have made them partially assimilated and psychologically identified with the dominant group, Japanese Americans, as members of a subordinate or minority group, will not be fully accepted by the dominant group.

In light of this situation I would like to make three proposals to Japanese Americans. Instead of total assimilation, Japanese Americans should first affirm their Japanese-American identity while frankly acknowledging their marginality; second, they should develop strategies of solidarity and common action with other marginalized ethnic groups; third, they should work for the coming of the reign of God on the global level.

Roy I. Sano, the first Japanese-American bishop in the United Methodist Church, speaking of the Japanese-American heritage, suggests:

> The resurgence of ethnic minority consciousness encourages two distinct treatments of Asian cultural heritage for Japanese Americans. First, developments in recent decades require a conscious recovery of elements in our cultural heritage which have been rejected. Second, because strong cultural forces persist despite our acculturation and assimilation into this society, honesty calls for an uncovering of a heritage hitherto unnoticed.[9]

My experience of being interned in America's concentration camps during World War II and my search for my identity as a Japanese American on the margin of the American society have led me to ask: "What is the purpose of life and history?" My marginal journey has been a blessing as it has inspired and spurred me to develop faith in God and to seek a universal purpose for existence as well as for history and creation. There are hidden blessings in being at the margin in America. From my perspective as a Japanese American, I feel called not only to develop a community of Japanese Americans in the United States, but also to help shape the future of Asia where history is rapidly being made.

---

[9] Roy I. Sano, "A Sword and a Cross: Japanese American Christians," *Pacific Theological Review* (spring 1982) 28.

# A Path of Concentric Circles: Toward an Autobiographical Theology of Community

*David Ng*

*The Master said,*
*At fifteen I set my heart on learning;*
*At thirty I took my stand;*
*At forty I came to be free from doubts;*
*At fifty I understood the decree of heaven;*
*At sixty my ear was attuned;*
*At seventy I followed my heart's desire*
*without overstepping the line.*

—Confucius

## Toward a Method: Autobiographical Theology?

Is this essay autobiographical theology? Or is it theological autobiography? Or perhaps this writing is no more than the reminiscences of a person of faith engaging in what gerontologist Robert Butler calls "life review," an irresistible developmental urge when one reaches six decades of life.[1] As I understand it, a person of faith is inclined to review

---

[1] Robert N. Butler, "The Life Review: An Interpretation of Reminiscence in the Aged," *Psychiatry* 26:1 (1963) 65–76. Also, Robert N. Butler, *Why Survive? Being Old in America* (New York: Harper and Row, 1975).

one's life in terms of faith, interpreting and extrapolating the events of life through the eyes of faith. One's life story becomes a lifestory, a way of relating the events to providence. "Life" is connected into a reasonable (and sometimes paradoxical) series somehow taking on a story structure, informed by faith. The stories of faith in the Bible serve as models for a Christian person of faith. One's life is seen as a story that is part of a larger story. The story is social and includes the other persons and groups of one's life. A person's story connects with tradition: it is a continuation of the story of God's grace, redemption, call, and mission. The prototypical story is the Bible story. This Word offers a way of explaining one's life.

While theological, a lifestory told in terms of faith is not necessarily a systematic theology. Systematic theology is an enterprise or even a vocation for a gifted few, who perform this task on behalf of the Church as one way of explaining our faith and our beliefs. This writer does not feel called to such a task and is not qualified anyway. Further, I have scant interest in such a task, particularly because my cultural heritage and upbringing nurtured me in another form of explanation. My parents and teachers did not explain life to me as propositions and abstract philosophies, or as metaphysical and ontological rationalizations. Actually, life was hardly explained at all. But I was told myths, fables, and stories. Eventually I came to know life itself as stories and as a life story.

Consequently my autobiography is in the shape of a story, shaped by story. Stephen Crites sees life as having a "narrative quality of experience."[2] I cannot help but explain my life not just as a pot-full of happenings, as though life is "one damned thing after another." I have found my life to have sequences and connectors that make some sense. The sense is derived from faith. As faith would see it, my pot-full of happenings takes on the same sense that the Bible makes. Crites articulates story-shaped life this way: "It is significant that the early Christian preaching was largely a story-telling mission, offering people a new story, the Christian kerygma, to reorient their sense of the meaning both of historical time and of their own personal life-time."[3] A life story takes shape not only as the development of a "somatic" identity that is basically a physical entity, but also as a "personal" identity which integrates a person's inner and outer world with the person's experiences and behavior. Also, the person's identity has a "social" quality to it, in which the person shares a geographic and historical setting with other

---

[2] Stephen Crites, "The Narrative Quality of Experience," *The Journal of the American Academy of Religion* 39:3 (1971) 291–311.

[3] Ibid., 308.

persons.[4] Erik Erikson rightly emphasizes that human identity is psychosocial; life is situated at all times in a setting that is at once personal and social. We are persons-in-community.

Be it autobiographical theology or theological autobiography, my biography is not a solo, isolated life story. It is communal and of necessity includes the lives of other persons and of my own life-in-community.

Especially within the bounds of one chapter in one book, an autobiography cannot be comprehensive. It will be very selective. James William McClendon Jr., in his seminal book *Biography as Theology,*[5] provides a method for a selective biography. Using the examples of Dag Hammarskjold, Martin Luther King Jr., Clarence Jordan, and Charles Edward Ives, McClendon sketches each life-story and identifies in each life a dominant, integrative *theme*. In each life he describes McClendon finds a "dominant image" that characterizes the person and dominates or drives that person's behavior. Hammarskjold was haunted by the notion that Christ was his brother and so his own life was lived as a sacrifice for the sake of others. King was possessed by the Exodus story. He understood his mission as one who would lead his people out of bondage to a new crossing of the Red Sea. King could see the Promised Land from the mountaintop even though he would not be privileged to enter that land himself. And indeed, King's life was true to that story.

I find much encouragement in McClendon's method. Without having to tell one's whole life story one's life can nevertheless be explained by key images or themes. These images and themes serve as metaphors that "contain" and "convey" faith.[6] These images "manifest" doctrine. The "controlling motif" identifies how a certain life, a person, is lived in the light of doctrine.[7] McClendon claims that the lives of these exemplary persons provide images, analogies, and models that are a form of theology. He actually claims that theology can *only* be conveyed this way.[8]

There is one more realm of thought that informs my attempt at a theology arising from my life story. I am a Chinese American, and my Asian and Chinese culture and heritage affirms and advocates the use of story as a way of conveying meaning and of expressing theology. A

---

[4] Erik Erikson, *Life History and the Historical Moment* (New York: W. W. Norton and Co., Inc., 1975) 46.

[5] James William McClendon Jr., *Biography as Theology: How Life Stories Can Remake Today's Theology* (Nashville: Abingdon Press, 1974).

[6] Ibid., 97.

[7] Ibid., 101.

[8] Ibid., 110.

story illustrates this point. As the director of a large study on Asian North American ministry, I despaired over the lack of progress by a project team of twelve very different Asian North American scholars and pastors. We were getting nowhere toward putting together the book we were committed to writing. Then, typically, a group of the team members stayed up quite late one night talking about the impasse. They caught on to the obstacle preventing us from doing what we wanted to do. We were trying to design a rational, logical, systematic book to analyze the situation of Asian North American congregations and to prescribe remedies. This was not a natural way for us to think or to write! The next morning at the team meeting a new consensus was formed for writing *People on the Way: Asian North Americans Discovering Christ, Culture, and Community*.[9] Each writer would begin one's chapter with a story. Then some analysis would be offered, to suggest the issues and to move toward potential ways to deal with them. Then each chapter would invite the readers to join the writers as "companions on the Way," seeking understandings and solutions together. We Asian North American Christians saw ourselves as companions on the Way—the *Tao*—telling stories to each other and helping each other on the way. *People on the Way* is praxis—a melding of theory and practice. Its theology is a "theology on the Way" rather than a systematic theology. And the theology often is expressed in story form. The reader is left to ponder the story and to draw one's own conclusions or to contribute one's questions to the community's search for answers.

A story theology or narrative theology seems fitting for Asians and Asian North Americans such as me. I recall an informal seminary faculty discussion in which I tried to share with some colleagues at the Graduate Theological Union my emerging theological method: experience, story, and then theology. C. S. Song's gentle response was, "David, if you have told your story, you have already told your theology."

Professor Song is himself a practiced and proficient story theologian.[10] Many other Asian theologians share his method and/or style. Korean theologian A. Sung Park uses Korean folk stories to illustrate how *minjung* theology is expressed. In the stories of the people theologians can hear the situations of the people and learn how they experi-

---

[9] David Ng, ed., *People on the Way: Asian North Americans Discovering Christ, Culture, and Community* (Valley Forge, Pa.: Judson Press, 1996).

[10] See, for example, Choan-Seng Song, *Third-Eye Theology: Theology in Formation in Asian Settings* (Maryknoll, N.Y.: Orbis Books, 1991), and Choan-Seng Song, *Tell Us Our Names: Story Theology from an Asian Perspective* (Maryknoll, N.Y.: Orbis Books, 1987).

ence transformation. Particularly in the Korean sense of *han,* of recognition of the reality of deep suffering in life, Korean theologians can find a dominant motif and prevailing theme that affects their thinking and behaving. "One of the important tasks of Minjung theologians is to be Minjung storytellers."[11]

While not strangers to *han,* Chinese persons who would be theologians could recognize other images or themes that are characteristic of their culture, history, and religious perspectives. A case could be made for *li,* propriety. Infused into this one word are two or more thousand years of understanding of what enables people to live in community. Much more than formal acts in social settings, *li* symbolizes a whole way of thinking about how people relate to each other and practice respect, reciprocity, mutuality, and, ultimately, community. Albeit gratuitous to say so, to understand more deeply what *li* is and why it is so important to the Chinese, one would need to hear the innumerable stories of how *li* has been practiced. For every treatise on *li* there must be a thousand stories.

Confucian scholar Tu Wei-ming of Harvard University understands all the principles of Confucian teachings, including *li,* to be ways in which the Chinese (and most East Asians) practice community.[12] The history of China—its lifestory—is a story of how people relate to each other. The Confucian project is a series of concentric circles of relationship in which the individual relates to family, neighborhood, state, and cosmos. Until China and the Chinese came under the influence of Western ideas, every Chinese person's life image or life theme was *community.* In this essay I claim community to be my life theme too.

John England, a New Zealander who has worked many years in Asia to foster Asian approaches to theology, provides a theological process that serves to summarize what is attempted in this essay. England, in some informal comments at the Pacific Rim Theological Conference held in 1991 at the School of Theology at Claremont, suggested one way, among many, for "doing theology":

- What is happening to people—how are they surviving?
- How are people responding, in the *stories* that they tell?

---

[11] Andrew Sung Park, "Minjung Theology: A Korean Contextual Theology," *Pacific Theological Review* 18:2 (1985) 17–9.

[12] Tu Wei-ming emphasized the significance of community in Chinese and Confucian thought most strongly in his *Centrality and Commonality: An Essay on Confucian Religiousness* (Albany: State University of New York Press, 1989), a revised and enlarged edition of *Centrality and Commonality: An Essay on Chung-yung.*

- What shapes their stories; what are the jagged realities? (What are they finding from within their experiences?)
- Where is Jesus' story in their stories?
- How does this become "shared food for the road"?[13]

In this theological method I find people (the *minjung*) as the source for theology. Theology begins with their stories from within their social and cultural contexts. The faith story, centered on the biblical story of Jesus, serves to define the people and their experiences. And their stories—their theologies if you will—become shared resources for everyone on the Way, the *Tao*.

On the other side of the world, German systematic theologian Jürgen Moltmann expresses a similar approach to doing theology. In the preface to *The Way of Jesus Christ: Christology in Messianic Dimensions*[14] Moltmann describes his personal journey to the eventual title of his book. To think of theology as "the Way of Jesus Christ" is to acknowledge that theology is always "in process." A "christology of the way" suggests that every theology is historically conditioned and limited. And "every way is an invitation." Anyone who follows the way of Jesus will discover who Jesus is and will follow the way of Jesus in the ethical sense. Moltmann calls his book a "narrative christology."[15]

We Asian North Americans are grateful that Moltmann chooses to be a companion with us on the Way, the *Tao*.

In the vignettes, stories, and reflections that follow, my attempt at autobiographical theology or theological autobiography is a telling of my story and a sharing of a dominating image or theme in my life and my theology: *community*.

## Stories of Being in Community

### Reaching Sixty Years of Age

The Chinese do not wait until a person dies to eulogize that person; after all, by then the deceased is not around to enjoy the good stories and good words spoken about her or him. Rather, when one reaches the age of sixty, a celebration is held to honor the person and to acknowl-

---

[13] From my notes of John C. England's comments at the Pacific Rim Theological Conference, Claremont, California, November 5–9, 1991. Mr. England was at one time an associate of the Programme for Theology and Cultures in Asia.

[14] Jürgen Moltmann, *The Way of Jesus Christ: Christology in Messianic Dimensions* (London: SCM Press, 1990).

[15] Ibid., xiv–xv.

edge the completion of a full cycle of years[16] and the attainment of wisdom and maturity. So my wife and two sons invited a host of friends, colleagues, and relatives to celebrate my sixtieth birthday. The Confucian poem about life stages quoted at the beginning of this chapter was the central motif and was displayed in large script. Each of the stages became the focus a of poster collage of photographs, leaflets, and memorabilia representing that decade of life. A film-slide and audio show that was made when the Association of Presbyterian Church Educators honored me as the Educator of the Year was played continuously, and an album of the family Christmas newsletters for the last thirty years was on display,[17] along with letters and cards from people who could not attend.

Going through photograph albums and boxes stored in closets to find items to attach on the poster collages of my life constituted a life review. This was an occasion to recall places, events, and especially persons that had an impact on the sixty years of my life.

For example, the poster depicting my teen years reflected not only my involvement in sports but, not surprisingly, the influence of being a part of the worshiping community of faith at Cameron House Community Center and the Presbyterian Church in Chinatown. Not that photographs were available of prayer cells, small discussion groups, or gatherings around a fireplace on a weekend retreat. There was no camera available during the times of intimate sharing, of listening, disagreeing, forgiving, reconciling, affirming, and bonding together. How do you photograph a moment of grace? But by attaching whatever photographs were available, my wife Irene and I were reminded of those people and events that formed, through participation in community, our faith and our lives.

At the sixtieth birthday party the speeches by family and colleagues contributed to my life review, telling the good stuff, of course. A special gift was a beautiful large framed Chinese calligraphy rendering of Ephesians 4:11-16, my favorite passage which I often refer to as "the

[16] Given a twelve-year cycle in the Chinese horoscope (recall the twelve animals such as the dog, ram, ox, serpent, etc., each animal representing one year) and the five elements of the world (wood, metal, fire, water, and earth), a person who has reached sixty years has lived the full cycle of 12 years, times 5 elements, or 60; 12 x 5 = 60.

[17] The Ng family is noted for creating Christmas newsletters that have two characteristics: each newsletter is of a different format, usually a parody of some popular form of communication such as a TV Guide or tee shirt catalog, and the word "busy" is never used. These newsletters would make an interesting book in itself, telling the story of the Ngs.

Christian Education Manifesto," particularly because it calls for "equipping the saints for the work of ministry" as one of the main tasks of Christian education, and of my own vocation.

A communal life review upon reaching sixty years of age helps a person recall many life events or stories that have shaped identity and formed values. Such stories are too numerous for one chapter in one book. A few recollections will have to suffice.

### *A Son of Chinatown*

Growing up in Chinatown, San Francisco, the son of immigrant parents and a resident in the only ghetto which is also a tourist attraction (although now tourists have "discovered" Harlem too), was a rich and wondrous experience. Every time my parents told me to go to the corner grocery store for a quarter's worth of pork, a bundle of bok choy, and two salted duck eggs, the grocery clerk would also throw in as a bonus a piece of ginger root. And he would never fail to gently feel the bumps and shape of my head and predict great accomplishments by me in the future. I could not figure out how he could tell, but I enjoyed his affirmation and affection nevertheless. In the village called Chinatown, even as a little boy I was esteemed and the villagers had high expectations of me.

During World War II we often had as a dinner guest, whenever he was in port, a young Filipino sailor named Gene. I do not know how my father met him and it did not matter that he was not Chinese. He was, in those war years, a member of the family. After the war our family sponsored two cousins from China, who lived with us and joined us daily in the most significant event of the day, the family dinner. They too were "family." My father died while I was a student in seminary. When I looked at one of his Chinese notebooks I saw a meticulous list of about three hundred names and sums. A few of the entries were crossed off but most were intact. Over the years friends, relatives, and associates of my father had "touched him" for a few dollars, here and there, now and then. Over the years he seldom collected on these loans. Apparently if someone needed a bit of help, my father tried to help.

I do not recall ever having heard a lecture on Confucian values, certainly not from my father or mother. There were no lectures about inclusive hospitality or generosity. The lofty concepts of family, loyalty, mutuality, reciprocity, filial piety, and such were not taught, at least not in so many words. I simply grew up in the Ng family who lived in Chinatown. Fifty years later while watching Bill Moyers interview Tu Weiming, a Confucian scholar, I knew immediately what Tu meant when he said that Chinese have a "Confucian DNA." I do.

### The Community Practiced at Cameron House

My adolescent years of identity formation were spent as a full (many hours every day) participant in the Cameron House Community Center, an adjunct of the Presbyterian Church in Chinatown. In other writings I have tried to describe the power and genius of the youth ministry at Cameron House.[18] As young persons we experienced a wide range of club activities, study groups, work projects, retreats, discussions, corporate worship and small group prayer cells, etc. What was especially formative to many peers and me was our study, virtually paragraph by paragraph, of Dietrich Bonhoeffer's early writings, *The Cost of Discipleship* and *Life Together*.[19] Through these books we were introduced to the concepts of discipleship and its personal cost (which we knew firsthand as young persons who became Christian within non-Christian homes), cheap grace versus costly grace, the reality of sin and the artificiality of humanly created community versus the *koinonia* of community mediated in and through Christ. These teachings from Bonhoeffer, modeled on his own life and martyrdom, gave voice to what we were experiencing in the program at Cameron House.

Today I can be classified as a "worship nut," especially regarding corporate worship and liturgy, and I can be identified as being consumed by the search for community in and out of the Church. The roots of this identity include not only my Chinese Confucian upbringing in Chinatown, but more so my being rooted in the realized experiences of Christian community at Cameron House which Bonhoeffer's writings helped us to articulate.[20]

### A Village Church Nurtures Its Young Pastor

When the Ng family of pastor, wife, and a two-year-old son (and another child on the way) came to the northern California village of

---

[18] David Ng, *Youth in the Community of Disciples* (Valley Forge, Pa.: Judson Press, 1984).

[19] Dietrich Bonhoeffer, *The Cost of Discipleship*, trans. R. H. Fuller (New York: Macmillan Co., 1957), and Dietrich Bonhoeffer, *Life Together*, trans. John W. Doberstein (New York: Harper and Brothers, 1954). These were the English versions which we high school and college-aged youth studied at that time.

[20] It is clear from the titles of my writings that the themes of community and inclusiveness have been the "dominant image" (McClendon) in my life: *Children in the Worshiping Community, Youth in the Community of Disciples,* and *People on the Way: Asian North Americans Discovering Christ, Culture, and Community* obviously use "community" as a major theme. My recent articles in various journals advocate a multicultural church in a multicultural society, i.e., the desirability of an accepting, inclusive *community*.

Mendocino, we integrated the town and the church. There had been a colony of Chinese immigrants living and working in Mendocino a hundred years prior, but they were run out of town by the whites and the village had been pretty much all white since then. But a large part of my sense of call to the Christian ministry was to proclaim the message of acceptance, of inclusion, or, in negative terms, of combating racism. Mendocino was a good place for a marginalized person to draw ever larger circles to bring people into an inclusive community. In the 1860s Mendocino was a booming redwood lumber and salmon fishing village settled by New Englanders. Then it fell asleep for fifty years, only to be rudely awakened in the 1960s by an influx of middle class southern Californians seeking a rustic life, artists (and then hippies) who discovered the beauty and isolation of the area, and then by a social activist Chinese American Presbyterian pastor and his family.[21]

The evening before the first worship service I conducted, I called the clerk of session to explain why I was clearing the communion table of all flowers and other bric-a-brac. Only a communion cup and a plate would be on the table. Difficult as it was to explain, I wanted to rescue that little table that had been functioning as a flower stand to make the Lord's Table the focal point of the worship and the community.

The people also taught me a few things early on. During my first week on the job I visited a dying old-timer in the hospital. I asked (and his devout wife was pleased that I did), "Would you like me to say a prayer?" Old Cecil bolted up, looked me in the eye, and said, "As long as you keep it short." A few days later I told this story to the crowd gathered at his funeral—they loved it, and they got the sense that this pastor was one of them—one of the folks who had a sense of what this community was about.

The Mariners Club of young and middle-aged couples taught my wife and me the joy of potlucks and having fun together. They supported me in the establishment of "Exploration," a monthly discussion group where any question on any topic could be discussed. Agnostics, skeptics, and Church dropouts came and enjoyed the give and take. One time we met in the cabin home of Emil Hamm, the notorious town atheist and general curmudgeon.

Children were welcome in the Sunday corporate worship, and they got into the habit of sitting together in the front pew and laughing at

---

[21] A sociological report and analysis of the Mendocino Presbyterian Church in the 1960s and 1970s can be found in Stephen R. Warner, *New Wine in Old Wineskins: Evangelicals and Liberals in a Small-Town Church* (Berkeley: University of California Press, 1988). In the book my name is disguised but I am the "liberal" referred to in the title.

the preacher's jokes. The youth group was ecumenical. (How else could the church bring fifteen kids together?) One of their favorite activities was, to everyone's surprise, Israeli folk dancing, which is more communal than the usual so-called "social dancing" between exclusive couples. To assist the black churches that were burned in Mississippi, the church and townsfolk joined together to sponsor an art and music festival which drew people from San Francisco as well as from the local area. Old-timers, newcomers, artists, Ladies Aid members, and hippies worked side-by-side to raise money to send local carpenters to Mississippi to rebuild the churches.

A church leader who was a real estate agent and I toured the north coastal area debating the California fair housing proposition. Through it all we were on opposite sides yet remained friends. And as controversy developed over the growing involvement of the United States in Southeast Asia, the session of the church voted to have their pastor preach on the Vietnam War.

One of my closest parishioner supporters did say, "One more sermon on social justice and I'm walking out of here!" But she did not walk out; she and many other members felt a bond with each other forged through worshiping and praying together, eating and laughing together at potlucks, and working together scrubbing the church kitchen or digging holes to put in plants, and searching the Scriptures together. The church officers knew something about the real basis for community and relationship, which transcended politics and race— they had to read *Life Together* and discuss it in their officers' meetings. The members who paid attention to the sermons knew the meaning of *koinonia,* having heard it explained so many, many times. When the congregation shared bread and wine, they were sharing life together in Christ.

For its first one hundred years the Mendocino Presbyterian Church existed with a session of "ruling elders" but with no Board of Deacons. When such a board was formed the newly-elected deacons supposed the pastor would have them go through the Book of Order to learn their duties and responsibilities in decency and order. To their surprise they too were given copies of—perhaps not so surprising after all—Bonhoeffer's *Life Together*. Although none of the deacons had studied beyond high school, we waded into this book about the nature of Christian community and how we are to minister to one another, bearing with each other, proclaiming the forgiveness of Christ to each other, and supporting each other through intercessory prayer. Visiting church members and villagers in the hospital or in their homes took on deeper significance for these deacons. Precious gifts of love, concern, and community were shared during these visits.

### Finding Grace in a Bureaucracy

Can a staff worker in a large denominational or ecumenical organization find happiness in a large bureaucracy? Perhaps, if she or he realizes that organizations are composed of people and have purposes beyond churning out organizational charts and institutional reports. When I joined the Presbyterian Board of Christian Education as a junior high program and curriculum developer I was immediately embraced and often held up and supported by "a team of wild horses." That was what the shy, fragile, but brilliant Norman Langford, senior editor, called the five of us on the junior high ministry team when we all jumped into the same elevator he was in on our way out for a coffee break. As always, Norman was right. The five of us were crazy, and we did a lot of crazy things together. We were like the junior high kids we were supposed to educate. But I also knew the other four to be professionally competent, creative, talented, and to care very much about junior highs and about the Church. These team members challenged, supported, and listened to me. From them I learned new understandings of call, covenant, and of being a caring community. Developing curriculum, leading workshops, and designing approaches to youth ministry requires good theology and creative methods. Most of what I know about Christian education I learned from the team; they taught it to me by doing it with me.

The wildest horse was Jim Simpson, a creative genius in Christian education and numerous other topics. Often Jim and I would return to the office after a lunch break with our pockets filled with street findings such as nuts and bolts and scraps of things. Jim would say, "I just know that there's a use for this thing." Jim also never met a piece of styrofoam he did not like. It was from Jim that I learned how to construct the styrofoam sculptures and picture frames I made in later life. Rooming with him at a conference was a test of stamina as he would talk excitedly into the night and early morning about Christian education, curriculum development, and, of course, his latest invention for styrofoam or whatever else could be recycled. Jim always had a theological foundation and an educational principle that rationalized his teaching strategies and methods. That was the part of his mentoring that most impressed me. I learned a theology of Christian education from Jim.

Jim, Chad, Ed, and Fritz were a community for me. Within the life of this community within a large bureaucracy, my own sense of Christian mission, ministry, and community were nurtured.

### The Vision of a Global Community

At mid-life I had the opportunity to run a bureaucracy! After several years of teaching at a seminary in Texas (which will be dealt with in the next section on seminary community life), I returned to the East Coast to the "God Box," as the huge cube-shaped Interchurch Center at 475 Riverside Drive, New York, was called. This building had nineteen stories of Church offices, and nineteen thousand stories of bureaucratic machinations happening each day. As the Associate General Secretary for Education and Ministry of the National Council of the Churches of Christ in the U.S.A., I experienced community at the two extremes of local and global manifestations. Having worked as a Church bureaucrat before, I knew how important it was for individual staff workers not only to have a sense of call and to see mission goals in one's functions and roles, but also to be valued as an individual and as a member of the team. Human and spiritual values are necessary for Church bureaucrats; the alternate is eventual burn-out. In our twenty-five person division each person—clerk, executive, and secretary—was considered "a valuable person" and was treated as such. Much effort went into division activities such as worship, birthday celebrations, and other recognitions of journeys and passages. Our movements may have been awkward to an observer who walked into our suite at lunchtime, but we on the inside believed that our attempts to do t'ai chi were good for the spirit and for the corporate body as well. Occasional workshops and presentations were available for all the staff. One occasion proved deeply significant for several secretaries when representatives from the Network of Biblical Storytellers, including founder Tom Boomershine, came to demonstrate the use of storytelling in Christian education and in personal development. My wife Irene and I hosted an annual Twelfth Night Dinner Party in our Brooklyn apartment. In some respects this was simply a party. But in terms of personal and group dynamics, this party was a meaningful expression of the care we had for each other and the good times we could enjoy together.

Group activities such as t'ai chi or learning how to tell stories and share lifestories were matched by deeper level activities of listening, support, and pastoral care. At the National Council our division behaved as though we were a community of faith bound to each other. It was as though we were trying to live up to the vision of life together in Bonhoeffer's book!

Working within the confines of an institution of the Church tested the will and patience of the staff. Time and money were always in short supply. Developing educational programs and resources that would suit the needs and interests of forty member denominations was impossible unless staff and constituents were skilled politicians and artists in the craft of compromise and consensus. At one of the endless committee meetings that was our institutional way of life, one of my suggestions served to push a colleague off the edge and she told me so with the verve and color of language that reflected her Irish upbringing. It took some in-office, closed door conversations and a willingness for each of us to ask forgiveness of the other to restore the peace. I still treasure her gift to me of a copy of Hammarskjold's *Markings* as a symbol of reconciliation. For us community was very dear and did not come cheaply.

In the eighties the National Council of Churches was an exciting place. Every division engaged in social justice and advocated the solidarity of all peoples. Governing Board meetings brought together several hundred Church leaders twice a year to be the ecumenical Church at work. We joined hands to fight racism, militarism, sexism, and similar forces that would deny our humanity, peace, and community. The efforts and results of the council's work are recorded in numerous other places. The National Council of Churches was a grand attempt to be a cooperative, corporate, global "community of communions." Here I offer a personal observation of my encounter with some of the great leaders in Christian education and the mission of the Church throughout the world. To my pleasant relief these women and men who headed denominations or whose pioneering projects and writings galvanized the Church around the world were themselves humble, friendly, and collegial. It was easy to be in community with them.

## In Seminary a Teacher Learns Twice

I recall how irritated I was when I was a professor at Austin Presbyterian Theological Seminary and an upperclass student stated during orientation that a seminary is not a church, it is a school. She was trying to help the new students get over any sentimental expectations they may have about life in a theological seminary. My own view is that the seminary community does focus on academics but is in its own way very definitely a community of faith. Students, faculty, administrators, and staff are together in numerous ways. Worship is for real, not just a learning exercise. Learning takes place beyond the classroom as well as within it. Professors learn from students as well as teach them.

I remember how distraught I was the first week of my teaching career when a student asked a question I did not understand! All Steve wanted to know was if the approach to Christian education I had proposed in my presentation was a "phenomenological approach." When I confessed later that day to another student that I felt quite inadequate to teach, the student was like a pastor to me, encouraging me and helping me to go forward. There were many other times in that first year of teaching at the seminary level when a colleague or student would say the right thing or simply "be there" to help this novice learn how to teach and what to teach. I learned new lessons in humility. I learned how to ask for help, realizing that there was so much I did not know even though I had been called to the school to be a teacher. The experiences of community I was privileged to have were gifts to me from the others in the community.

Achieving community often requires facing up to difficulties. To do so requires that we help one another. As a person of color I had grown up with the reality of being, in our nation, a "racial/ethnic minority person." While I would not accept a white person calling me a "Chinaman" or some even more distasteful name, I have used the term facetiously and jokingly among friends, especially among us "Chinamen" ourselves. Sometimes humor is what saves us from becoming mentally ill. One day in class I used a racist term referring to blacks. The one African American student in the class took great offense. It was not easy for me to apologize, especially in front of the whole class, for what was said in jest to make a point. The point was completely lost. I apologized, asked the student to forgive me, and to share with the class her concern over what I had said. She was gracious enough to help me, and the rest of the class, become more sensitive to what excludes and hurts people, and what includes and heals people.

During our Austin years our family worshiped at Trinity Presbyterian Church, a neighborhood congregation. The primary character of this church was its friendliness and plain-folks-style of operation. If some churches are task-oriented, this one was relationship-oriented. This style held true during the monthly potlucks. These were low-keyed affairs with a minimum of planning. Families just showed up with some food, placed it on the serving table, and then after saying grace we'd get in line, load up our plates, and sit down to enjoy a nice meal. We sat by families. When the meal was over we'd help clean up and then go home with our families.

Our family felt there could be more to this monthly get-together. We offered to plan the next potluck. When the people arrived, they were invited into the sanctuary, a nice space when the individual chairs were set aside to open up the room. We played some get-acquainted games, culminating in a lively game that put us into groups of eight. Then we went to the social hall for dinner, sitting in our newly formed groups of eight. Members of the same family were separated. More get-acquainted activities and table conversations took place during dinner, and then a program appropriate for the season (Advent) was presented. For us Ngs it was of small value to go to the church just to sit as a nuclear family and eat as a family and then come home again. We wanted the church to be a place for being in touch with others, and for being not just the Ng family but a part of the family of God. Does Christian community just happen? Or must there be some intentionality?

Maybe there is something about Texas that enhances personal relationships. All I know is that even today, twenty years after those wonderful times, my family and I can go back to Austin and visit the congregation we attended, or run into a former colleague at Luby's Cafeteria, or sit with a pastor in the seminary lounge, and it will be as though only a day had passed and our Christian friendship is as strong as it was the day we left Austin in 1981. What really is it that enables us to share community even now?

There came a time when the leadership at the seminary changed. The new leader was an unbelievably bad fit for the institution. Although Texan by birth, he comported himself in an extremely arrogant, elitist, and unsocial manner. Perhaps because my serving on the faculty without a Ph.D. embarrassed him, and I suspect because I symbolized on campus the importance of being in community, he was cold and even mean in his dealings with me. For example, he never came to my office and the few times he wanted to speak with me he telephoned me from his office nearby. The opportunity came to join the National Council of Churches as head of the Division of Education and Ministry. At the time I believed I was responding to a call to do educational ministry in an ecumenical and global setting, and to work on very significant projects including the Inclusive-Language Lectionary, the New Revised Standard Bible, the Uniform Lesson Series, Friendship Press, multicultural education, etc. Looking back on this now I must admit that the lack of community at the seminary at that time was a strong if barely conscious factor in my choosing to leave Austin for New York City. Community—or the lack of it—drove my decision. (Some of my experiences of community at the National Council were described above in the section on working in bureaucracies.)

### The Return of the Native

After service in the Church bureaucracies I returned to my home region and alma mater to teach at San Francisco Theological Seminary. This call provided opportunities to be in contact with scholars and Church leaders who were deeply immersed in "racial/ethnic" and multicultural studies and ministries. The San Francisco region is a mixing bowl (not a melting pot) capable of incorporating many ingredients, gaining flavor from each with panache from the whole. In this region I could be among any of many ethnic and cultural communities, and could be in conversation with thinkers and innovators seeking ways to go beyond the obsolete American ideal of the melting pot. This region is already the tossed salad/stew/mosaic/tapestry/orchestra that is the cultural diversity and solidarity our American society and Church needs to become.

Teaching at San Francisco Theological Seminary allows much academic freedom and encourages exploration of new ideas and configurations. Being part of a nine-seminary consortium of Graduate Theological

Union opens up the possibilities even more. As good as the faculty (and student) community is at SFTS, I have found my affiliation with the Racial/Ethnic Faculty Association at GTU even more supportive and stimulating of explorations in the areas of multiculturalism and cultural affirmation. This affiliation is not without cost. We find ourselves in wide disagreement at times, and we have endured times when African Americans have refused to participate, or Hispanic Americans find no common ground, or Asian Americans have failed to reach out to the other ethnic groups. But for all the difficulties, it can still be claimed that the fifteen of us "professors of color" feel more solidarity with each other than with any other affiliation at the schools. Our connectedness includes common experiences of suffering from racism and common needs for affirmation and esteem. At the risk of establishing a common "enemy" we at least can state what we are up against in trying to teach in a society and in schools dominated by a majority culture and infected by institutional racism.

After much agonizing discussion, the Racial/Ethnic Faculty Association is putting together a book reflecting our perspectives on theological education. We are concerned that the overall curriculum is based on a "Western canon."[22] Even though the vast majority of the faculty members of the nine seminaries recognize that the Christian movement is global, and that Christian theology can be African, Asian, etc., as well as European or American, we still labor within a curriculum that reflects one culture and subordinates the realities and contributions of other cultures. A transformation of the curriculum is needed. The association also anguishes over the reality that so-called racial/ethnic minority students can receive a fine education at any of the GTU seminaries and yet not be adequately prepared to minister among their own ethnic or cultural group. An African-American student, for example, upon graduation and appointment to an African-American church, would then need to learn how to preach in the African-American tradition and idiom.

The Racial/Ethnic Faculty Association sponsored a course I taught entitled "Multicultural Theologies for Ministry." Expecting perhaps fifteen to twenty students we were pleased that the classroom was filled and additional chairs had to be brought in to accommodate the nearly

---

[22] This term is explained and examples given in James A. Banks, *Multiethnic Education: Theory and Practice,* 3d ed. (Boston: Allyn and Bacon, 1994). As one example, Banks points out that most textbooks on American history offer an east to west movement of events and teach history from a Euro-American point of view. The Racial/Ethnic Faculty Association at GTU is concerned that theological education has this same monocultural slant. James A. Noel, a professor at SFTS/GTU, points out that when the history of the churches in Europe or North America is considered, it is "church history," whereas when that of the churches in Asia, Africa, or Latin America is considered, it is "missions."

forty students. Expecting this course to be primarily of interest to "racial/ethnic" students, we were pleased that over one-third of them were "Euro-Americans." In this course there was freedom to try new ways of doing theology and expressing it. One guest presenter, Professor James Noel, moved the students with his powerful evocation of black theology symbolized in "the moan and the shout." Professor Edmond Yee, a Confucian scholar and theologian, brought the students nearly to a point of frustration when he refused to answer their questions about his religious commitment, repeating time and again that he is Chinese, he is Confucian, he is a follower of the Way of Jesus, and he is several other "things." Not only was he eclectic in his theology, so was the whole Christian religion! In other words, Christianity was born in an Asia Minor stable, nurtured in a Greco-Roman temple, and formed in a Euro-American school. And now Christianity is being further shaped in a global house or *oikos/oikumene*.[23]

I gratefully continue to receive community and to learn from colleagues and students in my present teaching position at San Francisco Theological Seminary and Graduate Theological Union. The topic of multicultural congregations and educational approaches is so new that were it not for the wisdom and creativity of the students, the courses I teach on that topic would be abstract, theoretical and untried, and static. I reported to one class that I would be leading a workshop on multiculturalism in a Korean-American congregation. A Korean student reminded me that such churches are not, as I had said, monocultural. If there are adults, parents, and young people in a Korean-American congregation then that congregation is multicultural. This student and the rest of the class helped me to revise my workshop plans to be more appropriate to the congregation.

In this class students and teacher participated together in various exercises and in cultural practices and rituals. We shared with each other our ethnic and cultural identities and also our ambivalences. One time, each of us drew a coat-of-arms that depicted personal and family values and hopes. We witnessed to each other concerning the integrity of our personal being and the issues of identity that we continue to struggle with. Another time, instead of a lecture we set a table with a nice tablecloth, lit candles, and shared *pan dulce*—a Mexican bread. We celebrated the Day of the Dead. We each recalled a loved one who had died and told each other what that person meant to us. We joined hands around the table and offered prayers of gratitude for the persons who had died. We helped each other to renew our faith in the resurrec-

---

[23] This image was offered by Cain Hope Felder of Howard University in a television program, *Voices from the Village,* Public Broadcasting System, June 1996.

tion and our sense of the communion of saints. In this and in other ways the class bonded together into a learning community.

A multicultural church in a multicultural society is an ideal not universally shared. This reality was vividly impressed on me several years ago when I eagerly began to read a Fourth of July issue of Time Magazine that dealt with multiculturalism in the United States. The lead article was by one of my heroes from the days of the Kennedy Camelot era, Arthur Schlesinger Jr. The further I read in his article the angrier I got! I found Schlesinger paying token tribute to the idea of a multicultural America but gravely warning that America would end up "balkanized" into separate ethnic groups that would tear apart the American fabric. I resisted the temptation to rip up the article. (It would have been misunderstood by the people seated around me on the airplane.) Instead, I snuck the magazine into my briefcase and later used Schlesinger's article in my multicultural Christian education class.

In the class we tried to deal with the reality Schlesinger and others were concerned about. But we were committed to working toward a multicultural society and Church, in the light of our understanding of what God intended for God's creation. Indeed, our ideal is a multicultural society in which every person is accepted for what she or he is, and finds self-actualization by affirming one's ethnic and cultural heritage and identity. Further, one's identity, including the unique blend of ethnicity, culture, and experience, becomes the gift each of us brings to the community. We hope not just for a multicultural society which recognizes differences. We reach beyond that for a society where our differences become gifts enriching the society, leading beyond separatism to a new form of solidarity with one another.

Nowadays it seems I wear multicultural eyeglasses when I read the Bible. These lenses cause me to see the Bible as I had not noticed before. Everything comes up multicultural! When God establishes the covenant with Abraham (and Sarah) as reported in Genesis 17, I see that the covenant is for the benefit of a "multitude of nations." The story of the Tower of Babel continues to be a lesson regarding the futility of human efforts to reach heaven. But I now notice the verse that states that the people who spoke those different languages got scattered "to the four corners of the earth." To me this is an etiology telling us that from before history the people of the earth spoke diverse languages and were multicultural. Babel, for us Christians, is answered by the account of Pentecost when everyone hears, understands, and responds to the gospel in one's own language. Whatever our ethnicity, we can receive and respond to the gospel in our own way.

I have been influenced by experiences even from childhood that uphold the value of inclusiveness and hospitality. I have been formed by a lifetime of ministry and writing about acceptance, forgiveness, and community. All this I incorporate into my understanding of multiculturalism as the life-blood of community. When I read about the Lord's Supper in 1 Corinthians, I see a multicultural celebration. And I borrow from Bonhoeffer's *Life Together* to try to articulate my vision. In simple terms, using some simple names as examples, a multicultural community comes about this way. Christ calls Andre, accepts him, forgives him, redeems him, and brings him into community. Andre is in the community because Christ has called him into it. Christ calls Teresa, accepts her, forgives her, redeems her, and brings her into the community. Christ calls Wah-mun, accepts and forgives him, redeems him and brings him into community. Each person is in the community because of Christ, who calls, enables the person to overcome one's sin (including broken relationships and alienation), and thus enables the person to be in communion with Christ. Andre, Teresa, and Wah-mun each has relationship and communion with Christ. Through Christ they have relationship with each other. This relationship is not of their own doing, but is mediated through Christ. Nor is this relationship a "cheap grace" or a "cheap community." It has been made possible because Christ has enabled each person to deal with the sinfulness of self-centeredness, self-gratifying relationships and alienation.

The community enabled by Christ is not based on human, sentimental notions of how people can learn how to get along and come to like each other, overcoming personal differences. The only thing Andre, Teresa, and Wah-mun have in common in the new community is their common experience of the saving grace of Christ. That is what ties them together. The community they have is not what they have created on their own. Community is a gift of Christ.

Christ calls each person to the community that is realized at the Lord's Table. But when Christ beckons Andre and Teresa and Wah-mun to the table, Christ does not say, "You must give up who you are to come to this table." Rather, Christ says, "Bring who you are to the table. If you, Andre, are an American of French heritage, that is what God intended and created you to be. Bring that to the table, and be fulfilled as the best French American Andre you can be." The same is true of Teresa and Wah-mun, who are called to be the best they can be incorporating and integrating all aspects of their persons. And at the table, who and what we are becomes the unique gift each can offer to the others at the table. In this Christ-formed community, we can be who we are in all our glorious differences, and our differences become the gifts we share with one another.

### Discovering Christ, Culture, and Community

While striving to articulate the idea of a Christ-formed multicultural community as described above, I became director of a project sponsored by the Lilly Endowment. A dozen Asian North American scholars, educators, and pastors came together to acknowledge our East Asian Confucian roots and to put these values in dialogue with the Christian gospel. The project proposed that Christians of East Asian heritage (China, Korea, Japan, and to a degree Vietnam) have a Confucian background which includes a profound sense of community. This is in contrast to Western, Euro-American Christians who for the most part have a profound sense of individualism. The Confucian sense of community is similar to the New Testament sense of *koinonia*. When Asian North Americans come into the Christian Church they bring with them their sense of community. This sense of community is their contribution to the Church and calls the Church away from an individualistic faith back to a corporate faith.

The very first hours of an international conference our project team conducted were exhilarating. Upon arrival and before anything had happened many of the conferees were already thanking the team for the conference. The conferees had been thinking thoughts about their Asian heritage and identity, and asking questions similar to ours. They knew in their hearts that being Korean or Chinese or Japanese in North America was no disgrace, and that our Asian religion and culture was worthy. They did not have to lose their identities in a melting pot that would melt them into a large, bland American mush. But they thought and pondered in isolation. It was deeply confirming and affirming to come to a conference of a hundred Asian North American Christians who were on the same journey. For a few days we walked the way together, singing, praying, discussing, and inquiring together (and of course, doing t'ai chi together). We were family, we were community, we were *koinonia*.

At the conference the project team led a dozen workshops on various aspects of our Asian heritage and Christian commitment, and the implications for community and mission. The discussions and feedback generated in the workshops helped the leaders to refine the chapters they wrote for the book, *People on the Way: Asian North Americans Discovering Christ, Culture, and Community.*

In the workshop on Confucian values I had the opportunity to tell a story about some discoveries I made concerning an Asian sense of community. During a sabbatical study leave I sought to learn more about Confucian understandings of community and how this compares with Christian and Western understandings, particularly understandings about *koinonia*. Colleagues in the Asian-American community had alerted me to the dearth of terms for "community" in Chinese and other Asian languages. Perhaps it is because community is so prevalent that it is taken for granted, and "it goes without saying." There are Chinese terms that refer to groups, organizations, assemblies, associations, and other structural forms of community, but no word that compares to the English words "community" or "fellowship" in the conceptual sense.

To do research in the library of the Chinese University of Hong Kong and Chung Chi College I was required to fill in a long form and attach a photograph of myself. Further, I had to obtain the signature of the head of the department in the area of my research. When I asked Dr. Allan Chan, Head of the Theology Division, for his signature, he signed the form without even looking at it. Then he asked, "What are you studying here at the university?" "The Chinese and Confucian understandings of community." Dr. Chan replied, "But there is no word in Chinese for 'community.'"

His somewhat casual response could have torpedoed my study project, and I could have packed up and returned to San Francisco! But perhaps the Holy Spirit was at work in our little conversation. I mustered enough sense to ask Dr. Chan, "But what about in the Chinese version of the New Testament? How is 'koinonia' translated?" "Oh, that is *tuen kai*," he responded in Cantonese. (In Mandarin it is *tuan qi*.)

Dr. Chan graciously invited me into his office to explain how recent translations of the New Testament from Greek into Chinese now use the words *tuen* and *kai* in combination to connote *koinonia*. To capture the richness of the New Testament sense of community the Chinese borrowed terms from Chinese understandings of family and community. These terms carry no sentimental sense of camaraderie and unity of like-minded agreeable folks who choose and create their own "fellowship," as is often the case in North American churches. (In *Life Together* Bonhoeffer criticized such communities as idealistic human creations.)[24] *Tuen* means solidarity; *kai* means responsibility. Indeed the Confucian sense of family is that this communal unit is bonded together. But the bond is not by choice—we do not choose our parents or siblings, we are simply family and always will be—family is a "given." Were we to disagree or fail to get along, or even if one of us is a horse thief (or a heretic), we continue to be related to each other and continue to be in solidarity. And as family, we are responsible to each other and for each other.

Solidarity and responsibility! What a fine rendering of the biblical concept of *koinonia!*

[24] Bonhoeffer, *Life Together,* 31–9.

# "But Who Do You Say That I Am?" (Matt 16:15): A Churched Korean American Woman's Autobiographical Inquiry[1]

*Jung Ha Kim*

> Theology is autobiographical, but is not an autobiography. . . . Theology is certainly autobiographical, because I alone can tell my faith story. . . . If theology is contextual, it must certainly be at root autobiographical.
>
> —Jung Young Lee, *Marginality: The Key to Multicultural Theology*, 7.

> I have come to believe that theologians, in their attempt to talk to and about religious communities, ought to give readers some sense of their autobiographies. This can help an audience discern what leads the theologian to do the kind of theology she does. What has been the character of her faith journey? What lessons has this journey taught? What kind of faith inspires her to continue writing and rewriting, living and reliving theology in a highly secular white-and-black world paying little or no attention to what theologians are saying?
>
> —Delores S. Williams,
> *Sisters in the Wilderness: The Challenge of Womanist God-Talk*, ix.

For a large number of people worldwide, notions of origin, nationality, residence, and home may shift several times over the course of a

---

[1] I would like to dedicate these autobiographical reflections to the memory of Professor Jung Young Lee, who walked his life as a churched Korean American and who taught me lessons of intergenerational respect and collaboration.

103

lifetime. And those who have had to come to terms with moving and re-settling as ongoing experiences of life are convinced that self-identity is a matter of politics rather than inheritance. Their autobiographical accounts would bear witness to understanding and experiencing self-identities that are simultaneously both personal and global. "Origins are never quite what they seem, never quite offer the foundational stability and identity that is desired, and are never quite as unadulterated or unmediated as the historicism of the 'once upon a time' would have us believe."[2] As an expatriate Puerto Rican writer puts it, identity is determined not so much by "where are you from?" as "where are you between?"[3] This between-ness can be documented by delineating a set of postmodern characteristics, such as a dramatic increase of people's mobility on the global scale (as in forms of migration, emigration, traveling, etc.) via advanced means of transportation; surreal encounters of different peoples and cultures through the relentless innovation of communication technology; and a robust production of surplus people thanks to the globalizing (late-capitalist) market economy. It is not an exaggeration to say that by virtue of being alive at this particular juncture in human history, each and every one of us occupies multiple and complex social locations where boundaries and identities become increasingly uncertain, displaced, and fused into one another.

Given the global impacts of post-modernism and late capitalism, a set of selected social categorizations and memories became salient and instrumental for my entry into the increasingly contested discourse on the politics of identity. And since it is now a truism that a person's identity is socially constructed and situationally contingent upon the political agendas of the present, the first section of this paper will be devoted to discussing how I (and other Asian Americans and women of color in general) struggle to grapple with the displacement, uncertainties, and fusions in the context of living in the late-twentieth-century United States. In the second section of the paper, selected ancestral resources of my life/identity will be shared as a way to illustrate how an auto-biographical account is inherently and inevitably fused and juxtaposed with biographies and memories of others who have influenced my everyday life. Indeed, an autobiographical account is a testimony to how deeply human life is grounded in and through relationships with others. By sharing this autobiography I attempt to reiterate both the

---

[2] Shelley Sunn Wong, "Unnaming the Same: Theresa Hak Kyung Cha's *Dictee,*" *Writing Self, Writing Nation,* ed. Elaine H. Kim and Norma Alarcon (Berkeley, Calif.: Third Woman Press, 1994) 126.

[3] Luis Rafael Sanchez, "The Airbus," *Village Voice* 39–43 (1984) 41.

need and importance of doing theology that is inherently autobiographical in nature on the one hand, and, on the other hand, to disclose various contours of the (Western) cult of mutually exclusive autonomy that is embedded in the field of theology.

## I Am a Churched Korean American Woman

I often find myself in a peculiar cultural milieu in which people's chances and life stories are largely determined by various configurations of racial, ethnic, class, gender, and religious identities in the United States. Certainly, I am much more/beyond/other than a combination of these contingencies and constructs. As long as a peculiar cultural milieu is not seen to pop up from a vacuum, I would like to give an autobiographical account by utilizing these historically constructed variables. More specifically, since I have already highlighted venerable constructs such as race, ethnicity, gender, and nationality for articulating my self-understanding in some of my previous works,[4] I would like to weave my autobiography centering on my spiritual journey. Not that different components of my identity can be neatly compartmentalized into mutually exclusive dimensions and categorizations, as they are analytically distinctive, but for heuristic purposes all interlocking parts of my lived experiences can be consciously remembered by focusing on one or more aspects.

I am more churched than Christianized. Christianity, as name of a religion, carries various connotations that are historically rooted as well as "dangerous memories" that are engraved in different people's souls. Having been born into a "typical" Korean family whose spirituality most often than not drew no clear boundaries between "popular" and "organized" religions, I learned early on what I needed to know about Christianity: that a religion for worshiping a Western god has no business being in Korea. My paternal grandmother who raised me in the Buddhist temple had said so; and I had no reason to question how she freely adapted a religion from India and China as her own and mix-matched it with other practices of indigenous Korean spirituality. Her devotions

---

[4] See Jung Ha Kim, "Ancient Sources Outside the West: 'Accidental Tourists' and Matchmakers of Spiritual Marriage," *Spirituality and the Secular Quest*, ed. Peter Van Ness (New York: Crossroad, 1996) 53–71; Jung Ha Kim, "A Voice From the 'Borderland': Asian American Women and Their Families," *Religion, Feminism and the Family*, ed. Ann Carr and Mary Stewart van Leeuwen (Louisville, Ky.: Westminster/John Knox Press, 1996) 343–57; and Jung Ha Kim, "The Impact of National Histories on the Politics of Identity," *Journal of Asian and Asian American Theology* 1:2 (1997) 113–8.

were sincere and her spiritual journey needed no formal explanations using Western rationality. Notions such as superstition, syncretism, and shamanism did not have much influence, if any, on her experiencing a holistic life that was deeply spiritual.

When my parents took me to Japan to live with them, I became exposed to at least three different religious sites and sets of practice simultaneously. On the one hand, I was drawn to Japanese temples of Buddhism and Shintoism; on the other hand, I became increasingly curious about a small Christian (Protestant) church located on the outskirts of a market. With the pointed cross erected on the horizon, the presence of that church sent out an aura that was exotic and un-Japanese at the same time. Though my parents sent me to an all-Japanese school with a newly assigned pseudo-Japanese last name, my daily experiences at school and at home did not save me from highly fluctuating anxieties and contradictions between my desire to fully fit in and my reluctance to erase the memories and habits that made me feel different and foreign. Hence I patronized all three places of devotion—the Buddhist temple, the Shinto shrine, and the Christian church—by taking much needed refuge and solace anywhere I could find them.

What I remember distinctly about these three sites was not so much that they belong to three different religions (most Japanese are both Shinto and Buddhist at the same time) but that physical activities that I experienced as a form of devotion at the church seemed far less strenuous and demanding than what I remembered as forms of devotion at the Korean Buddhist Temple: no early morning veneration of lighting candles for a hundred consecutive days and no bowing down low before a statue of the Buddha for three, thirty, fifty, and a hundred times were required. Adherents of the church just sat still for an hour with a minor variation of standing up and sitting down to sing one or two hymns and a prayer in between. At times, I had to stop by the Zen Buddhist temple on the way back from the church, just to ensure that God/the Lord/the Spirit/the Master/the Buddha had seen and heard my devotional sincerity. Neither did I feel anything inherently contradictory about performing religious rituals at all three places, nor do I remember anyone making an issue of my multireligious practices. From time to time, my home-bound younger sister, struck by polio, commented on my insistence of going to designated religious places/buildings. "Why can't you stay home and pray? Do you not think that the Spirit can hear prayers if you pray at home?"

While I made myself busy hopping from one religious service to another, which made me feel more or less a Japanese, a Korean, none-of-the-above, and sometimes all at the same time, my parents made a decision for the whole family to immigrate to the United States. We arrived in New York City when I was thirteen. There was no invitation of any kind for the family from the United States. There were no relatives or friends waiting for us at the airport to introduce life in "America." (Un-)Fortunately, I have no recollection of the first thirty-some hours of resettlement of the family in the new "homeland." I had such a strong combination of severe airsickness and a stomach virus while crossing the Pacific Ocean that I had to be literally carried out on a stretcher by the medical staff. When I opened my eyes, I was on my parents' bed and my new life had already begun on this side of the Pacific. In retrospect, at least these two memories became poignant and instrumental for understanding and naming the process of my being a 1.5 generation Korean American living in the States: that I personally did not make the decision to come to America; and that my first crossing of the Pacific Ocean was more surreal than real, for it literally took place while I was sub-/unconscious.

Once the family had crammed into an apartment, each and every one of us, alone and together, had to learn to swim in the gigantic pool that was the so-called American melting pot. Kids were sent to public schools within walking distance with their only grammatically correct English sentence, "I cannot speak English," and parents were off to long hours of physical labor for the first time in their occupational history. And of course being "religious" as I was/am, I eventually ventured into the only Korean Christian church in the area which happened to be a twenty-minute walking distance from my new home in America.

To be honest, I have no clear recollection why I started to attend the church rather than look for a Buddhist temple. Perhaps I was searching for a religion in a new place or a community of people with whom I could feel a sense of belonging or maybe both. I just remember how ecstatic I was to find a sign that says the Christian church in Korean—"Kyo-whe"—posted on a church wall. Even after my "discovery" of the Korean church in Queens, New York, it took me another two months to actually walk into the building. The first several months of my new life in America took place without my parents' close guidance and a set of clear cultural norms that can be taken for granted. I clearly remember a keen sense of the helplessness of constantly being uprooted. Once I walked into the church, however, a whole different world of all-Korean and of all-too-familiar aura of kim-chee was waiting for me. I felt comforted and reassured that a community outside of my own family was also going through what I had been going through. People at the church seemed strangely very "Korean" in America. I was no longer alone. I started to attend Sunday worship services regularly. I also enthusiastically participated in Wednesday Bible Study sessions, Sunday early morning prayer meetings, Sunday Bible Study classes, youth group activities, and volunteered for clerical assistance at the church on weekends. I needed all the religion I could get. My life in America pushed me to rely more desperately on the omnipotent and omnipresent power beyond all human and realistic possibilities. And I brought my younger sister, younger brother, mother, and father, in that order, into the church over a period of two years. My whole family has been churched since and that is how I became a Christian.

## I Am a Spiritual Person Who Believes in the Resurrection

My religious identity as a whole makes little sense without reclaiming life sources from my ancestors, especially my paternal grandmother. I remember her as a devout Buddhist and, later on, as a sincere Christian. She was the one who taught me the ever fluid and complex nature of human life and how to allow and anticipate changes in life for both myself and others. She also demonstrated a viable way to live life as a woman in her own historical context. For these and other reasons I light candles and offer food and drink in memory of her as a small token of my deeply felt love and gratitude for her presence in my life. I do not perceive and experience these acts of libation and seeking guidance and strength from her (and from other ancestors) as a form of worship. For my own life testifies that ancestors are more than mere memories of the dead and that there exist clear links between and among the past, the present, and the future. But I am getting ahead of myself here. Allow me to briefly share how understanding my paternal grandmother's biography gave way to understanding my own autobiography.

My grandmother was born in 1911, the year of the pig, under the Japanese colonization of the Korean peninsula. Three months after her first menstruation, she was married off to my grandfather. She did not lay eyes on her husband-to-be until their wedding night. Two years after their marriage, at the age of nineteen, she gave birth to her only child, my father. As the (first) wife of one of the most successful businessmen in town, who also bore a son to pass down the family heritage, she was a proud, no-nonsense, straightforward mistress of the influential household which provided daily staples and shelter for more than fifty people in town. Despite her social status, hardly anyone remembers her as a woman of smiles or hearty laughter. My grandfather had many "other wives" (i.e., concubines) who lived all over the town, and my grandmother was forced to accept and endure much of her unspoken pain as the high price she had to pay for her family's social status.

She is also a member of the particular generation who lived through all the national tragedies and crises in Korea: the Japanese annexation of Korea for thirty-six years, national independence, the Korean War, the division of Korea, the April 19 Student Uprising, the May 16 Military Coup, military dictatorship for nearly four decades, the Kwangju massacre, and the nation's election of its first civilian president. I cannot even imagine what she must have had to go through just to survive in her own homeland. What I know with some clarity is that she had lost her only son [my father went to Japan before the war broke out] and the rest of the family migrated from North Korea to Seoul during the Korean War. She did not know whether her son was alive until three years after the Korean War had ended.

With the baggage of pain that was both personal and national, she turned to religion. She went to the nearby Buddhist temple, offered food and prayers to household gods, performed rituals according to the shamans' advice and warnings, and sought out famous fortune tellers to discern her son's whereabouts. Ghosts and gods took pity on her; and my father returned to South Korea to carry out duties and responsibilities as the eldest and only son. He married my mother, and I was born exactly a year after their wedding. Thirty days after my birth, however, my grandfather died, and after elaborate funeral services that lasted forty-nine days, my grandmother took me with her into the Buddhist temple. And that is how I remember her as a devout Buddhist who took me under the care of compassionate Kwan-in (a feminine manifestation of the Buddha) and the community of Buddhist nuns.

After I left her to join my parents in Japan, I did not get to see her until she came to the States to live with us. I was already in college. And one summer day when I went back to my parents' house to spend a few weeks of my summer vacation, she taught me a lesson I would not forget. I heard her chanting a familiar Buddhist tune when I passed by her room. I stopped and listened. She was singing/chanting the Christian Lord's Prayer to a Buddhist tune! With a keen sense of confusion and uneasiness, I opened the door and interrupted her. She was trying to memorize the Lord's Prayer, she told me. "I need to know at least a few basic prayers and songs before I go to church with rest of the family. Don't you agree?"

"But you are a Buddhist; at least that's what I thought you are. Why would you want to go to a Christian church? Did any one of the family ask or force you to go to church with them?" I do not remember clearly how many questions I asked and how many of my questions were indebted to the Western conceptualization of reality based on the mutually exclusive "either/or." My grandmother did not deny that she was a Buddhist, but she also told me that she had come to live in a new country to be reunited with her family.

"When you start a new life in a new place, you need to learn to respect the ways of life of that place. I am now in America, and Christianity is an American religion. [Therefore] I would like to go to the Christian church with the rest of the family on Sundays. I do not want to stay home by myself, even on Sunday. Now, would you please help me memorize the other prayers that I need to know?" And that is how she started to attend church and became a Christian. Even after her return to Seoul, I was told that she would faithfully attend Sunday services at a local Christian church until she died in 1996.

There are many unanswered questions that still linger in my mind: about her understanding of religion in general and of Christianity in particular; how she made almost intuitive assumptions about life; how she dealt with being constantly uprooted and resettled; reasons and forces that pushed her to turn to various religions/spiritualities; her understanding of the family and of being a woman; and her opinions about Japan, the United States, and the division of Korea. I did not ask these questions partly because I knew I had neglected her wishes for me to live with her, but mostly because I knew that these questions bore no particular importance to her but rather to me. She faced head-on whatever life opened up for her and lived fully according to her ways and means of survival. If I had forced her to answer these questions or to name herself as a Buddhist or a Christian, a Korean or a Korean American, she would have resisted, I am sure. For her, a self-understanding is not so much a matter of how or what to name one's self, but how one experiences life. And since none of us really know what courses our lives will still take, none can articulate or impose a constant and stable self-identity until we die. And even after our death, different people will remember and resurrect selected memories about us based on their own political agendas at a particular time.

## Some Theological Implications

I am aware of the hermeneutical arguments against putting too much emphasis on autobiography in academia. To quote an eminent scholar:

> Self-reflection and autobiography are not primary and are therefore not an adequate basis for the hermeneutical problem, because through them history is made private once more. In fact history does not belong to us; we belong to it. . . . The focus of subjectivity is a distorting mirror. The self-awareness of the individual is only a flickering in the closed circuits of historical life.[5]

---

[5] Hans-Georg Gadamer, *Truth and Method,* 2d rev. ed., trans. Joel Weinscheimer and Donald G. Marshall (New York: Crossroad, 1990) 276–7.

Just as exclusive claims of the so-called universal truth and epistemologies based on Enlightenment rationality had to undergo a crisis of legitimacy in the post-colonialism era, an articulation of unexamined "Western"[6] assumptions about autobiography is in order. To a person or community in need of recovering a sense of subjectivity due mainly to historical erasure, invisibility, and constant misrepresentation, self-reflections and autobiographies are viable means of reclaiming wholeness, rather than producing privacy. To a people or culture that resists drawing clear boundaries between the dead and the living, the past and the present, self-reflections and biographies reveal stories of people, rather than of an autonomous self.

Furthermore, in order to reassess the forces that are already established as the only viable references and as legitimizers for constructing realities for everyone, un- and under-represented people have to learn to take their own autobiographies and the stories of their own communities seriously. For no social being is an isolated island; and no autobiography is completely divorced from other biographies. Indeed, human identities are grounded in and through relationships with others. To borrow an African scholar's words, people "must cease to go along with the notion that the West alone can define whose and what thought qualifies as philosophical, whose belief is worthy of the term religion, and whose way of life can be deemed as developed, advanced or civilized."[7] Thus, though the cult of an autonomous self is rather pervasive and rampant in the United States, I would argue that my autobiographical account offered here is both personal (mine) and communal (ours) at the same time. They point to a complex overlapping and intertwining of an autobiographical account of my becoming who I am and the community's struggle to form itself as a member of a multicultural and multireligious society under a tremendous pressure to melt into the dominant group.

As more and more people and communities reflect upon themselves and (re-)claim the importance of autobiographies, theologians will have to face pressing questions and challenges to reflect upon what it

---

[6] The word "West" and "Western" are used mainly to refer to a historical construction made by both Enlightenment and post-Enlightenment rationality. Recognizing both the complexities and contradictions of the term "the West," Chandra T. Mohanty nevertheless defines it as "various textual strategies used by particular writers that codify Others as non-Western and hence themselves as (implicitly) Western." See her "Under Western Eyes: Feminist Scholarship and Colonial Discourse," *Boundary* 2:12 (1984) 59–67.

[7] Elleni Tadla, *Sankoma: African Thought and Education* (New York: Peter Lang, 1996) 218.

means to do theology on the basis of people's lived experiences. Depending on what is at stake and for whom, a churched Korean American woman like myself in particular and other Asian-American Christians in general are pressed to struggle with further questions. What concepts and categories enable us to faithfully articulate our lived experiences and spiritual journeys? Which of the so-called main- and male-line Christian doctrines, which interpretations of the Bible and of rituals need to be dismantled and/or reconstructed in efforts to take seriously our own communal struggles and issues? What makes a person or people Christian? What "dangerous memories" are worth remembering in doing theology?

As I alluded in the introduction, I raise these questions as a way to reiterate the importance of doing theology that is inherently autobiographical. For only through a critical assessment of autobiographies does one learn to remember life sources that are deeply rooted in the stories of one's ancestors and the legacies of one's community. And it is through the political act of remembering in the midst of relentless cultural amnesia and the cult of autonomous self that our eyes may be opened to identify "new tools that are actually passed down from our ancestors and communities for ages." For

> survival . . . is not an academic skill. . . . It is learning how to take our differences and make them strength. For the master's tools will never dismantle the master's house. They will allow us temporarily to beat him at his own game, but they will never enable us to bring about genuine change.[8]

---

[8] Audre Lorde, "The Master's Tools Will Never Dismantle the Master's House," *Sister Outsider: Essays and Speeches* (Freedom, Calif.: The Crossing Press, 1984) 112.

# Betwixt and Between: Doing Theology with Memory and Imagination

*Peter C. Phan*

To be betwixt and between is to be neither here nor there, to be neither this thing nor that. Spatially, it is to dwell at the periphery or at the boundaries. Politically, it means not residing at the centers of power of the two intersecting worlds but occupying the precarious and narrow margins where the two dominant groups meet and clash, and denied the opportunity to wield power in matters of public interest. Socially, to be betwixt and between is to be part of a minority, a member of a marginal(ized) group. Culturally, it means not being fully integrated into and accepted by either cultural system, being a *mestizo*, a person of mixed race. Linguistically, the betwixt-and-between person is bilingual but may not achieve a mastery of both languages and often speaks them with a distinct accent. Psychologically and spiritually, the person does not possess a well-defined and secure self-identity and is often marked with excessive impressionableness, rootlessness, and an inordinate desire for belonging.

However, to be betwixt and between does not bring total disadvantage and negativity in its wake, as past psychological and sociological studies seem to have suggested. Paradoxically, being neither this nor that allows one to be *both* this and that. Belonging to both worlds and cultures, marginal(ized) persons have the opportunity to fuse them together and, out of their respective resources, fashion a new, different world, so that persons at the margins stand not only between these two worlds and cultures but also *beyond* them. Thus being betwixt and between can bring about personal and societal transformation and enrichment.[1]

---

[1] For this understanding of marginality, see Jung Young Lee, *Marginality: The Key to Multicultural Theology* (Minneapolis: Fortress Press, 1995) 29–76. For an

113

Doing theology betwixt and between is thinking religiously from both sides of the boundaries. Theology on the boundaries, whose horizon is the "global village," is by its nature an intercultural theology. Such a theology is predicated on the conviction that no culture is totally devoid of divine presence since God has truly and really communicated God's self to all peoples in truth and love, in Word and Spirit, at least in the form of a genuine offer.[2] Hence, there is the need of developing a theological method that can take into account expressions of God's message that are different from those that have grown out of one's own philosophical, religious, political, and ethical traditions. Such a theological approach will remove the dangers of prejudice, racism, colonialism, and ethnocentrism on the one hand, and inferiority complex and loss of cultural identity on the other. Intercultural theology does not dispense with the methods of rational sciences and their analytical tools that the West has developed. However, such research methods and scientific models cannot be regarded as exclusively and universally normative but must be enriched by alternative forms of acquiring knowledge.[3]

Put differently, theology betwixt and between is theology done with both memory and imagination; it is contemplating the past and creating the future at the same time. Memory anchors the theologian in the ocean of history and tradition, the Church's and one's own; but the stability and security it affords is impermanent and illusory. Remembering is not reproducing reality exactly as it happened (Leopold von Ranke's *"wie es eigentlich gewesen"*) but re-*creating* it imaginatively; it is re-*membering* disparate fragments of the past together and forming them into a new pattern under the pressure of present experiences, with a view to shaping a possible future. Like powerful undercurrents, the imagination thrusts the theologian into a new world or at least a different way of being in the world. It empowers the theologian to break out of the limits of the past and bring human potentialities to full flourishing. Like a pair of wings, memory and imagination carry the theologian aloft in the

---

evaluation of this work, see the review by Peter C. Phan in *Dialogue & Alliance* 11:1 (1997) 146–9.

[2] This ontological self-offer of God in human history has been described by German theologian Karl Rahner as the "supernatural existential." For a brief explanation of this concept, see Peter C. Phan, *Eternity in Time: A Study of Karl Rahner's Eschatology* (Selinsgrove, Pa.: Susquehanna University Press, 1988) 59.

[3] For reflections on intercultural theology, see, for example, Robert J. Schreiter, *The New Catholicity: Theology between the Global and the Local* (Maryknoll, N.Y.: Orbis Books, 1997); Stephen Bevans, *Models of Contextual Theology* (Maryknoll, N.Y.: Orbis Books, 1992); and Kosuke Koyama, *Buffalo Theology* (Maryknoll, N.Y.: Orbis Books, 1976).

work of linking past and future, east and west, north and south, earth and heaven. Both memory and imagination in their mutual interaction are indispensable tools for theology. Without memory, theology would be empty; without imagination, it would be blind. They are the epistemological equivalents of *yin* and *yang,* ever in movement, ever transmuting into each other, ever complementing each other, to capture reality in its wholeness.[4]

## At the Margins: Poised Between East and West

One of the many lessons life has taught me is that very few momentous and decisive things which shape one's destiny are within one's planning and control. One's birth, genetic makeup, race and ethnicity, family connections, language, culture, and even religious affiliation are basically inherited or are the result of the fortuitous confluence of unpredictable and uncontrollable factors. They are, to use Heideggerian language, the "world" into which we are "thrown."[5]

In my case, a theological career was not something I would have chosen.[6] Like most of my classmates, I undertook theological studies primarily because they were a requisite of the preparation for my ministerial "vocation," which in turn was something thrust upon me. Some are born theologians; others strive to become one; still others, among them myself, have theology thrust upon them. When I left Rome in July 1972 after my four-year theological study, I thought I had closed the

---

[4] For attempts at doing theology with imagination, see Choan-Seng Song, *Third-Eye Theology: Theology in Formation in Asian Settings,* rev. ed. (Maryknoll, N.Y.: Orbis Books, 1990), and Choan-Seng Song, *Theology from the Womb of Asia* (Maryknoll, N.Y.: Orbis Books, 1986).

[5] See Martin Heidegger, *Being and Time,* trans. John Macquarrie and Edward Robinson (New York: Harper & Row, 1962) 135–48.

[6] Perhaps it is appropriate to explain here how a Vietnamese like myself bears the Western-sounding name of Peter. Actually, my original Vietnamese name is Phan Dinh Cho. Phan is the family name, which is placed first. Dinh is the middle name, often used to indicate maleness. Cho is my first and own name, which is always placed last and often bears a meaning, in this case, to give. Vietnamese parents always give their child a name with a meaning, hoping that it will be the distinguishing mark of his or her life. In Vietnam, a person is always referred to by his or her first name, whether a friend or not. At their baptism Catholics are given, in addition to these names, the name of a patron saint (Peter). When I came to America, I took my patron saint name as my first name, used my name Cho as the middle name, and placed my family name last, according to the Western usage.

pages of theological tomes for good. If academic achievements during my undergraduate days were any indication, a teaching career in classical and modern languages or in philosophy would be more in line with my tastes and abilities.

My destiny as an accidental theologian was preceded (though not necessarily prepared) by a series of events quite beyond my control. In retrospect, one could say that the hand of Divine Providence was guiding my life, but that is a faith statement I would be willing to wager only in fits of piety and not one susceptible of rational verification. In another respect, even those early events foreshadowed my later betwixt-and-between status. Unlike most Vietnamese of my age, I was given a French education, something that was, to use an anachronistic expression, politically incorrect in the late fifties, in the aftermath of Vietnam's independence from France. While the government was promoting the Vietnamese educational system as a means to remove its colonial past, I was among a very small minority sent to study at the few surviving *collèges* that were still allowed to function after the country's declaration of national independence in 1954. There I not only had to use French as my mother tongue, but also to study French literature, history, geography, art, and way of life. Textbooks were the very same ones approved by the French Department of Education and used throughout France and its colonies. I memorized the names of all of France's kings and queens, military victories and defeats, rivers and mountains and valleys that every French schoolchild must know. My native tongue was only the second "foreign language" in the curriculum, after English. It was even taught in French! In the examinations we had to translate Vietnamese texts into French and comment on them in French as proof of our comprehension.

I was trained to think and behave like a French boy and to live, vicariously, in my adopted fatherland *(patrie)*. I climbed the Alps and the Pyrenees, cruised on the Seine and the Loire, toured Notre Dame de Paris and Chartres, admired Gothic architecture, ate escargots and drank Bordeaux, dressed in thick woollens, basked in the glory of Louis XIV's the *Roi Soleil,* sang La Marseillaise, celebrated Napoleon's military conquests, and even recited French prayers. All this, of course, without ever setting foot outside the flat land of Saigon, during monsoons and in wilting heat, in the company of snub-nosed, yellow-skinned people who did not even know what snow looks like, let alone savoring buttered snails and vintage wine! Dead French heroes were more real to me than my own living Vietnamese compatriots.

Meanwhile I learned nothing of Vietnam's history and geography and literature and art. Ancestors that gave birth to our nation were nameless ghosts to me; heroes that died to save my country from the

Chinese and the French were total strangers; I could not name the mountains and the rivers and the valleys that were home for me and my people for millennia; and I could not recite any of the poems that from time immemorial nourished the souls and spirits of the Vietnamese people. Worse, I was subtly brainwashed to look upon anything Vietnamese as uncouth and barbarian. I was betwixt and between two cultures and worlds, belonging to neither and yet somehow being part of both.

This bleaching out of my own culture and mimicry of anything Gallic was so successful that I could take the *Brevet* examinations three years before the legal age. My father had to procure a birth certificate that changed my year of birth from 1946 to 1943 so that I would be old enough to sit for the examinations. The only blight of this second birth of mine, which my father did not foresee, was that it made my mother pregnant with me before her marriage, which was a source of great scandal to my religious superiors when they noticed it. Since my coming to the United States, however, the stigma of my out of wedlock birth has been amply made up by a double birthday celebration every year and the prospect of early retirement!

My philosophical studies distanced me further from my cultural roots. From 1962 to 1965, at Don Bosco College in Hong Kong, I followed a course of neo-scholastic philosophy. Textbooks were in Latin, lectures delivered in Latin, and students required to speak Latin in the examinations. I do not remember whether I understood much of philosophy at the time, but I do recall that I was absolutely certain, on the basis of the truths we were taught, that Descartes, Leibniz, Locke, Hume, Kant, and Hegel, and of course, Nietzsche and Marx, were all dead wrong. Ironically, even while we were living in Hong Kong, with the Chinese people all around us, we were not introduced to the writings of any Chinese philosopher nor were we given the opportunity to learn Chinese. Eastern philosophies and cultures were not deemed worthy of study because they were judged not to contain any truth which would not have already been known through Christian revelation.

Once again, I was poised between two worlds, East and West, even as Hong Kong itself was a symbol of this cultural schizophrenia, then a British colony at the very gate of China. At any rate, however inadequate my philosophical preparation was, the faculty were sufficiently impressed with my academic performance, so that after my graduation, at the age of eighteen, I was appointed to teach philosophy to first-year students. To my dying day I must apologize to them for teaching them the "truths" with such certainty and self-assurance as only an unfortunate combination of blissful ignorance and innocent youth could muster.

My theological studies in Rome from 1968 until 1972 placed me again, in more ways than one, at the margins of two worlds. For the first time in my life I came into contact with the world I had known only through books. There was, of course, an initial stage of adjustment to the Italian, or more precisely, Roman way of life. Happily, I did not suffer any severe cultural shock, though there were moments of loneliness, especially during the Christmas and Easter holidays, when most of us Asian students could not go home to our families and had to remain on the deserted campus by ourselves. Moreover, student life at the international Salesian Pontifical University was closely regulated. Life was centered on academic studies and there was little room for extracurricular activities, such as going to museums or visiting sites of historical interest.

In one respect, however, studying theology in Rome in the late sixties was a unique and exciting experience of living at the boundaries, scarcely imaginable to those born after the 1960s. The Second Vatican Council, the most important event in the last four hundred years of the Catholic Church's history, had just concluded in 1965 and had set the Church on an unchartered and tumultuous journey into a new era. The fresh air of reform that Pope John XXIII wanted to let into the dusty and moldy church turned out to be a tornado of convulsive changes threatening to blow it apart. The council was literally a watershed event; beliefs and practices in the Catholic Church could be dated as pre-Vatican II or post-Vatican II.

During the four years of theological studies, I was again placed between two worlds and epochs: between the pre-conciliar and the postconciliar, between the conservative and the liberal, between the old and the new, between the right and the left. For one thing, classes were no longer conducted in Latin but in Italian and clerical garbs were discarded in favor of civilian clothes, but this linguistic and sartorial mutation is but a symptom of the sea changes then taking place in the Church. Every facet of Church life was subjected to revision and renewal: liturgy and sacramental celebrations, hierarchy and laity, religious life, ecumenical unity, dialogue with non-Christian religions, relationship between the Church and the modern world, ethical norms, biblical studies, and theological education.

Of course, during the brief interval between the council and my arrival in Rome these momentous reforms had not yet come to full fruition. At our university we only saw trickles of them, but what we experienced there gave us a clear and distinct awareness that things in the Church would never be the same again. One small incident may serve as an illustration. In 1970 two of our professors were dismissed from the faculty because of their alleged unorthodoxy. In protest against such measure, a majority of the theology students went on a hunger strike (as president of the second-year class I had voted in favor of the action). Our superiors and professors were stunned since protest, let alone hunger strike, was something utterly unthinkable for people bound by the vow of obedience. Public hearings were held, academic freedom asserted by students, religious obedience reaffirmed by superiors, unrepentant students marked out for dismissal. In retrospect, our hunger strike, which did not last long, was perhaps nothing more than a jejune version of student protests fashionable in those days, and it did not succeed in reinstalling the two dismissed professors. For us, however, it signaled an irreversible transformation insofar as the myth of unquestioned obedience was broken once and for all: religious authorities are not sacred, their orders should not be uncritically accepted, and actions in favor of justice must be taken.

While residence in Europe and theological studies in Rome vastly expanded my intellectual horizon, they removed me further from my own cultural roots. Cultural and religious pluralism was an unknown category in the theological language of the day, at least at our university, and no course was offered in Asian theology and history. I remained as ignorant as ever of Vietnamese and other Asian cultural and religious traditions. Fortunately, one thing seemed to remedy my heavily Roman Catholic and Eurocentric theological education. One of the requirements for the licentiate degree in theology was writing a thesis on a topic of the student's choosing. As I was searching for a theme I gravitated toward the theology of Paul Tillich. I was interested in him because he was a Protestant; studying him would afford me the opportunity to connect the "Catholic substance" with the "Protestant Principle" with which I was until then vaguely familiar. Furthermore, of all contemporary Protestant theologians Tillich appealed to me the most because he made a systematic use of metaphysics and did not follow the *sola scriptura* principle.[7] But most of all, I perceived a sort of intellectual and spiritual kinship between the German theologian and myself because he explicitly described himself as standing "on the boundary line," exploring connections among different worlds through his method of correlation. My thesis investigated Tillich's understanding of Jesus the Christ as the New Being overcoming human estrangement by bridging the gap between what he terms "essence" and "existence."[8]

---

[7] Tillich's work that most influenced me is his *Systematic Theology,* 3 vols. (Chicago: University of Chicago Press, 1967).

[8] See my "Jesus the Christ, the New Being," unpublished S.T.L. thesis, Salesian Pontifical University, Rome, 1972.

## The Aftermaths of War

When I returned to Vietnam in July 1972, the Paris peace talks had been going on for some time; on January 27, 1973, a peace accord was signed. As a result, the American military personnel was gradually withdrawn, and the prosecution of the war against the Communist North Vietnam assigned exclusively to the southern armed forces. After my ordination to the priesthood in August 1972, I was stationed near Saigon (now Ho Chi Minh City); my work consisted mainly in youth ministry, high school teaching, occasional lecturing on philosophy and theology to ministerial students, and chaplaincy to a women's prison and a police academy (what an ironic combination!) on Sundays.

This uneventful life was shattered in April 1975. Despite the peace accord, war between the North and the South went on unabated. In March 1975 the Communist army invaded the South and took over most of the northern and central parts of South Vietnam. Without my knowledge, my parents, who lived in Nha Trang, had abandoned their home and escaped, first by walking some thirty miles and then by way of the sea, to the Phu Quoc island south of Saigon. I had no contact with them until, some weeks later in the middle of April, they showed up one day, empty-handed, at my school. Meanwhile, rumors of the eventual invasion of Saigon and capitulation of the southern government were rampant as waves and waves of soldiers deserted their posts. Pictures of dead adults and children lying abandoned on boats and barges filled the newspapers and television. One man was shown crushed by the wheels of a plane, trying to cling to them, as the plane lifted off. My mother told me that as people jostled to climb from their little boats up the ladder to board the big ships, some of their children dropped into the sea and could not be rescued because of the waves and the darkness of night. Reports of wealthy and powerful people trying to leave the country were also in the air. I even saw the picture of an airplane carrying Vietnamese children, allegedly orphans but possibly children of wealthy families, to the United States that burst into flames after it fell into a field not far from our school.

My parents, my younger brothers and sisters (apart from my older brother and his family, there were eleven of us), and I had no intention of leaving the country. Even if we had, we could never have afforded seats on planes or boats; everything my parents had ever owned—land and houses—had been lost. Only my older brother, who was working for the American consulate, was allowed to leave with his wife and four children. My parents agreed to let three of my younger brothers go with him (should he be permitted to take them along) for fear that the Communists would conscript them after their victory. On Thursday,

April 24, 1975, we said a tearful goodbye to them, hoping that they could leave sometime later, as there was no means of communicating with them after our farewell. On the following Friday and Saturday, every time our family saw a plane in the sky, we said to each other: There they go!

On Saturday night, it was reported that the new president had permitted everyone, except military and police personnel, to leave the country. But by then we no longer had the means to do so, since my older brother had already left. We did not know that due to a shortage of planes, he, his family, and our three younger brothers had not been able to leave and still remained in Saigon. On Sunday morning, as my parents and family were attending Mass, one of my younger brothers who had been with my older brother came to tell them that they must leave immediately and join my older brother at the American Embassy. They stood up, all fourteen of them, right in the middle of the homily, and quietly walked out (the poor priest must have thought that his sermon was the reason for my family's walk-out protest!). Normally on Sundays I would have been inside the women's prison by six o'clock in the morning and there would have been no way of contacting me. For some reason that Sunday I was taking a late breakfast near the church, and one of my sisters spotted me and told me that our family was leaving the country and that my parents wanted me to join them.

While my family was arranging transportation to the American Embassy, I rode my motorcycle back to my school some twenty miles away. Before crossing the bridge where there were beggars I stopped, took out my wallet, and dumped the whole contents into the hands of one of them. Never in my life had I seen eyes sparkle with astonishment and happiness as that beggar's. It was not an act of charity on my part; I simply wanted to get rid of all my money because I knew it would soon be useless. At my office I took a quick look at all my possessions (among which there was a copy of my dissertation on Tillich!), decided to take nothing with me, walked up the four flights of stairs to my room, took a change of clothes, said goodbye to my friends, and was driven to the American Embassy.

At the embassy my family started filling out papers for departure. There was, however, a problem. Only my older brother and his family were on the list of those allowed to leave the embassy for the airport; eleven of us were not. At the last minute, miraculously (providentially?), my older brother could add our names to the list because our uncle, whose last name was also Phan, and his family of eleven could not come to the embassy as planned because his wife fell and broke her leg as she boarded the bus that morning. My older brother, still working for the consulate, crossed out their names and substituted them with ours. Thanks to this clever maneuver, all of us could get on the bus and left for the airport around noon. Only then did I see total chaos in the streets; rivers and rivers of people with huge mountains of luggage were attempting to get to the airport too.

At the airport we began filling out forms to board the plane. More complications arose. Our eleven names, which had been substituted for those of our uncle and his family, did not match with those on the list which the American official at the airport had. Explanations and protestations were useless; only my older brother and his family were allowed to leave. Once again, we said a tearful goodbye to them and stayed behind. Only then were we seized with terror, for with our older brother, who had connections with the American embassy, gone and with no possibility of going back, eleven of us were stranded at the airport with no money, food, or shelter. In the meantime we made friends with a young official-looking American man. He assured us that those who were already in the airport would be able to leave sooner or later. Our fear was abated, but not by much. Strangely, the fact that there were hundreds of people stranded like we were kept our hope up. Strangely too, with nothing to eat and drink the whole day, and standing in the scorching sun for hours, most of us felt neither hunger nor thirst. We just wandered around, and waited and waited. Happily, at about seven o'clock in the evening, we were told to get in line and board the plane.

It was a military plane. All the seats had been removed to accommodate as many people as possible, and passengers were told to sit on the floor. Two soldiers, armed to the teeth, stood at the doors, holding machine guns pointed outward. The plane jerked violently and lifted off. As the plane made a few circles around the city, I could see, through its doors, gathering darkness below, tiny houses with their flickering lights, streams of cars moving like ants, and long rivers snaking their ways among the villages and fields. We did not know what our destination was. There were no flight attendants we could ask. None of us, I suspect, thought that this was a journey without return, a permanent farewell to our country and home; otherwise, we would not have had the courage to board the plane. Deep in our hearts, we hoped that it was just a temporary trip to avoid casualties. The deafening roar of the engine prevented us from talking. We sat there in silence, lost in our private thoughts. There was a sense of relief in that finally we could leave the airport, but there were no signs of joy and celebration. Seared indelibly in my memory was the image of my father squatting, his head cradled between his hands, praying silently. My mother had the rosary beads in her hands, the source of her consolation and strength throughout her life.

## A Refugee in the United States

After what seemed an eternity our plane landed and we were told that we were on the island of Guam. We were taken to a huge, well-lit hangar. Lo and behold, there, among hundreds of fellow refugees, my older brother and his family were waiting for us. How they knew that we would be able to fly out, how long they had been watching out for us, and how we could spot each other out from among the huge crowd was a mystery. We were given a tent to settle in, all eighteen of us. The marines were putting up tents around the clock to accommodate endless streams of refugees that kept pouring in. Everyday, early in the morning, we queued up for food. It usually took about three hours to reach the food stands; so right after breakfast, we would stand again in line for lunch; and after lunch, for supper. In a way, this all-day standing in line was a blessing since it afforded us a chance to meet newcomers and learn from them the latest developments in Vietnam. I remember as clearly as yesterday that on April 30, when it was announced on the public address system that the government of South Vietnam had capitulated to the North, and as the national anthem was being played, people, young and old, men and women, especially soldiers, shamelessly broke into loud weeping. Prayers were said and songs sung for Vietnam. It was then that I clearly realized for the first time that a new page had been definitively turned in my life and that I would never be able to call my country home again.

The following Sunday before daybreak our family and others were ordered, with no advance warning, to leave the tent and board the bus for the airport. This time it was a large and comfortable commercial plane. No one told us where we were going. During the flight, when the stewardesses asked us if we wanted food, at first we politely said no because we thought we had to pay for it and we had no money. After a stopover in Honolulu we arrived at our final destination, which we later found out to be San Diego, California. We were taken to the Marine Corps Camp at Pendleton. Each of us was given a huge army coat, the same size for all. I recall watching with amusement my youngest sister, then six years old, wrapped in one of them and trailing it on the ground, like a cope-wearing bishop in a procession, as she walked around the camp. Once again, our family was given a tent with eighteen cots to settle in. At night it sometimes was so cold that we had to wear every piece of clothing we had to bed to keep ourselves warm.

Life at Pendleton was more orderly and better organized than in Guam. The line for food was much shorter, and there were all sorts of recreational activities. Unfortunately, together with calm and order, the psychic numbing of the first days of exile began to wear off. People came to realize the enormity of what had happened to them and were seized with homesickness and anxiety about their uncertain future. Meanwhile, refugees kept coming day after day, so that by the end of May there were some ten thousand people in the camp.

The American Catholic chaplains asked me to head the group of Vietnamese priests to respond to the religious needs of the refugees. It was in this capacity that I witnessed immense pain and suffering. One day I was summoned to help a young woman who had literally gone berserk and attempted to chop herself to death. She had lost her husband whom she married just a few weeks before the fall of Saigon. Another time I was roused out of my cot after midnight by a marine and driven to the camp's hospital because a mother refused to let the doctor take care of her newborn baby. The tiny girl had high fever, and the doctor attempted to lower the temperature by placing her in a basin of cold water. The mother, who did not know any English, was convinced that the doctor was killing her baby, and kept howling and howling until I could calm her down by explaining to her, amid the ear-piercing shrieking of the baby, the purpose of the procedure. Even my father, who missed his daughter and her family who had not been able to leave the country with us, demanded to be allowed to go back to Vietnam, and there was a group of older men who wanted the same thing and asked me to communicate their demands to the American authorities. I also had to mediate a dispute between an older Vietnamese priest and a Buddhist monk because the latter's service tended to exceed the allotted time and cut into the time for Mass. Nerves were frayed and tempers exasperated. One crisis followed another.

Not everything was tragic, however. One young couple whose wedding had been canceled because of the exodus wanted to get married in the camp. So I organized the biggest wedding possible, with traditional ceremonies, costumes, and music. Local TV reporters showed up to film the event. After the wedding, the American chaplain asked me what I had planned for the newlyweds' honeymoon. I told him that the refugees were not allowed to leave the camp. Undeterred, he said that something must be done for the newlyweds, so he requisitioned a tent to be set up on top of the hill so that they could spend a few days by themselves.

After about two months in the camp, my family and ten others were sponsored by the now defunct University of Plano located in the north of Dallas, Texas. There, after proper interviews (something quite strange to us since in Vietnam people usually get jobs because they know someone), we were given temporary employment in a summer job program. I worked in the Street Department of the City of Plano as a garbage collector for about two months. We did not know the name of the man who recommended us for these jobs, so we nicknamed him "Mr. Two-

Ten" because we were paid two dollars and ten cents an hour, the minimum wage in 1975.

## An Icon Between Two Worlds

My somewhat detailed account of how I came to the United States is not intended to be a trip down memory lane but to illustrate the two points I made earlier, namely, that most life-transforming events are often beyond our planning and control, and that my career as a theologian was accidental. For historians, my coming to America was but the result of a serendipitous combination of chance occurrences: a shortage of planes, a late breakfast, an aunt who accidentally broke her leg, a shrewd substitution of names, and a last-minute flight. Like most unimportant lives, mine is like a story without plot, a poem without rime, a quilt without a pattern. Only in the light of faith can my coming to the United States, which was totally beyond my wildest dream and yet radically changed the direction of my life, appear, in retrospect, as an event of the mysterious design that Divine Providence has conceived for me.

As for my taking up teaching theology, it was at first simply a way to earn a living to support my family. Furthermore, my career as a theology professor came about in a rather fortuitous way. After a brief stint as a garbage collector, I had to look for permanent employment and was introduced to the University of Dallas, a Catholic liberal arts school. In the interview for a position in theology, the academic dean recommended that I look for a teaching position in high school, possibly because he deemed that I was unqualified. Nevertheless, since I preferred college teaching, I applied for admission and was accepted into the doctoral program in philosophy offered by the University of Dallas. As I was filling out necessary forms, the registrar noted that I had a degree in theology; then and there she called the chairman of the Department of Theology and suggested that I be hired as an adjunct instructor. Thus began my saga as an accidental theologian. With the hope of obtaining a tenure track position I undertook doctoral studies in theology rather than in philosophy at the Salesian Pontifical University in Rome. Because of my special circumstances, the Salesian University kindly allowed me to complete the course work at the University of Dallas and then write the dissertation under the direction of a professor in Rome. Professor Achille Triacca was assigned as my mentor and he proposed three topics for my dissertation, one of which was on the thought of the Russian Orthodox theologian Paul Evdokimov (1901–1970).

Like Tillich, Evdokimov attracted my attention because there seems to be an existential and spiritual kinship between him and me. Like Tillich and myself, he too was a refugee. Born in St. Petersburg, he emigrated after the Bolshevik Revolution, first to Constantinople and finally to Paris. After obtaining a doctorate of letters with a dissertation on the problem of evil in Dostoevsky and a doctorate in theology with a work on Orthodoxy, Evdokimov taught theology at several institutions, in particular at the Institut Saint-Serge, an Orthodox theological school in Paris. Besides being an active participant in ecumenical dialogue, Evdokimov was a prolific writer.[9]

What unites his manifold writings is the conviction that finite reality, human and cosmic, is authentic and can be fulfilled only if it is open to the divine, only if transcending itself, it contains and manifests God. This is so because, from the beginning and in view of the end, the whole of created reality is destined to participate in the divine life and because, by reason of the incarnation of the *logos* and by the power of the Holy Spirit, nothing in reality can be closed upon itself or profane but is suffused with sacredness. Thus, in Evdokimov's vision, protology and eschatology are two powerful beams illuminating the meaning of creation. In this sense, human culture, and especially the human person, must become an icon of the heavenly kingdom.

Icon, as is well known, is a particular form of two-dimensional painting representing sacred personages. It is highly popular in the Orthodox Church, which defended its veneration in the Seventh Ecumenical Council at Nicaea. As a symbol of culture, the icon is the expression *par excellence* of the eschatological nature of culture and is itself the supreme instance of the eschatological transfiguration. It is a colorful profession of faith in the reality of the incarnation, an eloquent affirmation that nothing in culture, art included, can have a neutral function but must contain and manifest God. The icon, containing in itself the whole material world and the fruit of humanity's noblest cultural endeavors, is a window through which we can glimpse and anticipate the kingdom of God; it is the paradigm of culture-in-transfiguration.[10]

In many ways Evdokimov's theological vision has deeply influenced my own theological development. Exile and the resultant state of being betwixt and between had particularly impressed upon me the fragility of things and the ephemeral character of time. Ironically, this sense of the rootlessness and transitoriness of human existence is well expressed by the mobile home, a ubiquitous and distinctive feature of the Ameri-

---

[9] Evdokimov's most important works include *Dostoievsky et le problème du mal* (Lyon: Éd. Les Ondes, 1942); *Orthodoxie* (Neuchâtel-Paris: Delachaux et Niestlé, 1959); *Les âges de la vie spirituelle: Des Pères du désert à nos jours* (Paris: Desclée, 1964); and *L'Art de l'icône: Théologie de la beauté* (Paris: Éd. du Seuil, 1973).

[10] My study on Evdokimov was published as: *Culture and Eschatology: The Iconographical Vision of Paul Evdokimov* (New York: Peter Lang, 1985).

can landscape and yet a cultural oxymoron for Asians, for whom home means a permanent place, rooted in the earth, where one is born and dies. Familiarity with Evdokimov's theological corpus enabled me to articulate this existential awareness in terms of Christian eschatology in which the kingdom of God remains the predominant symbol.

Paradoxically, this heightened sense of the eschatological nature of reality, coupled with faith in the resurrection of Jesus and of the dead, intensified my awareness of and appreciation for these very earthly realities, because the cosmos, which is our permanent home and not a roadside motel to stop by on our pilgrimage to heaven, and diverse human achievements, however humble, are not destined for destruction in a universal conflagration at the end of time but will be preserved, purified, and perfected in the kingdom of God. Our eternity is not something that comes after time but is time itself, in which God has entered and which God has assumed into God's own trinitarian life, made final and definitive. This theme, which can be termed "eschatology," has become and remains the leitmotif of my theological thinking. I explored it again in the thought of Karl Rahner in my dissertation for the doctoral degree in philosophy from the University of London as well as in other contemporary theological movements in my later writings.[11]

## Doing Theology with Imagination and Memory

As a branch of theology which deals with betwixt and between events, eschatology is theology done with imagination. It is not an advance historical report of events that will transpire in the beyond, after our death and at the end of time, as fundamentalists are wont to taking the Scripture's apocalyptic texts to be. Rather it is, as Karl Rahner has said, an imaginative "extrapolation" *(Aussage)* into the future or a reading from the present into the future.[12] What is extrapolated is the

---

[11] My writings on eschatology include *Eternity in Time: A Study of Karl Rahner's Eschatology* (Selinsgrove, Pa.: Susquehanna University Press, 1988); *Responses to 101 Questions on Death and Eternal Life* (New York: Paulist Press, 1998); "Woman and the Last Things: A Feminist Eschatology," *In the Embrace of God: Feminist Approaches to Theological Anthropology,* ed. Ann O'Hara Graff (Maryknoll, N.Y.: Orbis Books, 1995) 206–28; "The Eschatological Dimension of Unity: Paul Evdokimov's Contribution to Ecumenism," *Salesianum* 42 (1980) 475–99; "Contemporary Context and Issues in Eschatology," *Theological Studies* 55 (1994) 507–36; and "Eschatology and Ecology: The Environment in the End-Time," *Dialogue & Alliance* 9:2 (1995) 99–115.

[12] See Karl Rahner, "The Hermeneutics of Eschatological Assertions," *Theological Investigations,* vol. 4, trans. Kevin Smyth (Baltimore: Helicon, 1960) 323–46.

*present* situation of salvation brought about by the ministry, death, and resurrection of Jesus into its future, definitive and final, stage of fulfillment. In other words, eschatology is an imaginative construal of christology in its future mode of final and definitive fulfillment. Whatever we know about eschatology, we know it only in and through what happened to Jesus in his death and resurrection. Eschatology is christology conjugated in the future tense by means of the imagination. Thus, far from being a harmless appendix of systematic theology to be treated at the end of the theological curriculum, or a treatise providing answers to our curiosity about when the end of the world will come or how long purgatory lasts, eschatology or apocalypticism is, in Ernst Käsemann's memorable phrase, "the mother of all Christian theology" without which the Christian faith would be robbed of its forward-looking and world-transforming thrust.[13]

However, as we have said above, theological imagination must be nourished by memory, otherwise it is empty phantasmagoria. In my case, this memory was first recovered through a study of the early Christian writers. Thanks to my study of Evdokimov and Orthodox theology I acquired some familiarity with what is known as patristic literature. When I was invited by Professor Thomas Halton of the Catholic University of America to contribute two volumes to the series "Message of the Fathers of the Church" I took the opportunity to research patristic teachings on social, political, and economic issues as well as on anthropology.[14] This *"ressourcement"* provided me with a fresh appreciation for the necessity of Tradition for theology, or to use Hans-Georg Gadamer's expression, of the need to take into account the *"Wirkungsgeschichte"* in interpreting texts.[15] Because of this background I would be reluctant to agree with proposals made by some Asian theologians to bypass the development of Western theology in constructing a theology appropriate to the Asian context.

But doing theology with memory is more than archaeological digging into a dead past, forgotten and irrelevant. For humans, time is not only *chronos* but also *kairos,* not only measurement of change but also moments pregnant with the promise of transformation. We who live in time do not experience the past as something irretrievably lost and gone but as truly present, effectively shaping our identity and our des-

---

[13] See Ernst Käsemann, *Exegetische Versuche und Besinnungen,* vol. 2 (Göttingen: Vandenhoeck & Ruprecht, 1960) 100.

[14] See my *Social Thought* (Wilmington, Del.: Michael Glazier, 1984) and *Grace and the Human Condition* (Wilmington, Del.: Michael Glazier, 1988).

[15] See Hans-Georg Gadamer, *Truth and Method,* trans. Joel Weinscheimer and Donald G. Marshall, 2d rev. ed. (New York: Crossroad, 1990).

tiny. Similarly, we do not experience the future merely as something empty and unreal; rather, we experience it as a lure and a challenge, inviting us to move forward to actualize our potentialities. In this human time, the past is gathered up and preserved in our *memory,* and the future is anticipated and made real in our *imagination.* In time our soul, as Augustine puts it, is "distended," turning backward to embrace the past, and reaching forward to anticipate future possibilities.[16] Our identity is achieved by this capacity to somehow fuse the three layers of time—past, present, and future—into a personal unity and to possess all three dimensions of time wholly and together.

This anthropology of time is verified for me in my attempts to re-create the past for the future, to do theology with memory and imagination, to think religiously betwixt and between. As Hans-Georg Gadamer and Paul Ricoeur have pointed out, when we attempt to understand a text, a work of art, an event, or anything at all, we bring to the hermeneutical task some *preunderstanding* or *prejudgment* of it. This preunderstanding is formed by the tradition of (often conflicting) interpretations of this subject matter and gives us a handle on it. Approaching the subject matter to be interpreted with a preunderstanding means that the interpreter is neither totally passive, docilely absorbing the "objective" meaning and truth of the text, nor totally active, arbitrarily creating meaning and truth at will as if the text were completely unstable. Rather, as David Tracy has argued, the classic to be interpreted and the interpreter interact with each other in a give-and-take, back-and-forth process that has been likened to conversation or game. The interpreter interprets the classic, and the classic interprets the interpreter; neither remains unchanged in the process.[17]

Having been schooled in the historical-critical method I appreciate the usefulness of historical criticism with all its sophisticated tools to retrieve the world *behind* the text, in order to *explain* it, which functions as a *window* through which we can have a glimpse of the past. To *understand* the text as adequately as possible, however, requires more than reconstructing the meaning intended by its author(s). We must also enter into the world *of* the text by seeing ourselves in its stories, its plot, its characters, its rhetorical strategies, its styles, its linguistic usages. Here the text functions as a *mirror* in which the reader discovers himself or herself, so that an objet d'art can become a work of art; a sheet of scores, music; a script, drama; a text, the Word of God.

---

[16] See Augustine, *The Confessions,* trans. John K. Ryan (Garden Day, N.Y.: Image Books, 1960) 285–6, 298–302.

[17] See David Tracy, *The Analogical Imagination* (New York: Crossroad, 1981) 99–153.

Finally, the worlds *behind* and *of* the text project a world *in front of* the text, that is, a new way of being and acting in the world which we have to *appropriate* in our lives. Only then are we *transformed* by the meaning and truth of the text; only then will the interpreting process come to full fruition: from exegesis to criticism to hermeneutics. Of course, at this point, the whole interpreting process begins anew, like an ever-ascending spiral, because *appropriating* the world *in front of* the text will lead to a new *explanation* of the world *behind* the text, which in turn brings about a different *understanding* of the world *of* the text.

## In Solidarity With Those Who Suffer

Doing theology with imagination and memory in this way, however, can lead to solipsism, if it is not accompanied by an explicit attention to the sociopolitical and economic dimensions of human existence and to what Gustavo Gutiérrez calls "the underside of history."[18] Thus, together with the hermeneutics of retrieval and reconstruction, there must be a hermeneutics of suspicion, to be practiced with fairness and humility, to unmask forms of repression and oppression embedded in the text and in the social and ecclesial structures.

In addition to Paul Tillich with his method of correlation, Paul Evdokimov with his iconographical vision, Karl Rahner with his transcendental anthropology, and philosophers of hermeneutics such as Hans-Georg Gadamer and Paul Ricoeur, liberation theologians, first Latin American and later Asian, have profoundly informed my theological thought.[19] Not that I am worthy of the title of liberation theologian; to be a liberation theologian is far more demanding in terms of personal sacrifice, solidarity with the poor and the oppressed, and even willingness to risk one's life at the hands of dictators than thinking and writing and waxing eloquent about economic exploitation and political and gender oppression in an air-conditioned and computer-equipped office (rather than in the slums), surrounded by books and journals (rather than by poor and hungry people), and assured of a monthly income (rather than worrying about where the next meal will come from).

[18] See Gustavo Gutiérrez, *The Power of the Poor in History,* trans. Robert Barr (Maryknoll, N.Y.: Orbis Books, 1983) 169.

[19] See my "The Future of Liberation Theology," *The Living Light* 28:3 (1992) 259–71; "Peacemaking in Latin American Liberation Theology," *Église et Théologie* 24 (1993) 25–31; "Experience and Theology: An Asian Liberation Perspective," *Zeitschrift für Missionswissenschaft und Religionswissenschaft* 2 (1993) 99–121; and "Overcoming Poverty and Oppression: Liberation Theology and the Problem of Evil," *Louvain Studies* 20 (1995) 3–20.

Nevertheless, theologians such as Gustavo Gutiérrez, Jon Sobrino, Leonardo and Clodovis Boff, among Latin American theologians, and Aloysius Pieris, Samuel Ryan, Choan-Seng Song, *minjung* theologians, and Asian feminist theologians among Asians have taught me the centrality of the kingdom of God, God's preferential love for the poor, the liberating message of Jesus of Nazareth, personal solidarity with victims of oppression of every kind, Christian life as discipleship and martyrdom, and the uselessness and even perniciousness of theology unless it helps transform society into a community of freedom, justice, peace, and love.

## "Come Back and Bathe in Your Home Pond"

There is a Vietnamese proverb which says: Come back and bathe in your own pond; clear or muddy, the home pond is always better. This saying, seemingly an egregious instance of boorish chauvinism, is at bottom a confident invitation to all people to trust their own resources, personal and national, and to make use of them in their quest for understanding reality, or, to use the title of one of Gustavo Gutiérrez's well-known books, to "drink from our own wells."[20]

Having been deprived of my own cultural wealth throughout most of my education, I have tried of late to rethink certain fundamental Christian articles of belief in terms of Asian, and in particular Vietnamese, cultural resources (e.g., the kingdom of God and christology). These resources include myths of origin, everyday stories, religious texts and rituals, spiritual traditions and practices, literature and art, philosophy and worldviews. Theologically, this project is known by the neologism of inculturation. Ideally, in the process of inculturation all three levels of culture, that is, its basic forms (the *who, what, when, where, how,* and *what kind*), its systems of meanings (the immediate *whys* which relate the basic forms together into a pattern), and its philosophical and religious worldviews (the basic *whys*) are engaged in, if not simultaneously, at least ultimately.[21] Inculturation is the process whereby the Christian faith is integrated into the culture of the people to whom the Good News is preached in such a way that *both* the faith is expressed in the elements of this culture and transforms it from within *and* the culture in turn

---

[20] See Gustavo Gutiérrez, *We Drink from Our Own Wells: The Spiritual Journey of a People,* trans. Matthew O'Connell (Maryknoll, N.Y.: Orbis Books, 1984).

[21] For this understanding of culture see Louis L. Luzbetak, *The Church and Cultures: New Perspectives in Missiological Anthropology* (Maryknoll, N.Y.: Orbis Books, 1988) 225–39.

enriches and transforms the previous expressions of the faith brought in from outside. Essential to inculturation is the *mutual* criticism and enrichment between the local culture and the Christian faith. Both the understanding of the faith and the elements of the indigenous culture are challenged, corrected, transformed, and enriched.

To achieve this task of inculturation I was fortunately able, through a grant from the Research Enablement Program, to immerse myself in the cultural, religious, and spiritual streams that have refreshed the minds and nourished the hearts of my people for thousands of years before the coming of Christianity and have continued to sustain them ever since the Good News was preached to them in the seventeenth century. This second *ressourcement* was already sparked by my earlier interest in Asian liberation theology. As Pieris has convincingly argued, Asian liberation theology must take into account both poverty and religiousness.[22] Whereas Latin American liberation theology has focused on economic poverty, a properly Asian liberation theology must reflect upon the two fundamental features of the Asian situation: its massive poverty and its widespread religiousness. In Asia, where all world religions originated, in addition to enforced poverty, there is the voluntary poverty taken up by the religious in order to liberate the poor from their enforced poverty. Thus, far from being the opium of the masses, religions in Asia, in spite of their potential for escapism and otherworldliness, have assumed a social, political, and economic role in the transformation of society, a fact that Karl Marx could not appreciate and a Marxist social analysis cannot uncover. Hence, political and economic liberation in Asia as well as inculturation of the Christian faith must go hand in hand with interreligious dialogue. Those are the three pillars upon which an authentically Asian theology must be built: liberation, inculturation, and interreligious dialogue.[23]

## *Nel mezzo del cammin di nostra vita . . .*

"In the middle of the journey of our life, I came to my senses in a dark forest, for I had lost the straight path," so began Dante in his *Divine Comedy*.[24] Dante's spiritual purification and final attainment of

---

[22] See Aloysius Pieris, *An Asian Theology of Liberation* (Maryknoll, N.Y.: Orbis Books, 1988) 74–81.

[23] See my *Mission and Catechesis: Alexandre de Rhodes and Inculturation in Seventeenth-Century Vietnam* (Maryknoll, N.Y.: Orbis Books, 1998).

[24] Dante, *The Divine Comedy*, trans. H. R. Huse (New York: Holt, Rinehart and Winston, Inc., 1954) 7.

eternal happiness, symbolized by his journey through hell, purgatory, and heaven, was guided by reason and philosophy (Virgil) and faith and theology (Beatrice). Dante himself represents humankind, his journey is everyone's journey, and so his two guides must be everyone's guides as well. Faith and reason are like the sun and the moon illuminating our path toward enlightenment and salvation.

In my journey so far as an accidental, if not reluctant, theologian (or, more modestly, teacher of theology), there were dark forests, crooked paths, unexpected turns, deep valleys, sun-lit clearings, and high mountains. Most often, it was a journey between worlds, betwixt memory and imagination. But as Dante himself acknowledged at the end of his masterpiece, understanding how the human image is conformed to the divine model, which is the task of theology, is like attempting to square the circle, an impossible mission: "My own wings were not enough for that—except that my mind was illumined by a flash through which its wish was realized. For the great imagination here power failed."[25] In front of the divine incomprehensible Mystery, all human speech about God is nothing but stammer and stutter that must end in worshipful silence and awe-struck adoration. But again like Dante, all that one can hope is that in the end "my desire and will were turning like a wheel moved evenly by the Love which turns the sun and the other stars."[26]

[25] Ibid., 481.
[26] Ibid.

# From Autobiography to Fellowship of Others: Reflections on Doing Ethnic Theology Today

*Anselm Kyongsuk Min*

## From Seoul to Southern California

Names identify people, and so does my name, Anselm Kyongsuk Min. When I introduce myself with this name, I am frequently asked where I got the name Anselm. A Korean bearing the name of the great eleventh-century archbishop of Canterbury, a Benedictine monk and the father of scholasticism, is strange enough to provoke surprise, curiosity, and increasingly nowadays pity at me as a victim of Western colonialism. Let me, therefore, begin with the story of my name.

I was born Kyongsuk Min, or rather Min Kyongsuk in proper Korean order, Min standing for my clan, Kyong for my generation and shared by my brother and three sisters, and Suk for me as an individual, although the generational and individual components are usually combined—Kyongsuk—to make up the equivalent of the personal name in Western languages. When I was born in Korea in 1940, my family had not yet become Christians; they were Confucian in human relations and shamanist in times of crisis. The country was under Japanese domination, well noted for its brutality, to the point of forcing Koreans to adopt Japanese names and drafting teenage girls for sexual service to front-line troops fighting an imperialist war in the Pacific.

One day in 1944, one of my two uncles was away on a trip through Kangwondo, the province directly east of Seoul, on his mission, according to a family legend, of delivering funds collected at home to the Korean troops fighting the Japanese in Manchuria. He was crossing a bridge, fell, and drowned to death. Like all mothers, my grandmother was inconsolable with tears for days and weeks. Finally, my father suggested that she join a church. When she was baptized and received into the Catholic Church, so were all in the family under her matriarchal authority, my mother, aunt, myself, and my brother, but not the adult males, my grandfather, father, and uncle, who joined the Church many years later. It was and still is a Korean custom to give the newly baptized a *bonmyong,* a name "proper" for a person born into a new, true life in Christ. This was different from the *sogmyong* or "secular" name given at birth. The "proper" name was taken from that of a saint, often the saint whose feast day coincided with one's own birthday. I was born on April 21 (according to the lunar calendar), so I was named after St. Anselm, whose feast fell on the same day (according to the solar calendar).

My earliest and most indelible memory of Church life is that of the Sunday Latin Mass followed by the Benediction of the Blessed Sacrament in the evening. I still remember the scent of incense, the Kyrie and Gloria to the Credo to the Agnus Dei, as well as the Tantum Ergo and O Salutaris Hostia. As I joined the altar boys I went to Mass not only on Sundays but also on weekdays, especially during the summer and winter holidays. Serving the 6:30 Mass under the dim light of candles, even on freezing winter mornings, was an experience of divine presence complete with mystery, silence, awe, and grace. Also deeply etched in my memory is the spectacle of the annual National Eucharistic Congress that would begin at the seminary and proceed, in a public display of Catholic faith, to the Myongdong Cathedral across town. Again I remember the seminary choir singing eucharistic hymns in Gregorian chant, so uplifting, angelic, and mystical.

Korean Catholicism dates back to 1784, when a government official named Sunghoon Ri, baptized Peter in Beijing, returned and baptized fellow Confucian scholars. The first hundred years were years of persecution, producing over 10,000 martyrs, of whom 103 were canonized by Pope John Paul II in Seoul in 1984. Originally a Church of the scholar-official class, as persecution intensified it became largely a Church of the poor and uneducated. As a mission of the Foreign Mission Society of Paris, Korean Catholicism was a transplant of the French in its theology, liturgy, and spirituality. Receiving its freedom of religion in 1886, the Church spread its roots among farmers, concentrating on parochial work rather than, as did Presbyterians and Methodists, on medical work and education, out of which came the predominant majority of Korean leaders of the first half of the twentieth century.

June 25, 1950, is an unforgettable day for every Korean over fifty. On that day began the Korean War (1950–1953) that would shake Korean life to its very foundation for decades to come. Some three million people out of a population of less than thirty million were killed, maimed, wounded, or displaced. Whole cities were razed to the ground through street battles and saturation bombing from the air. It was a period of universal, unrelieved suffering for Koreans. It was also a period of religious awakening and conversion for many. The war was an existential demonstration of the vanity of all things, the fragility of life, and the radical perversity of human nature. I too felt there was no hope for this world, apart from God.

It was my grandmother's simple piety that nourished my faith. She was the one who insisted on our going to church every Sunday, our saying morning and evening prayers, our going to confession regularly, and our fulfilling other obligations of traditional Catholic piety. She was most active in the parish, involved in women's activities, never failing to visit the sick and the dying. She was also a most devoted wife, mother, and grandmother at home, even receiving an award given to devoted wives. Without the persistence of my grandmother, I would not have become a Catholic; without the enduring example of her piety, simple and unsophisticated, perhaps I would not have remained a Catholic even to this day.

As I entered high school (tenth to twelfth grade) in 1954, I became active in the parish, serving as president of the high school students' association, and in general hanging around in the parish on weekends. The three seminarians from the parish, each about ten years my senior, took special interest in me and served as my counselors on theological questions I was then beginning to ask, from God's existence to the problem of evil to the "true" church of Christ, as well as on the possibility of my vocation to the priesthood, of which I was increasingly convinced. They would come home for the summer and winter holidays, and I would join them in their get-togethers, picnics, and longer trips. At their suggestions I read Cardinal Gibbons's *The Faith of Millions;* Fr. O'Brien's history of the Reformation from the Catholic perspective (I forget the exact English title); the lives of many saints, especially St. Gemma Galgani of Italy; histories of the church; and biographies of famous twentieth-century converts such as Gertrud von Le Fort, Jacques and Raissa Maritain, Paul Claudel, G. K. Chesterton, Claire Booth Luce, Ronald Knox, Gabriel Marcel, and others whose names I no longer remember.

Unforgettable from this period was the experience of attending the ordination liturgy at the cathedral. The Veni Creator Spiritus in solemn Gregorian chant at the beginning made one almost feel the breath of the Holy Spirit. The litany of saints and the invocation of divine blessing on the ordinands completely prostrate on the floor brought home in a most moving way the truth of the communion of saints: separated though we are in time and space as well as by death, we are not alone but remain in fellowship with one another across the generations and cultures. Pope Pius XII was on the papal throne then, and Bishop Paul Ro, the first Korean bishop, was the Vicar Apostolic of Seoul. Each was projecting the majesty, the durability, the sacredness of the church, a church totally secure in her identity, a bulwark of truth against all the evils and errors of the modern, secular world, confident in the divine promise of protection, "Tu es Petrus, et super hanc petram . . ." ("Thou art Peter, and upon this rock . . ."). One was proud to be a Roman Catholic.

Upon graduation from high school in 1957 I decided to join the Jesuits because they were known for their intellectual apostolate, missionary work, and obedience to the Holy Father. *Omnia ad majorem Dei gloriam!* All for the greater glory of God! At that time the Jesuits— Americans from the Wisconsin Province—were in the process of establishing themselves in Korea, buying a house, looking for land on which to build a college, and establishing contacts with the Korean clergy and the government. They did not yet have a novitiate in Korea that I could immediately join, nor was I, at seventeen years of age, allowed to go abroad without completing my military service. I was thus invited to live with the Jesuits until I was ready to go to the novitiate in the United States, going to college and completing my military service in the meantime. For two years I attended the newly-founded Hankuk University of Foreign Studies, where I concentrated on English and general education. At home the Jesuits taught me Latin and English, in addition to all the basics of Jesuit religious life: the three-day retreat, the daily routine of the morning Mass, meditation, spiritual reading, and evening prayer, the weekly confession and conference with the spiritual father, etc. I began my life with the Jesuits with a three-day retreat. It was my first, and perhaps best, retreat according to the Spiritual Exercises of St. Ignatius, directed by Fr. Peter Jin, a Korean Jesuit. At the most impressionable age, this pre-novitiate with the Jesuits was to have the most enduring and profound impact on me.

On February 10, 1961, after two years of college and twenty-two months of military service, three other Korean candidates and I flew to the Minneapolis-St. Paul airport and entered the newly built novitiate at St. Bonifacius. I still remember the first community Mass I attended; it was the same Mass, same Credo, same Pater Noster that I used to pray back home in Korea but with a singular impact on me, a Korean novice among Americans in Minnesota, ten thousand miles away from home. It was a most moving expression of the universality, the catholicity of the faith we shared. The novitiate was a year and a half—reduced from two years in view of my years already spent with the Jesuits in Korea—of concentrated spiritual discipline, of immersion in Jesuit spirituality and tradition as well as of initiation into the entire Christian tradition of religious life from the Desert Fathers to Augustine and Benedict to Therese of Lisieux.

After I completed the novitiate in September 1962, I became a Junior, a Jesuit scholastic studying the *litterae humaniores* for two years according to the famous Jesuit *Ratio Studiorum*. It was two years of intense intellectual discipline, without neglecting the spiritual, of course, devoted to the study of the Western humanistic tradition, fifteen hours of Greek and Greek literature from Homer's *Iliad* to Plato's *Republic* to the Greek New Testament, many more hours of Latin and Latin literature from Virgil's *Aeneid* to Horace's *Odes* to Cicero's *Orationes,* and many courses in English and English literature from *Beowulf* to Shakespeare and Milton to the prose of Newman and Carlyle. I was immersed in the riches of the Western classical tradition, and I enjoyed the experience thoroughly.

My study of philosophy, the next phase in my Jesuit training, began in September 1964 at the College of Philosophy and Letters, the seminary for Jesuit philosophy students, which was part of Saint Louis University. The first two years were devoted to the mastery of the philosophical system of St. Thomas Aquinas, from logic and metaphysics to natural theology, epistemology, and philosophy of nature to philosophy of "man" and ethics, all according to the mind of the Angelic Doctor. We would also take courses at the university to complete other requirements for the B.A. in philosophy, like cultural anthropology, personality theories, and history of ancient philosophy. At the end of the curriculum we would take oral exams in Latin. The third year was devoted, for those like me destined to go into philosophy, to pursuing a master's degree in philosophy. This was the first time I was exposed to the modern (Western) world, history of modern European philosophy, modern philosophies of religion, Bergson, Whitehead, and the Existentialists.

No Catholic living in the 1960s could have escaped the impact of the Second Vatican Council, the major event of twentieth-century Catholicism that opened its first session on October 11, 1962. Opening up to modernity, critique of her closed and polemical past, and an enthusiasm to return to the spirit of the Gospel were sweeping through the Church in a "new Pentecost." Once the council began we were living from week to week, anxious to hear the most recent theological debates of the week from news and church weeklies. As we moved from the idylls of rural Minnesota to the urban, university atmosphere in St. Louis, and as we were better acquainted with "modernity" through courses/readings as well as through living in a modern city, all our studies were conducted in the light/shadow of the conciliar debates among the Ottavianis, Beas, Koenigs, Legers, Suenens, and Fringses, among the Rahners, Congars, de Lubacs, Daniélous, Küngs, and Ratzingers. We were increasingly gripped by a self-conscious spirit of criticism directed at the *whole* of Catholicism: the dualism of its Greek heritage, its Constantinian past, its withdrawal from the world, its ahistorical stance toward history, the monolithic papacy, the imposed uniformity of its language and liturgy, its endemic clericalism, the "static" approach of its official, Thomist theology and philosophy, its illusion of triumph.

The radical, dissenting critique of the Church also put into question my own Catholic past, which I was beginning to realize was *not* the eternal form of the Church but a contingent, Korean, authoritarian version of post-Tridentine, French, Western Catholicism. Ironically, all these criticisms did not disillusion me of Catholicism as such but expanded, deepened, and thus confirmed my Catholic faith. All such criticisms were from within, motivated by love of the Church, and based on the retrieval, not negation, of the Catholic tradition. Catholicism had not been Catholic enough. They also made it possible for me to accept so much of modernity along with its critique of Christianity from Hume and Kant through Marx and Feuerbach to Russell, Dewey, and Sartre. Catholicism had room for whatever authentic elements there were in them, including the element of protest in their "protest atheism."

During the summer of 1965, and then during the two subsequent summers, I was one of the few among my classmates allowed to study in a non-Catholic institution. I studied Hinduism and East Asian religions at Columbia University in 1965, the *Bhagavad Gita* and analytic philosophy of religion at the University of Chicago in 1966, and a typology of modern philosophies of religion (dialogical, pragmatist, process, humanist, etc.) and New Testament christology at Union Theological Seminary in New York City in 1967. While at Union, it was exhilarating to hear Harvey Cox and Maurice Friedman, a Buber scholar, debate the "secular city." The summer sessions were invaluable opportunities to study the Asian traditions, at a time when I was beginning to develop a strong interest in comparative religion. The non-Christian religions were, I was told at first, varieties of "natural" mysticism (Daniélou, Maritain, Cuttat), and then "supernatural" mysticism, albeit in "implicit" and "anonymous" forms (Rahner, Schlette). In any event, the council declared, in a most momentous and liberating statement, that salvation was possible even for non-Christians provided they followed the dictates of their own conscience. The grace of the Holy Spirit was operative in history, in the secular city, in other Christian denominations, and in other religions. It was glorious to be alive then and experience the radically expanding horizons of the postconciliar Church.

After the summer session at Union in 1967, I returned to Seoul for three years of teaching at Sogang Jesuit University, equipped with the master's degree in philosophy and plenty of youthful enthusiasm. I taught philosophy and worked with students. After two years of teaching and after many years of spiritual discernment going back to the days in St. Louis, I decided to leave the Jesuits, who asked me to continue on the faculty. It was part of the mass exodus of clergy and religious leaving the priesthood and/or religious life in those days. The world and the flesh were not evil. The laity too had an equal vocation to holiness and the mission of the Church. Why bind oneself to celibacy and other restrictions of religious life? I left the Jesuits in August 1969 and married my wife, Soonja, in February 1970. At this time I was also involved in a Church-funded survey of Korean Catholicism, past and present, critiquing from the postconciliar perspective its endemic authoritarian clericalism, its dualism of sacred and profane, its historical and political indifference, its self-enclosed institutionalism, and its false triumphalism. This resulted in two related works, *The Spiritual Ethos of Korean Catholicism,* a survey of the theology and spirituality of the Korean church from 1784 through the 1960s, and *Korean Catholicism in the 1970s* (which I co-authored), a sociological survey of attitudes of different Catholic groups on major issues.[1]

In September 1970 I entered the doctoral program in philosophy at Fordham University in the Bronx, New York. My ultimate goal was to go into theology, but given the constitutive role of philosophy in theology, I thought I should do more work in philosophy. Concentrating mostly on (European) continental philosophy, I took courses in Heidegger, transcendental Thomism, Phenomenology, Hegel, Marx, Kierkegaard, classical American philosophy, Royce, British Empiricism, and others. My horizon was deepening and expanding. It was at this time that I acquired a relatively thorough knowledge of Karl Rahner's philosophy and theology. I asked Quentin Lauer, S.J., a Hegel scholar, whom I should work on for the dissertation, given my theological interest, and was told, not unexpectedly, that I should work on Hegel, which I did.

Hegel was the first one to teach me to take history and society seriously. Both the Catholic tradition of social doctrine, the neo-Thomist

---

[1] *The Spiritual Ethos of Korean Catholicism* (Seoul: Sogang University Social Research Institute, 1971); William Biernatzki, S.J., Luke Jinchang Im, and Anselm Kyongsuk Min, *Korean Catholicism in the 1970s* (Maryknoll, N.Y.: Orbis Books, 1975).

theory of human rights, and the Existentialist critique of contemporary culture sensitized me to the plight of the workers, oppression of human rights, and the dehumanization and alienation in Western and increasingly in westernized societies of the world. These theories, however, remained abstract, often moralistic generalities without a sense of the historical change that generated such plights, oppressions, and alienations. As idealistic as anyone in his commitment to the self-transcending dynamism of the spirit, both human and divine, Hegel was also the most realistic philosopher in insisting on analyzing the concrete dialectic of socio-historical contradictions for the real possibilities of freedom in community. It was also precisely in and through this dialectic that the divine Spirit was immanent in the world. Hegel's thought was a philosophy/theology of liberation based on the reconciliation of the divine and human, the individual and social, freedom and community. After the shock of Hegel, I could not look at history in the old, ahistorical way any longer.

In 1974, when the oil crisis shattered the hopes of many a Ph.D. graduate for jobs, I was lucky enough to land a position at Belmont Abbey College, Belmont, North Carolina. I would stay here for the next eighteen years, teaching mostly philosophy and every conceivable area within philosophy from introduction and logic to ethics and philosophy of religion to modern and nineteenth-century philosophies to Existentialism, American philosophy, and political philosophy. I would also occasionally teach "Oriental" philosophies dealing with the classics of Hinduism, Buddhism, Taoism, and Confucianism.

In 1976 my Hegelian historical consciousness was deepened by an eight-week summer seminar in contemporary Marxism at the University of Kansas, funded by the National Endowment for the Humanities. It was an opportunity to expand my knowledge of the varieties of contemporary Marxism including critical theory, but especially to wrestle in some depth with the major texts of Marx and Engels. Along with Existentialism, Marx deepened my critique of capitalism. Marx also made me sensitive to the conditioning role of the economic conditions and the constitutive role of socialized matter in the totality of human life. All human ideality becomes actual and effective only when appropriately materialized. My social and sociological sensibility was deepened further when I attended another summer seminar in 1980 at Duke University, also funded by the National Endowment, a seminar in different schools of sociology such as functionalist, phenomenological, and dialectical.

The decade of the seventies was critical in so many respects. Revolutionary movements were afoot in many parts of the world. The United States was disengaging itself, rather ignominiously, out of its morass in Vietnam. The oil crisis and inflation were symptoms of the deepening crisis of capitalism. In the United States, Black and women's liberation movements were making disturbing waves. The liberation theology of Latin America was beginning to have its impact in the United States. The Call to Action of Detroit in 1976 was galvanizing the forces of reform within U.S. Catholicism. Dictators all over the world were making martyrs of thousands of people. The dictatorship of Park Chung Hee in South Korea was reaching its repressive climax when he was assassinated by his own intelligence chief in 1979. I was looking at the world with increasing concern, born of the mixed perspectives and sensibilities of Christian faith, Catholic social doctrine, liberation theology, Hegelian and Marxian dialectic. In the early eighties I also had an opportunity to participate in the labor-management dialogue sponsored by the diocese of Charlotte and in the drafting of the bishop's letter on labor, largely modeled on John Paul II's *Laborem Exercens*.

In 1984 I had my first-ever sabbatical leave and went to Vanderbilt to realize my original goal, a Ph.D. in theology. Peter Hodgson, Edward Farley, Sallie McFague, and Eugene TeSelle were outstanding scholars who were also kind enough to engage in extended theological conversations with me on all sorts of current topics. They were generous enough to allow me all the freedom to explore my own interests in the many courses taken with them, ranging from the Greek Fathers to Augustine and Aquinas to nineteenth- and twentieth-century Catholic and Protestant theologies, christology, theological method, and liberation theology. My overwhelming interest at this time was liberation theology, culminating in my dissertation "Praxis and Liberation: Towards a Theology of Concrete Totality" (1989) and the simultaneous publication of my *Dialectic of Salvation: Issues in Theology of Liberation* (SUNY Press, 1989), my Hegelian reconstruction of liberation theology partially based on the second part of my dissertation.

In many respects, 1992 has been a turning point in my life. Until then, I had been teaching only philosophy to the undergraduates at Belmont Abbey College. Since then, I have been teaching mostly theology to mainly doctoral students at Claremont Graduate University. Until then, I had lived in Charlotte and taught in Belmont, North Carolina, a mainly white, homogeneous society. Since then, I have been living in Southern California, a barometer of the pluralistic, multicultural, and conflictual society the whole world is increasingly becoming. Until then, my perspective was dominated by the theological vision of liberation based on Christian faith and the Hegelian-Marxian dialectic of history. Since then, under the cumulative impact of events and ideas going back to the eighties, the decline of liberation movements in Latin America, significant democratic victories in South Korea, the collapse of the Berlin Wall and Soviet Communism in 1989, feminism, womanism, mujerista theology, postmodernism, and religious pluralism, my vision has become more realistic, more complicated, and more open to pluralism.

I am no longer wholly committed to the Hegelian vision of totality or the Marxian vision of praxis and liberation, although I have by no means given up on totality and liberation.[2] I believe more and more in the necessity of a positively maintained tension between competing, total visions of life as well as between contemplation and praxis. From this more recent perspective I am completing two books, one on St. Thomas Aquinas, his contemplative vision of nature and reason within the framework of his trinitarian theology of creation, an attempt to reread Aquinas and retrieve the possibilities of contemplative theology; the other on solidarity of Others as a new theme of theology that combines the concerns of liberation and pluralism, along the lines suggested in the rest of this essay.

## In Search of Ethnic Theological Identity

Like most Korean Catholics of my generation I grew up and spent most of my youth liking and taking for granted Korean Catholicism in all its Western forms, in its theology, liturgy, and spirituality, which still largely remain translations of *Roman* Catholicism even after all the postconciliar changes and adaptations. Like most Koreans of my generation I also grew up liking and taking for granted American culture, its language, its commercial goods, its political ideologies of free enterprise, democracy, and anti-communism, Presidents Washington and Lincoln, even General MacArthur. Americans saved us first from the Japanese and then from North Korean Communism. We were all so eager to learn English and study in America. I remember, as a high school senior, memorizing Washington's Farewell Address and Lincoln's Gettysburg Address. In the fifties any questioning of Korean Catholicism for its Western form would have been simply unthinkable; to be Catholic was to be *Roman,* period. To question American presence in Korea would be tantamount to defending Communism.

It was only with the winds of change initiated by Vatican II in the early sixties that I began to acquire a certain ethnic theological self-

---

[2] For my modified Hegelian vision of totality, see Anselm Kyongsuk Min, "Liberation, the Other, and Hegel in Recent Pneumatologies," *Religious Studies Review* 22:1 (January 1996) 28–33, and "Towards a Dialectic of Totality and Infinity: Reflections on Emmanuel Levinas," *The Journal of Religion* 78:4 (October 1998).

consciousness, although only very, very gradually. Two books, George Dunne's *A Generation of Giants* and Jacques Leclerq's *Thunder in the Distance*, made me mad about the Roman bureaucrats whose narrowness brought to nothing the epochally significant Jesuit and other missionary attempts at inculturation of Catholicism in the seventeenth century and early-twentieth-century China respectively. Dom Aelred Graham's *Zen Catholicism* was an eye opener regarding the theological potential of Asia's own religious traditions. Until then, most books were triumphalistic stories of conversion to Christianity, such as Paul K. T. Sih's *From Confucius to Christ*, Lin Yutang's *From Pagan Back to Christian*, and John C. Wu's *Beyond East and West*. Graham's book was the first to awaken me to the possibility of an Asian religious contribution to Christianity.

I remember, as a student of humanities in 1963, listening to a Jesuit history professor saying in class that Western civilization is superior to Asian, and challenging me, one of the few Asian students in class, to refute him if he was wrong. With my youthful sense of humiliation at such an "ethnocentric" remark, I took up his challenge and spent the first half hour of the next class rebutting him with the best of my historical knowledge, although I do not now have the slightest idea of what I said then. I also experienced my first personal ethnic humiliation when one of my fellow American novices asked our novice master, right in my presence, but thinking that I would not understand him because he was using a very learned word, why Koreans were so "emaciated."

Studying the classics of Hinduism, Buddhism, Taoism, and Confucianism during the summers of 1965, 1966, and 1967 was my first exposure to my own Asian traditions in some depth in a systematic way. Until then, my exposure came simply from growing up and living in that culture, observing the Confucian rules and rituals of human relations, visiting Buddhist temples in the mountains while on picnics, and imbibing the Buddhist and Taoist ethos already there in the culture and especially in its language and literature. It is odd but true that a culture noted for its Confucianism and Buddhism has never provided any formal instruction in those religions anywhere in the first twelve years of schooling of its youths, as it still does not. The classic texts of Asian religions did reveal new worlds and new perspectives, but by then I had already learned to view things, including those religions, in light of my Christian faith. In the language of today's theology of religions, I learned to "subordinate" other religions to my own "inclusivist" vision. Besides, interest in Asian religions in American academic circles was just beginning; it was not yet on the agenda of mainstream theology and religious studies.

On a more practical note, I remember the confrontation between Korean and American Jesuits at Sogang Jesuit University in Seoul where I returned to teach in 1967. During the previous six and a half years in the United States I had really missed Korean food, as had other Koreans. When Koreans returned to Korea, they expected to eat Korean food at the community meals. With Americans in the majority, however, this was not to be. The food was American all the way. Koreans protested, and a compromise was reached: Korean food on certain days of the week, American food on other days. Another abnormality I began to note upon my return was the language of the faculty meeting. In the late sixties the university was a small institution, with slightly over a thousand students and perhaps about fifty full-time faculty. All the important positions from president to dean and important departmental chairs were taken by American Jesuits. The faculty met once a month, and the language of the meeting was English! I remember many of the Korean faculty, many of whom were not educated in the United States, complaining, sotto voce, about American colonialism. American Jesuits were both admired for their dedication and resented for imposing the American way from academic regulations to the language of the faculty meeting.

However, nothing that happened in the sixties was radical enough to challenge my theological identity that still largely remained comfortably Western. It was only in the seventies and increasingly in the eighties that my identity was shaken. Latin American liberation theology, black theology, the women's liberation movement and feminist theology, the *minjung* theology of Korea and other Asian theologies of liberation,[3] and French postmodernism: all these were truly radical in their critique and deconstruction of Christianity. Christianity was exposed as a product of totalitarian, imperialistic, and patriarchal Western logos. All the things I had grown up admiring in the Church has been subjected to a hermeneutic of radical suspicion and found to be tainted with the lust for power, ideology, and patriarchy. Christianity must be reconstructed on the new bases of non-Western, ethnic, and women's experiences as well as those of the oppressed. Theological revision and reconstruction was and still remains the order of the day. My publications of the last fifteen years, in the areas of liberation theology, pluralism, pneumatology, Asian theologies, and Emmanuel Levinas have been my attempts to reconstruct a more viable theological vision and theological identity in the postmodern world.

---

[3] For my interest in Asian theologies, see Anselm Kyongsuk Min, "Asian Theologians," *A New Handbook of Christian Theologians,* ed. Donald W. Musser and Joseph L. Price (Nashville: Abingdon Press, 1996) 22–48.

The political and intellectual changes of the last three decades have created truly critical dilemmas and challenges to the ethnic theologian in the United States. As a Korean theologian I am challenged to re-create a synthesis of Christianity, its Western form, and the Korean tradition. Christianity need not be identified with its Western form. The power of love of the triune God embodied in Jesus of Nazareth must always incarnate itself in a concrete language and tradition. In this sense, the Western form of Christianity is itself one of the possible incarnations of Christian faith. By the same token, Christianity must acquire appropriate inculturation in the particular languages and traditions of new nations, cultures, and continents where Christianity is preached. However, for those of us who received Christian faith from the West and in its Western form of institutional life, theology, liturgy, and spirituality, it is not valid—in view of the incarnational character of Christian faith—to separate Christian faith from the two thousand years of its Western tradition and try to return to the "pristine" and "original" Christian faith. Like it or not, the Western Christian tradition has become part of all non-Western Christianity evangelized by the West, including Korean Christianity.

The theological challenge for Korean Christianity is precisely to retrieve and incorporate the best of the Western tradition into its own theological reconstruction. In view of three decades of relentless hermeneutic of radical suspicion of the Western tradition, its classism, patriarchy, ethnocentrism, and imperialism, the same challenge also poses a dilemma. Is there still something authentic in the Western tradition left to retrieve after all the critiques of recent years? What is there for me, a Korean theologian, to retrieve in the colonialist, imperialist, patriarchal, and ethnocentric Western tradition without committing in the very act of retrieval a humiliating submission to Western theological imperialism and a betrayal of my own ethnicity?

The other challenge is to retrieve the best of the Korean tradition of religions and cultures not only as passive objects of critical theological reflection but, more importantly, as active sources or loci of theological insights for an authentically Korean Christianity. This retrieval means more than exegesis of classical Confucian and Buddhist authors in their contexts or reenactment of shamanistic rituals as these have been in their ancient tradition. Such exegeses and reenactments have been increasingly popular in recent years with the growing revival of tradition. True retrieval, however, entails the more delicate business of exposing the tradition to a hermeneutic of suspicion, bringing it into a dialectical encounter with the legitimate hopes and anxieties of our times, and rendering it effective as a critical and transforming power of the present. So much work on the tradition still remains at the level of exegesis, not retrieval.

The theological dilemma here, however, is the reverse of the earlier dilemma. Given the traditional simple identification of salvation history with the Western Christian tradition and so much traditional theological dismissal of "pagan" religions and cultures, can the Korean theologian retrieve the Korean tradition, which includes Confucianism, Buddhism, Daoism, and shamanism, without betraying the Christian faith? The overriding theological challenge and dilemma of the Korean theologian today, then, is to reflect on the theological status of both Western Christianity and the Korean tradition, and learn to retrieve the best of both for today.

I am, however, not only a Korean but also a Korean-American theologian, a Korean theologian doing theology in America, not Korea, which significantly complicates the theological task. The challenges facing Korean American theology include, first, the task of retrieving both the Western and the Korean traditions for the needs of the Korean communities in America, whose needs are new, complicated ones born of new circumstances. Korean immigration to the United Sates began in the early twentieth century when thousands of Koreans came as wage laborers to work on the sugar plantations in Hawaii, culminating in the late sixties and early seventies when a large scale immigration of entrepreneurs and professionals began. There are now almost a million Koreans living in the United States, most of them concentrated in southern California and New York City, and the rest scattered along the eastern and western seaboards as well as throughout the midwest.

The driving imperative of the first generation has been to survive, with hard work, in a highly competitive, alien, and hostile culture, with some sense of ethnic identity intact. Everything else had to yield to this categorical imperative of survival with success. As time went on, children grew up knowing only English and American culture, alienated from their own parents and grandparents. Women were forced to work full time both outside and inside the home. Not knowing the culture of white America or the ethnic cultures of other minorities with whom they were doing business, Korean Americans were more and more prone to conflicts and frictions with other groups. Concerns have been growing about the very meaning of life otherwise immersed in the making of a living, nostalgia for the home left behind in Korea, children no longer sharing traditional Korean culture, and alienation and fear of the ethnic other.

The Korean-American churches have been the only agencies dealing with these concerns and needs, providing symbols of transcendence for people exhausted with the struggle for survival, a space of identity and fellowship in a confusing and alienating world, hope and encouragement for people struggling with the disintegration of family, culture, and tradition. Most often, the churches were also the very arena in which personal and collective frustrations and contradictions of the Korean-American communities were aired and played out, leading to internal struggles, divisions, and alienations in the churches themselves. With no coherent and updated theologies available for their new life in America, the churches have been making do with whatever theological heritage they brought from home, largely evangelical, often fundamentalist, and generally conservative and exclusivistic. There had been no Korean-American theology systematically addressing the needs of these communities until recent years when there began to appear promising attempts by Protestant theologians such as Jung Young Lee, Sang Hyun Lee, and Andrew Sung Park.[4]

The second task of Korean-American theology would be to reflect on the theological significance of the Korean-American experience itself. I would like to single out four lessons as theologically important dimensions of this experience: separation, ambiguity, diversity, and love of the stranger, the other or xenophilia. The Korean-American experience is first of all the experience of separation from the old, familiar, ancestral ways of doing things back home in Korea. For a people so devoted to the tradition, living in America brings with it the pain of radical separation, the repression of nostalgia for the old culture and old identities, dying to the old self and being born again, born to the truth of human life as pilgrimage of the *homo viator,* the wayfaring human being. As the letter to the Hebrews put it, "here we have no lasting city, but we seek the city which is to come" (13:14). The Korean-American experience confirms the truth of Abraham as paradigm of faith ready to leave behind everything old and ancestral and venture into the new and the unknown, trusting in God alone.

The experience of radical separation is also the experience of ambiguity. Living in America means exposing oneself to different, even

---

[4] See Jung Young Lee, *Marginality: The Key to Multicultural Theology* (Minneapolis: Fortress Press, 1995); Sang Hyun Lee, ed., *Korean American Ministry: A Resource Book* (Princeton, N.J.: The Consulting Committee on Korean American Ministry, Presbyterian Church USA, 1987); Andrew Sung Park, *The Wounded Heart of God* (Nashville: Abingdon Press, 1993); and Andrew Sung Park, *Racial Conflict and Healing: An Asian-American Theological Perspective* (Maryknoll, N.Y.: Orbis Books, 1996). As a Korean American Catholic theologian, I have been editing, since 1993, an annual Korean-language journal of theology and opinion titled *Lumen Gentium* after the most important document of the Second Vatican Council, which has been debating practical issues facing the Korean-American Catholic communities, especially clerical authoritarianism, as well as trying to raise their theological self-consciousness still largely dominated by preconciliar mentality.

"bizarre" views and behaviors that relativize the norms of one's inherited tradition. It means no longer having the certainties of the home tradition available for every moment of decision and crisis, but rather meeting such a moment in a creative, inventive way, improvising, compromising, agonizing, and in any event learning to live with a large dose of ambiguity, the very ambiguity of life itself. One learns to be less attached to and less dependent on inherited tradition and more tolerant of uncertainty and contingency.

Equally painful as the pain of separation is the pain of diversity. Most Koreans have been brought up on the belief that the Korean people are one homogeneous ethnic group without much mixture of alien blood. They have been proud of their ethnic purity and most anxious to preserve it. Living in America means exposing oneself to and living with ethnic others, those who are different in ethnicity, language, culture, and religion. It means learning to respect and even welcome ethnic and cultural diversity as something positive. It involves the pain of overcoming and transcending closed nationalism and xenophobia and cultivating ethnic openness and xenophilia. In doing so, the Korean-American experience discloses and confirms the Christian truth and hope that there is "neither Jew nor Greek" (Gal 3:28) in Christ, who came to us precisely to "break down the dividing wall of hostility" (Eph 2:14) among human groups and races. The event of April 29, 1992, in Los Angeles, in which Korean businesses were systematically looted, burned, or otherwise destroyed by African and Hispanic Americans, must be considered a turning point in the collective ethnic consciousness of Korean Americans. They cannot live alone, still less for their sole interests; they must learn to live with others with some solidarity of interests.

The third task of Korean-American theology is to elaborate a political theology appropriate to Korean Americans as citizens of the United States who have both domestic responsibilities toward the common good and international responsibilities as the sole surviving superpower in an increasingly globalizing world. Unfortunately, recent ethnic theologies have tended to downplay the political dimension and withdraw into their respective ethnicity, with nothing to say about the politics of the *res publica* in which all ethnic groups are implicated, whether they like it or not, and which in fact determines the liberation/oppression, solidarity/conflict of the ethnic groups. As they are, Korean Americans are not just an ethnic group; they are also citizens of the United States and responsible, in a solidarity of responsibility with others, for the kind of laws, policies, and institutions that govern the country. Whether these will be liberating or oppressive, whether they will serve the common good of the nation, the basic political and economic rights of all, depends not on the power of any one ethnic group—no one group is powerful enough today to impose its own interest on the rest—but only on the political solidarity of ethnic others in collaborating for the creation of common conditions of life liberating to all. Apolitical withdrawal into one's own ethnicity, its culture, or its glorious past is not only to abdicate its political responsibility but also to abandon one's own ethnic destiny to the oppressors of the world.[5]

As citizens of the sole surviving superpower in a rapidly globalizing world, Korean Americans are also responsible, along with all other citizens, for what the U.S. government, its presidents, its diplomats, its armies, its nuclear missiles, its naval fleets, and its multinational corporations do for the good or ill of peoples in the world. As citizens of a country with the historic burdens of colonialism, slavery, and imperialism, Korean Americans too need particular sensitization to this international dimension of U.S. power. They cannot simply disavow all political responsibility for what their political, military, and economic representatives do overseas in their name. It is again unfortunate that there has been an increasing tendency for ethnic theologies to withdraw into their own ethnic preoccupations, creating a vacuum of prophetic theological criticism in the realm of international politics.

## From Ethnicity to Solidarity of Others

For good historical reasons we have seen, during the last three decades, a proliferation of deliberately "regional" theologies based on the needs and perspective of a particular ethnic group or gender as opposed to a "comprehensive" theology based on the universal needs and perspectives of all humanity. Traditional theology, which claimed to be precisely such a comprehensive, universal theology, has been exposed as being in fact a reflection of the particular needs and perspectives of those who are male, Western, and members of socially and ecclesiastically privileged classes. Although I do not want to "reduce" the whole of Western theology to such a reflection, it is also true that Western theology not only did not include but deliberately *excluded* the voices of others, those who are different in class, ethnicity, and gender, from the constitutive concerns and perspectives of theology, making itself guilty

---

[5] For insightful recent discussions of the problem of the one and the many in U.S. politics, see Martin E. Marty, *The One and the Many: America's Struggle for the Common Good* (Cambridge, Mass.: Harvard University Press, 1997); and National Endowment for the Humanities, ed., *A National Conversation on American Pluralism and Identity: Scholars' Essays* (Washington, D.C.: National Endowment for the Humanities, 1994).

of the many forms of historical oppression of the other. It is not only reasonable but also compelling that the oppressed, excluded, and marginalized others of history should claim their rightful places in theology as well. As a form of power, theology is too important to be left to its traditional Western masters. Each excluded group must do its own theology on the basis of its own needs, experiences, and perspective. Thus we have had an enriching and sensitizing proliferation of particular theologies based on gender, ethnicity, region, and sexual orientation, such as Native American, black womanist, Hispanic mujerista, white feminist, Latin American, black, Latino, Asian, African, and gay-lesbian theologies. Each regional theology has been busy retrieving its own cultural past and reconstructing a new theology from its own perspective and for the sake of its own liberation.

For many reasons, however, I submit that it is high time that we "sublate" *(aufheben)* the prevailing *particularism* of such regional theologies, not into a comprehensive, universal theology, which is not yet possible, but into a particular theology committed indeed to its own particular needs and perspective. This theology should also be self-consciously and constitutively open to the historical and theological solidarity of others in a globalizing world, a theology that does not cease to be particular in its needs and perspective but also tries to systematically incorporate the needs and perspectives of others into its own theology, making itself in the process less particular and more universal and regarding itself as an integral part of the emerging global solidarity of others and as contributing to a concretely universal theology of the future expressive of that solidarity.

Of the many reasons for this turn to a new paradigm, I would like to mention two: one historical and one theological.[6] Historically, we are living in a globalizing world, a world of intensifying economic interdependence in its complex dialectic with the political and cultural spheres. Ever since the European invasion of America in 1492, trade, transportation, communication, and technology have been bringing the different peoples, nations, religions, and cultures of the world closer together, culminating today, especially since the Uruguay Round of the General Agreement on Tariffs and Trade in the early 1990s, in the global extension of the free market that eliminates all barriers to trade and communication. The free market seems to reign supreme. National sovereignty, political or cultural, has become increasingly impotent and irrelevant.

---

[6] For a fuller discussion of these reasons, see Anselm Kyongsuk Min, "Solidarity of Others in the Body of Christ: A New Theological Paradigm," *Toronto Journal of Theology* (forthcoming).

This globalization of interdependence in the economic or material conditions of life in a world of unequal powers has always meant that some groups have been more dependent on others and thus more vulnerable to exploitation than other groups. Interdependence does not mean equal dependence of all groups on one another; such equality may be the goal of the future but neither the starting point nor the constant accompaniment of the process. From the first, interdependence has both brought about and been intensified by exploitations, conquests, slavery, wars, and certainly tensions among nations and human groups. Growing interdependence increases awareness of difference among groups, nations, and cultures, but, first of all, of difference in power, leading to colonial subjugation, imperialist domination, and self-assertive responses to such domination in the form of liberation movements and periodic revival of nationalism and national culture. Within the borders of a nation interdependence creates not only the consciousness of difference but also the need for living together with that difference. How can those who are different in gender, class, ethnicity, religion, and culture live *together* in common political space into which interdependence has brought them? How to achieve a solidarity of others sufficient to create common conditions of life liberating to all?

The process of global interdependence exempts no group from its universal impact. The unrestricted flow of capital across national boundaries and the rapidity with which new technology is invented make economic instability a permanent way of life for all. They make boom towns and ghost towns, create an economic tiger in one decade and an International Monetary Fund basket case in another, and make regimes rise and fall. They subject all nations, genders, races, cultures, and religions to constant mobility that displaces people from their native roots and places them among urban strangers, to constant competition that produces discrimination, loneliness, and alienation, and to constant commercialization that trivializes, relativizes, and impersonalizes all sacred values and subjects the totality of life to the rule of money. They respect no differences, ethnic, gender, cultural, religious, or even economic, but subject all to the uniformity of materialist culture now spreading across the globe. This is the universal condition and context of all life today, of all intellectual life and therefore of all theology.[7]

---

[7] For analyses of globalization as the central phenomenon of our time, see Richard J. Barnet and John Cavanagh, *Global Dreams: Imperial Corporations and the New World Order* (New York: Simon & Schuster, 1995); Robert N. Bellah, "Changing Themes in Society: Implications for Human Services: Social Change and the Fate of Human Services," Speech to Lutheran Social Services,

No theology today can credibly ignore this globalizing condition. Ethnic theologies used to justify their particularity by appeal to the particularity of their ethnic contexts. Such particularity still does exist insofar as it is constituted by the specificity of its ethnic history formed at a time when ethnic histories were relatively separate. Today, however, the context is no longer just particular but also drawn into the orbit of the common and the universal insofar as its context is co-constituted by the universalizing, globalizing condition of the contemporary world which has been growing interdependent in infinitely complex and intimate ways. No group can claim exclusive particularity for its own context. The context that creates the needs and perspectives specific to a particular group is no longer only the past of its particular history but also the present globalizing (dis)order of things. It is against this globalizing context and its often incomprehensible dialectic of power that each ethnic theology must reassess its needs and strategies of liberation as well as its own perspective. Any retrieval of an ethnic past must confront the universalizing context of the present into which *all* groups are compelled to enter. In such a context no particular group can liberate itself by its own power or claim universality for its own perspective. All are compelled by the pressures of the globalizing world to enter into a political solidarity of others in order to create conditions of common life that would both enhance the identity of each group in its particularity of tradition and culture and promote solidarity of such groups in their interdependence with one another as human beings with a common dignity and destiny. The context of an ethnic theology is no longer only particular but also in the process of globalizing itself, forcing all ethnic

---

San Francisco, April 28, 1995; Robert Gilpin, *The Political Economy of International Relations* (Princeton, N.J.: Princeton University Press, 1987) 364–408; Paul Kennedy, *Preparing for the Twenty-First Century* (New York: Random House, 1993) 329–49; the whole issue of *The Nation* (July 15/22, 1996) is devoted to an analysis of globalization; William Pfaff, *The Wrath of Nations: Civilization and the Furies of Nationalism* (New York: Simon & Schuster, 1993); Robert Wuthnow, *Christianity in the Twenty-First Century: Reflections on the Challenges Ahead* (New York: Oxford University Press, 1993); Peter Beyer, *Religion and Globalization* (London: Sage Publications, 1994); Robert J. Schreiter, *The New Catholicity: Theology between the Global and the Local* (Maryknoll, N.Y.: Orbis Books, 1997); the whole issue of *The Modern Schoolman* (January 1998) devoted to the topic of globalization, with essays by Jürgen Habermas on "Remarks on Legitimation through Human Rights," 87–100, James Bohmann on "Globalization of the Public Sphere: Cosmopolitanism, Publicity, and Cultural Pluralism," 101–18, and Enrique Dussel on "Globalization and the Victims of Exclusion: From a Liberation Ethics Perspective," 119–52.

theologies to enter theologically into the dialectic of particular and universal in its contemporary globalizing form. Contemporary ethnic theologies must express the emerging solidarity of others in all its dialectic; they can no longer remain content with celebration of their own ethnic past or bask in their merely proclaimed current identity, which would only lead to the vicious circle of fervor and disillusionment.

Besides this historical reason of a globalizing world that makes ethnic particularism impossible by rendering all human groups thoroughly interdependent, there is also the more important, theological reason for a turn to the new paradigm of solidarity of others. Christian theology is essentially universalist in its dynamism and ceases to be Christian when it is not. It is one thing to say that a theology must reflect the perspective and needs of a particular group, especially those of a group whose voice has been suppressed and absent, and another to say that God, Christ, salvation, grace, and the Church, objects of theological reflection, exist only for the needs of a particular group or can be grasped in their truth only from the perspective of a particular group. The first is a statement of the principle of embodiment or particularity, without which theology becomes a mere abstraction. The second is a statement of tribalism pure and simple, a most un-Christian negation of the principle of universality and transcendence. God, Christ, and the Church: these exist not only for a particular group but also for all humanity and all creation. They must be conceptualized and inculturated not only in the language and culture of a particular group but also in those of all groups.

The theological bottom line is that God is the universal creator of all reality, that Christ died and was raised for all. All Christian theology must live the tension between embodiment and transcendence, particularity and universality, and strive for concrete universality, a universality that is effectively concretized in the particular, a concreteness that seeks to transcend its particularity. Without this tension, theology falls into either oppressive tribalism or impotent universalism. An ethnic theology is Christian only insofar as it does not absolutize its own needs or perspective but regards itself as part of a global solidarity of others making a limited, particular contribution to the concrete universality of God and her Christ that animates all Christian theology.

The model I propose, solidarity of others, is an inherently dialectical model and must be grasped in all its dialectic. Opposed to all particularism and tribalism, it is not opposed to particularity as such. It advocates solidarity of others, not unity of the same. This is crucial, especially in view of the fact that global interdependence and universalization have historically been purchased by making victims of individuals, but most often of groups, based on gender, ethnicity, status, culture, and religion, by excluding and marginalizing them as others whose otherness must be either repressed or reduced to the same. In the foreseeable future of the globalization that is taking place now, oppression, exclusion, and marginalization are likely to continue although in different, unpredictable forms, and the theological need to defend the perspective of these others, promote their integrity, and struggle for their liberation will continue to be compelling. We live in a world where it is premature to talk of simply forgetting and transcending the particularity of ethnic needs and perspectives. I do propose solidarity, but precisely solidarity of *others* in their otherness and particularity. Until all are liberated, the voices of all the oppressed others must be lifted and heard. As long as there is oppression, the other must assert herself to protest, disturb, and interrupt. A universal theology will be possible only as a solidarity of these particular theologies in their complementarity and tension, just as the universal Church is not one local church imposed on all but the communion of local churches.

At the same time, I do propose and advocate *solidarity* of others. An ethnic theology cannot be only particular and exclusive without ceasing to be Christian. Just as each ethnic group must consider itself part of the universal theological solidarity of all humanity and all creation as created and redeemed by the triune God, so each group must work out its theological vision and identity in self-conscious appropriation of the needs and perspectives of the others. The culture and tradition of an ethnic group is valuable not as the self-sufficient source of a universal theology but as a particular contribution to the global communion of particular theologies, to the intrinsically differentiated universal theology of God, Christ, and the Church. These are universal in themselves, but *our* theologies of them are limited and particular, and must enter into the dialectic of solidarity with other theologies for mutual complementarity and correction. Without this dialectic, such theologies would fall into sheer tribalism. No regional or ethnic theology can remain content with its own particularity.

We need solidarity of others not only for the sake of the Christian integrity of each ethnic theology but, more important, for the sake of the very liberation of each group. No single group by itself can control the changing conditions of life in a rapidly globalizing world with all their liberating or oppressive potential. No group can liberate itself without the collaboration of other groups. Furthermore, genuine liberation does not mean liberation of each group for its own autonomy but precisely for a positive relationship or relationship of solidarity with others. Liberation in an interdependent world cannot mean mere juxtaposition of ethnic groups each liberated to do what it likes but entering into fellowship with others as human beings who share the same dignity and who are so destined as to depend on one another for the common conditions of life that alone can do justice to their respective dignity. Liberation today cannot mean the pursuit of ethnic selfishness but only the solidarity of others. Blacks in Los Angeles are not truly liberated unless the more powerful groups, such as whites and Asian Americans, are liberated from their own spirit of domination and are ready for solidarity with blacks, and unless blacks are ready in turn for solidarity with them. The liberation of each requires solidarity of others both as its efficient and its final cause.

That is why I am also advocating solidarity *of* others, not (merely) solidarity *with* others. Solidarity *with* others still implies a privileged center or normative perspective that regards the liberation of one's own group as the overriding concern and selects the relevant others with whom to enter into solidarity precisely for the sake of and around one's own agenda and goal. Others are not recognized as truly other, and solidarity becomes a tool of one's own liberation, one's own identity. It also tends to look on others as passive objects deserving *my* or *our* assistance from a privileged position, as in many expressions of solidarity with the "poor" and the "oppressed." Solidarity *of* others, on the other hand, implies mutual solidarity of others who are truly other to one another yet actively cooperate as subjects of a common destiny. It rejects the centrality of any one group, requiring each to consider even its own needs not from a privileged perspective but in the context of solidarity, the solidarity of all in their needs, praxis, and goal. It also implies the activity, agency, and responsibility of each for one another; "of" is not an objective but a subjective genitive.

Solidarity of others is a dialectical category and must be understood as a process of differentiation, contradiction, and movement to overcome the contradiction. "Others" must be taken not formally but materially, in all its intrinsic differentiation. African Americans, Native Americans, Hispanic Americans, Asian Americans: these are not just examples of the same class called other. They are other to others in different ways. Not all are equally oppressed; some are more oppressed than others and deserve preferential love from the less oppressed. There is the dialectic of tension and complementarity between particular ethnic theologies, as well as between them and the emerging vision of a global theology; between particular regions, as well as between them and the growing interdependence of the world; and between the theoretical particularity of ethnic theologies and the practical universality of their contexts. There is the ubiquitous dialectic of particular and universal, the local and the global, otherness and solidarity. Sometimes it is particularity that needs stressing, sometimes universality that does. Which needs stressing depends on the dialectic of the situation itself. Eventually, however, all dialectic aims at the achievement of ever higher and more adequate degrees of solidarity of others. What form this solidarity will take cannot be told a priori but depends on the dialectic of particular history. It is crucial to keep this solidarity of Others in all its dialectic and remain sensitive to the shifting contours of history for the concrete shapes and signs of such solidarity.

Autobiography is part of theology, but it cannot be the whole of theology. Theology is not reducible to autobiography, personal or collective, any more than philosophy is reducible to the Cogito of an individual philosopher or an individual school of philosophy. Autobiography shows the particularity of a theology in all its concreteness, but it does not show the dialectic of that particularity in its tensive interaction with other particularities in an increasingly universalizing, interdependent world. Autobiography is subjectivity, and the objective social, global dialectic increasingly forging and demanding global solidarity of others is simply irreducible to the autobiography of a particular theologian or ethnic theology. Theology as autobiography must be "sublated" *(aufgehoben)* into theology as fellowship of others, a theology that expands its own vision by incorporating the needs and perspectives of others and contributes its particular yet self-transcending contribution to the theological solidarity of others in the globalizing world.[8]

The requirements of an ethnic theology today are many and difficult. In the case of Korean-American theology it must reflect on the theological status of the Western tradition which after two hundred years has now become an organic part of Korean Christianity as well as of the indigenous Korean traditions of Confucianism, Buddhism, and shamanism as sources of theology. It must address the needs of the Korean communities in the United States, reflect on the theological implications of the Korean American experience, and enter into the solidarity of others with other ethnic groups and their theologies. Korean-American theology is only possible as a synthesis of these elements. Such a synthesis has begun on the part of Protestant theology as mentioned earlier, but

---

[8] I have been elaborating on this paradigm of "solidarity of others" in a number of essays: "Dialectical Pluralism and Solidarity of Others: Towards a New Paradigm," *Journal of the American Academy of Religion* 65:3 (fall 1997) 587–604; "The Challenge of Solidarity of Others: Philosophy of Religion after Kant and Kierkegaard," *Kant and Kierkegaard on Religion,* ed. D. Z. Phillips (New York: Macmillan, forthcoming); "Solidarity of Others in the Body of Christ," to appear in the *Toronto Journal of Theology;* "Solidarity of Others in the Power of the Holy Spirit: Pneumatology in a Divided World," to appear in the proceedings of the international conference on the Holy Spirit, Marquette University, Milwaukee, April 17–19, 1998.

not yet on the part of Catholic theology. Thoroughly authoritarian, Korean Catholicism has been preoccupied with the transmission of European Catholicism and Roman instructions. Even to this day, it has failed to produce a single creative theologian of significance capable of substantive reflection on the theological identity of Korean Catholicism. Korean-American Catholicism, now thirty years old, has been occupied with internal problems of individual communities, and failed to reflect even on the practical challenges facing Korean-American Catholicism as a whole, still less on its theological identity or its role in the emerging multicultural solidarity of others. At the present, Korean-American Catholic theology does not exist, not even as an idea or a need. I have only provided theological and historical prolegomena with regard to the formal elements of a Korean-American (Catholic) theology that is yet to be worked out. Honestly, my concern is that by the time Korean-American Catholic communities wake up to their theological identity, times may have changed so much and so fast as to require as yet unimagined new theological paradigms and do away with the present imperative of an ethnic theology altogether.

I started this essay by telling the story of my name and my identity. At the end of that story, I am still wondering whether I should keep or drop "Anselm" as part of my name. Is "Anselm" a sign of continuing Western colonialism naively and uncritically accepted and condoned? Can I, however, disavow it without disavowing part of my own identity? Is it possible to purify myself of all vestiges of Western influence without destroying myself? Could it also consciously be accepted as postcolonial, postcritical enrichment of my Christian identity? Perhaps these questions have been rendered obsolete by the emerging, new world of interdependence. Are we sure, however, that the West has ceased to be a global actor and that we need not bother with Western colonialism any longer? Are we really living in a "postcolonial" age? Or is "postcolonial" more a prescription than a description? What is the theological significance of the fact that when Asian theologians get together for a conference, they can communicate and relate to one another only in the Western language of English? Is this something only to be deplored as another unfortunate residue of Western colonialism, or is it a sign of a historical phenomenon whose theological significance is yet to be explored in all its dialectical ambiguity?

# Church and Theology: My Theological Journey

*Andrew Sung Park*

No one can choose his or her parents, gender, race and ethnicity. These things are given to us as part of our heritage. But we can choose how to live and with whom to spend our lives. I hope that sharing my theological journey may be of help to others in making choices for their own life journeys. In this essay, I will reflect on my ethnic background, the reason I chose theology as my lifework, the challenges facing me in teaching theology in the United States, some current theological issues, my theological positions, and, finally, some future issues for an Asian-American theology.

## From North Korea to an American Factory

My family originally came from North Korea. It belonged to the so-called "bourgeois" class. When the Communists took over North Korea, they confiscated all our possessions: the land, the house, and everything in it. Driven out of our home, my family escaped to a small town near Woolsan in South Korea, where my father served as pastor to a local church. In the early 1970s, my family immigrated to the United States.

In 1973, while serving a newly-founded Korean-American church in Colorado, I earned my living by working for the foundry of Denver Equipment Company, a mining-tool producer. My job was a molder assistant. All day long I shoveled dry sand up from a small square pit; I then hauled the sand in a wheelbarrow to the molders. My hands blistered from wheeling the sand-filled barrows for several hours a day and my back hurt badly from constant shoveling. Worse, I was continually

161

showered with dry sand; my whole body was covered with dust, and my mouth and lungs were filled with sand. Needless to say, it was a low-paying job. I came to understand what Marx meant by economic exploitation. My body could not take the tough job for long.

After a couple of months I found another job in Tom's Component Company, which made medical equipment. It was a small company with several employees, and my basic responsibility was assembling parts for machines. In the beginning, when I had to learn the necessary skills, the job was exciting, but soon it became monotonous and boring because it consisted of simple, repetitive acts and did not require much intelligence. I was just a part of the machine that assembled other machines. With other assembly workers I experienced the dehumanizing effects of this type of work. I also came to understand Marx's notion of the workers' alienation from their work. Work was separated from the worker's person, their doing from their being. I worked at the company for over a year until I enrolled in a seminary.

## No Need for a Korean-American Church?

After hard factory work, studying was a genuine pleasure. It stimulated and challenged my intelligence and way of thinking. While studying at the seminary, I continued to serve the same Korean-American (interdenominational) congregation in the city and the church grew in membership. We were using the facilities of the First Presbyterian Church in town. In the meantime, we had raised some funds, dreaming that we would have our own church building in the near future. One day the Presbyterian pastor met with our church leaders and strongly suggested that we join his church as a Korean mission. We would have to transfer our building funds and other financial resources to his Presbyterian church. His intention was sincere and genuine, not deceptive and manipulative; nevertheless, he was naive. The rational for the proposed merger was that, according to him, some day, perhaps within thirty years, the need for Korean churches would disappear. As examples he mentioned the churches of German, French, and Dutch immigrants which had all disappeared some three decades after their establishment. For him, having our own church building was superfluous and futile.

We rejected his argument by pointing out the fact that some Japanese-American and Korean-American churches, unlike European immigrant churches, had survived here over seventy years. Perhaps Asian-American immigrants are different from European immigrants in terms of their assimilation into the main culture. Asian Americans are not as meltable as European immigrants. Further, it is not desirable for us to abandon our ethnic identity and join the dominant culture. After a long talk, the pastor and the leaders of Korean-American church could not come to any agreement. Subsequently, we had to move out of the Presbyterian Church. Within a couple of years, our church purchased its own building.

Twenty-five years have elapsed since then, and yet the need for Korean-American churches has not diminished. On the contrary, there was only one Korean-American church in the city then, and now there are several in the same city. The multiplication of Korean-American churches may mean, among other things, that Asian immigrants and Asian Americans are not as meltable into this society as their European counterparts. Complete assimilation into the dominant church and culture is neither ideal nor viable for Asian Americans.

## A Pastoral Intern at a United Methodist Church

After completing my M.Div. degree, I went to Kansas to serve as a pastoral intern in a United Methodist church. The church was located in a rural city where the county seat was. The church was very gracious to me and I was well received by its members. With the intention of joining the conference, I applied for membership in the local church as soon as I started work. Toward the end of my one-year internship, I expressed my desire to join the conference as an ordained deacon. The district refused to recommend me to its conference on the ground that my membership in the church was short by one month, even though I had served the church as a pastoral assistant for almost one year. A minimum one-year membership in the church was required to join the conference. Deeply disappointed by the church's decision, I left for Claremont, California, for further studies.

While serving the church in Kansas, I was invited by a member of the church to attend an ecumenical charismatic service held in a Roman Catholic Church in a neighboring town. Several lay people of our church were also present at the service. During Holy Communion, people filed out to receive the elements. The priest gave out only bread. Sometimes only bread was distributed, and not wine, for fear that people might spill it. Our church members in front of me received the wafer and returned to their seats. When my turn came, the middle-aged priest refused to give me the wafer. Greatly shocked, I quietly returned to my seat. Out of deep shame, I told nobody about the treatment I received. I do not know why the priest refused me communion. In his eyes, I must have looked too foreign to receive Holy Communion.

The good news of Jesus Christ is that everyone is included in his community. When a person is excluded, especially at Holy Communion, the whole worship is perverted and the good news of Jesus is turned into bad news. In spite of this and other discriminatory incidents, I continue to believe that Christ's good news of inclusion will prevail over the bad news of exclusion in this society through our example and cross-cultural education.

## Vocation as a Theologian

My initial goal was parish ministry and I did serve a couple of churches for some time. But while studying at Claremont, my goal shifted from parish ministry to teaching ministry. As a result I pursued my theological education further. Several reasons underlie my choice of the ministry of teaching theology as my career.

The first was my conviction that Church and theology need one another. A theology that is separated from the Church cannot be genuine theology. This does not mean that theology must be subservient to the Church. On the contrary, it must keep its tension with the Church. However, it must work for the good of the Church. When I was working as a pastor I felt the need of theology to guide the Church's ministry. Consequently, my goal in pursuing a theological career was to develop a theology for the well-being of the Church.

The second reason was the need of Asian-American Christians to develop their own theology. Asian-American churches have drifted without the leadership of their own theology. They have adopted Western theologies and used them as if they were their own. A theology elaborated apart from its cultural context is not an authentic theology. A theology that ignores the Asian-American contexts cannot be a theology for Asian-American churches. I felt the urgent need for an Asian-American theology for Asian-American churches. Of course, Asian-American Christians can use the theologies of such Western thinkers as Barth, Bultmann, the Niebuhrs, and Tillich to articulate the gospel of Jesus Christ, but they must do so for their own contexts and for their own communities. Any theology that ignores its own culture and context is not theology but domesticated ideology. One of my goals is to articulate the Christian gospel in the cultural, sociopolitical, and religious contexts of Asian Americans.

The third reason was my interest in exploring the connections between liberation and mysticism. I am committed to the liberation of the oppressed and the downtrodden. But this liberation cannot be achieved through political and socioeconomic struggles alone. During my college years, I underwent a mystical experience. Since then, I have had a deep desire to explore the implications of the mystical dimension of the Christian faith. To me, being with the divine would provide the energy needed to challenge the oppressive state of affairs and transform it according to the ideal of a divine community. This does not mean that we can change our situation merely by seeking unity with God. We must also be involved in the work of transforming our world. The two traditions, liberation theology and mysticism, are indispensable to the Christian gospel. My goal is to show that these two currents are inseparable in doing theology. With regard to mysticism, I intend to include in it the perspectives of Eastern religions.

## Challenges in Teaching Theology in the United States

The challenges I face in teaching theology in the United States are manifold. The first is to enable the American society and its culture to become what they should and can be. Since our society generally considers theological worldviews trivial, theology has been marginalized. Part of the reasons for theology's current situation is that it has concerned itself with issues irrelevant to the life of most Americans. However, being relevant to the world is one thing; taking leadership in the world is another. Theology should direct the world with its fresh vision. Unfortunately, it has been a follower of other disciplines—philosophy, sociology, economics, biology, and physics. There is, of course, nothing wrong with learning from other disciplines, but it can be problematic when theology depends on other disciplines without its own vision. How can theology guide our society and its culture without a vision of what the community of God should be?

The second challenge is to enhance the Asian-American heritage by means of the gospel of Jesus Christ. The latter has been clothed in Jewish and Hellenistic categories, and traditional theologies have been constructed from Western cultural perspectives. However, the gospel of Christ cannot be identified with any one culture. On the contrary, the purpose of the gospel is to bring every culture to its fullest fulfillment, not to subjugate one culture or civilization to another. The task I am facing as an Asian-American theologian is not only to express the gospel of Jesus Christ in an appropriate way for the Asian-American community, but also to enhance the Asian-American culture and make it fruitful through the gospel. Jesus came into the world to serve people and their cultures so that through their own cultures they can maximize God's gifts. This is the reason why the gospel is good news to everyone and every culture. Each person and each culture can achieve their fullness in Christ. Consequently, the task of evangelization does not lie in "christianizing" cultures, but in enabling every culture to blossom and reach its perfection through Christ. Evangelizing the whole world does not mean forging all the different cultures into one uniform Christian culture, but enabling every culture to achieve its full potential in God through Christ.

The third challenge is to articulate an Asian-American theology. This task remains largely unfinished and there have been few works in this area. The goal is not just to construct an Asian-American theology, but to serve Asian-American and other communities with it. To do so, it is necessary to understand the agonies and the *han* of Asian-American communities. *Han* is the deep inner wounds of a victim that are at once conscious and unconscious, individual and collective. The deep pain of *han,* which is often indescribable, shapes our mode of thinking as well as our attitude. In this respect some of the challenging questions are: How can I keep my contact with the Asian-American communities and see reality from their perspectives? How can I authentically articulate a theology with them and for them? Can I still be sensitive to the needs of people while staying in an ivory tower? I truly need to hear the voice of the voiceless and the suffering and cry out with them through theology. Developing a theology from the perspective of victims is a challenge for me.[1]

The fourth challenge is to integrate intra-theological disciplines as well as interdisciplinary subjects. Within the theological discipline, we have various fields such as biblical, historical, constructive, ethical, pastoral, educational theologies. Currently, there is a wide gap between biblical and constructive theologies in particular. We need a certain level of integration of theological disciplines for the sake of providing theological visions for our culture and society.

Moreover, while seeking to integrate the various theological branches together, we must also strive to interrelate all the disciplines within the university with each other. Each discipline would suffer from reductionism if it is not in an effective dialogue with the others. Each department would pursue its own tunnel vision in separation from other departments. Since the Church is the place where various people of the university come together, the Church and theology can play a pivotal role in unifying their minds and articulating an integral and common meaning of all human pursuits.

Furthermore, studies at public universities deal with various penultimate problems of the human, and not the ultimate question and meaning of life. The task to dialogue with, challenge, and inspire university disciplines naturally falls to theology. Theology is inevitably engaged in the final aims of these disciplines. Theologians have to accomplish this task in humility and openness, without pretense and presumption.

---

[1] See my *The Wounded Heart of God: The Asian Concept of God and the Christian Doctrine of Sin* (Nashville: Abingdon Press, 1993).

## Theological Methodology

Theological methodologies should not be devised for their own sake. Rather, after a theological problem is identified and a theological goal is set up, a theological method will be formulated to achieve that goal. Consequently, no theological method can exist independently of specific theological problems or goals.

My own theological method requires first of all a diagnosis of *han*. How well we diagnose the pain of the world determines how well we are going to heal it. In investigating the problems of the world, we can make use of different disciplines. Also, we need sufficient time to diagnose correctly what is wrong with our society and world to avoid proposing premature solutions. In addition to *han*, the main theological problem we face is, of course, sin. The dual task of theology is to resolve *han* and to treat sin. The theological methods I employ are designed to perform this dual task. However, I do not limit myself to theological methodologies, but use all available scholarly tools to resolve the *han* of the oppressed and end the sin of oppressors.

Furthermore, theopraxis is part of the theological methodology. Praxis as the unity of theory and practice is important, and the direction of praxis is more important than praxis itself. Marx criticized philosophers for merely interpreting the world, without getting involved in the transformation of it. However, involvement by itself would not bring forth the necessary transformation. The world has been transformed by praxis, yet the world has not become what it ought to be. The direction of praxis itself makes a great difference in the outcome of transformation.

Marx's direction toward a classless society was not realistic because he underestimated the power of sin and the finitude of human freedom. Hence, his emphasis on praxis has not been fruitful in history. To me, to transform society, praxis should be a movement directed toward God. This praxis can be called theopraxis. Any praxis that is directed to a historical goal or object apart from God—a classless society, utopia, liberation—is doomed to failure. I recognize that the aforementioned goals do not necessarily exclude God. However, no reality can be the final goal of history except God—the final home of our destiny. When we bring out God's full presence in the world, various forms of an ideal society will come as gifts.

Theopraxis is living out God in our lives. The goal of theopraxis is to embody God's life. This means that we have to bring forth social and political changes until our society is filled with God's presence. Even liberation as salvation is secondary; "living out God" is primary. In the process of embodying God, we will experience liberation as a gift.

Liberation can mean different things to the oppressed and the oppressors. For the oppressed, it may mean being delivered from all kinds of oppression to be themselves. For the oppressors it may require renouncing their misuse or abuse of power. Thus, there is not a single way to praxis. However, both praxis for the oppressed and praxis for the oppressors converge on living out God in their ways of life. For the oppressed, theopraxis means moving toward God through restoring self-respect and self-confidence, healing oneself and one's fellow oppressed, confronting the oppressors, and transforming the evil structure of the social system which perpetuates injustice and oppression. For the oppressors, theopraxis implies turning toward God via self-negation, relinquishing power, redistributing wealth, converting fellow oppressors, and dismantling the evil social customs, traditions, and systems.

Theopraxis is not confined to the practice of theories but includes all movements of thought (vision, theory, reflection, and intention), words (dialogue, teaching, preaching, writing, and storytelling), and deeds (action, operation, practice, and the process of performance) toward the embodiment of God. The theopraxis of *sung* releases writers to write, teachers to teach, ministers to minister, farmers to farm, and laborers to labor, all for the well-being of the community, which is necessary for realizing the full presence of God. All their sincere efforts (thinking, expressing, and acting) which move toward incarnating God in history constitute theopraxis. My theological method includes all the means that embody God in our world and in this sense it is theopraxis.

## Current Theological Issues

First, while traditional theology has paid attention to the problem of sin from the perspective of sinners, Asian-American theology reflects on the *han* of the sinned-against. Influenced by Asian culture, Asian-American culture is shame-oriented, not guilt-oriented. Guilt is the reaction of regret by the sinner, while shame is the sense of recoil in the sinned-against. As both sinned-against and sinning, Asian Americans are in a position to see the whole spectrum of shame and guilt. In terms of racial discrimination, we are victims most of the time, but in terms of racial and sexual bias, we are offenders, too. We know both the act of sinning and the pain of *han*. Of the two, however, we experience *han* more acutely. Suffering from racism and sexism (for women), Asian Americans need to pay more attention to the struggle of the sinned-against and their problems. For this reason, I have been engaged in developing the notion of *han* and shame in addition to the doctrine of sin and guilt.

Second, while traditional theology has focused on the salvation of sinners, Asian-American theology can strive for the deliverance of the sinned-against. For two millennia, the Church has proclaimed the message of salvation for all. However, I believe that the destiny of sinners differs from that of the sinned-against. While sinners attain salvation through justification by faith, the sinned-against achieve liberation through justice. Even Gustavo Gutiérrez believes that salvation and liberation are identical. His agenda, however, is different from ours. He attempts to bring down the transhistorical dimension of salvation to the historical level of liberation. My understanding of salvation and liberation is historical without excluding the transhistorical dimension. As an oppressed group, we need to develop the doctrine of liberation for the sinned-against in contrast to the doctrine of salvation for sinners (oppressors).

Third, while traditional theology has stressed "faith seeking understanding" (Anselm), Asian-American theology develops "faith seeking seeing." Western theology has been rational and logical. It has treated faith as a means of understanding. Here "understanding" essentially refers to intellectual comprehension. Compared with Western theology, Asian-American theology, under the influence of Asian culture, is intuitive. It is primarily intuitive and perceptive. Of course, for Asian-American theology, faith is for understanding too, but understanding is achieved through seeing. Since the Asian culture prefers visualization to mental comprehension, I have been engaged in developing a theology of seeing.[2]

For me, how we see is intimately related to how the world is determined. How we see others shapes the way they themselves think and behave. In this sense, seeing is pivotal for understanding reality and transforming the unjust society. Seeing comprises being, doing, and envisioning. It is my hope that Asian-American churches pursue intuitive and visual theologies so as to be able to heal the *han* in our society.

## My Theological Positions

Whenever people asked me about my theological positions, I have always wondered what they are. When I entered the seminary, I had quite a closed worldview. After seminary, I became more open-minded. At this juncture, I want to go beyond the categories of liberal, radical, progressive, conservative, and evangelical. These categories have divided the Church and have sapped its energy. My position is a genuine boundary-less openness, yet within the boundary of Christ.

Unlike Karl Barth, I cannot say that I am "christo-centric" because I reject the separation of the center from its margin. It seems to me that

---

[2] See my *Racial Conflict & Healing: An Asian-American Theological Perspective* (Maryknoll, N.Y.: Orbis Books, 1997) 129–59.

the division between center and periphery is artificial, superficial, and arbitrary. Where God is, the center of the universe is. There is no place where God is not. That means that everywhere is the center of the universe. On the other hand, where God is, the periphery of the universe is, for God embraces the periphery which enfolds the whole. This means that there is no space which God cannot embrace. When we talk about space alone, we lose the dimension of time. The inseparability of space and time implies that discussing space alone is misleading. The symbol of space alone is inevitably incomplete. The literal interpretation of a center and its periphery is erroneous. In this sense, the term "position" is rather symbolic.

Consequently, my theological position is christo-centric and christo-peripheral, theo-centric and theo-peripheral, and pneumato-centric and pneumato-peripheral. To me, Christ is my center as well as the boundary of my identity. I belong to Christ, but the Christ whom I serve commands me to go beyond the boundary of Christianity. Christ as boundary includes all other centers and margins of love, trust, hope, peace, and justice. Jesus himself said, "Those who are not against me are for me." This inclusiveness is the open edge of Christ's boundary.

God is the center as well as the periphery of my existence. Theo-centric existence precedes christo-centric identity. God is for all peoples, not only for Jews or Christians. Whether people are Christian or not, God is their true center. God is also the growing edge of life. God stands where we experience the margin of life. From the width of God, God encourages us to grow to the brim of multicultural and multifaceted life.

The Holy Spirit is the center of our life, grasping the depth of our spirit, and is also the boundary that encompasses our total living. The Spirit searches the depth of our life, which we may not understand ourselves. The Spirit, however, lets us be and go for the abundance of life.

To express these paradoxical positions, the term "concentricity" might be useful. Concentricity has circles of centers; in it, centers become peripheries and peripheries become centers. Thus, my theological position is not christo-centric, but christo-concentric; not theo-centric, but theo-concentric; not Spirit-centric, but Spirit-concentric.

In this sense, I am defined by Jesus Christ, yet I am not constrained by the center of Jesus Christ, but transcend the circles of Christ: a particular church, Christianity, and christendom. So I am a Christian but am more than a Christian: a human being whom God intended to create in the beginning and an Asian American whom God has led me to be. I am surrounded by the Spirit, yet not delimited by the Spirit: the more I am enclosed by the Spirit, the more I am free in the Spirit. For the Holy Spirit is the very boundary of freedom. I am founded by God, yet not grounded by God; I am deepened, widened, and heightened by God's foundation.

## Future Issues for an Asian-American Theology

First of all, Asian Americans must ask what it means to be Christian in the United States. Are there any differences between being Christian as Asian Americans and as European Americans? I believe that there are. To be an Asian-American Christian is not to be a Westernized Christian, but an authentic Asian-American Christian. This might sound strange at first. But it is not unsound to say that we were not born to be Christians but to be the true human beings whom God intended to create. Thus, through Christ Asians must be true Asians; Africans true Africans; and Europeans true Europeans. At the outset, we were meant not to be Christians but to be authentic human beings in God. However, as we could not be what we ought to be, Christ came to enable us to be what we ought to be. Thus, to be true Asian Americans is for us to be Christians. Of course, we need to define what it means to be true Asian Americans. I hope that Asian-American theologians will wrestle with this issue.

Second, Asian Americans need to deal with racism without and sexism within their communities together. As much as we desire to transform racism in the society, we must transform sexism within our communities. The patterns of racial and sexual oppression are very similar. Both are forms of prejudice and discrimination. Sexism is the sin of Asian-American males whereas external racism is the *han* of our communities. We have suffered the pain of racial prejudice and discrimination because externally we look different from the dominant group. We know how unfair and unjust racism is. Asian-American men, however, use the same pattern of prejudice and discrimination against women in their communities. We practice prejudice and discrimination against women because they have a different gender. To the degree that we repent of our sin against women in our communities, we can raise an authentic voice against racism in our society. We need to challenge and transform the structure of the *han* of racism in the society and repent of our sin of sexism in our communities at the same time. I hope that Asian-American theologians will work on the issues of racism and sexism in tandem, unmasking their similar patterns of oppression, to promote liberation for both women and men.

Third, Asian Americans need to address the issue of eco-justice. Conjoined with racism, ecological exploitation has generated environmental racism. A high percentage of poor ethnic neighborhoods have been chosen for landfill and dumping sites for toxic chemicals. Environmental pollution will be the most urgent issue in the future, for it destroys our health, our home, our communities, the future generations, and other species. Some, Lynn White, for example, have blamed Christianity for the reckless destruction of the environment. Although the true meaning of the Bible does not allow mastering and abusing the environment, popular Christian culture has seized a few biblical passages to justify its misuse of the natural resources. To remedy this situation, Asian Americans can have recourse to their Asian religious heritage. For example, Taoism teaches that following the course of nature is the way to salvation. We can use Taoist insights to bring about the healing of nature and culture. Teaching Taoism and other Asian traditions of wisdom should be encouraged in the Asian-American churches, just as we have encouraged our children to learn about Jewish wisdom and history. Asian Americans are in a good position to perform the tasks of eradicating racism, sexism, and environmental pollution together, using their cultural and religious resources.

Finally, in North America as well as in Asia, science, rather than religion, plays the dominant role. There is then the pressing need of the dialogue between religion and science. Asian-American theologians should take up this challenge, especially from the viewpoint of interreligious dialogue.

It has been difficult for me to reflect autobiographically on my work as an Asian-American theologian, for I am still on my journey. My theological journey began with the desire to connect theology with the Church and to develop an Asian-American theology. My teaching of theology is geared toward leading the Church in its ministry of enabling each culture to achieve its full potential given by God. My theological methodology consists in analyzing the *han* of society in order to heal it through theopraxis. Current issues that have engaged my attention include the development of a theology for the sinned-against by distinguishing between sin and *han,* salvation and liberation. The theological positions I have taken are transcategorical and paradoxical, unfit for any usual label. Future issues for Asian-American theologians include defining the meaning of being Christian as Asian Americans, struggling against racism and sexism together, and overcoming ecological destruction by means of Christian/Asian resources.

The title of this book is *Journeys at the Margin*. Since margin and center depend on a specific perspective, I endeavor to see reality from a holistic view, transcending the division between center and periphery. True, I live in an unfamiliar and *han*-ridden society. In this sense I am journeying at the margin. However, in spite of its strangeness, ambivalence, incompleteness, and *han,* this country is my home—the consecrated space of my rest. My journey is not over yet, but I am at home; for home is everywhere God is and I am. And home is not only the place to relax, but also the place to struggle, challenge, and grow.

# Selected Bibliography

Brock, Rita N. *Journeys by Heart: A Christology of Erotic Power*. New York: Crossroad, 1988.

Ching, Julia. *Chinese Religions*. Maryknoll, N.Y.: Orbis Books, 1993.

____. *Confucianism and Christianity: A Comparative Study*. New York: Kodansha International, 1977.

____. *Religion, Philosophy, Politics in China: Mysticism and the Sage King Paradigm*. Cambridge, Mass.: Cambridge University Press.

Chung, Hyun Kyung. *Struggle to Be the Sun Again: Introducing Asian Women's Theology*. Maryknoll, N.Y.: Orbis Books, 1990.

Kim, Jung Ha. *Bridge-Makers and Cross-Bearers: Korean-American Women and the Church*. Atlanta: Scholars Press, 1997.

Koyama, Kosuke. *Mount Fuji and Mount Sinai: A Critique of Idols*. Maryknoll, N.Y.: Orbis Books, 1985.

____. *No Handle on the Cross*. Maryknoll, N.Y.: Orbis Books, 1977.

____. *Three Mile an Hour God*. Maryknoll, N.Y.: Orbis Books, 1980.

____. *Waterbuffalo Theology*. Maryknoll, N.Y.: Orbis Books, 1974.

Kwok, Pui-lan. *Chinese Women and Christianity, 1860–1927*. Atlanta: Scholars Press, 1992.

____. *Discovering the Bible in the Non-Biblical World*. Maryknoll, N.Y.: Orbis Books, 1995.

____. "God Weeps with Our Pain." *East Asia Journal of Theology* 2:2 (1984) 228–32.

____. "The Image of the 'White Lady': Gender and Race in Christian Mission." *Concilium* 6 (1991) 19–27.

Lee, Jung Young. *Cosmic Religion*. New York: Philosophical Library, 1973.

____. *Death and Beyond: The Eastern Perspective*. New York: Gordon and Breach Science Publishers, 1974.

____. *Death Overcome: Toward the Convergence of Eastern and Western Views*. Lanham, Md.: University of America Press, 1983.

____. *Embracing Change: Postmodern Interpretations of the I Ching from a Christian Perspective*. Cranbury, N.J.: University of Scranton Press, 1994.

_____. *God Suffers for Us: A Systematic Inquiry into the Concept of Divine Passibility*. Hague: Martinus Nijhoff, 1974.

_____. *The I: A Christian Concept of Man*. New York: Philosophical Library, 1971.

_____. *The I Ching and Modern Man: Essays on Metaphysical Implications of Change*. Secaucus, N.Y.: University Books, 1975.

_____. *Korean Shamanistic Rituals*. Hague: Mouton Publishers, 1981.

_____. *Marginality: The Key to Multicultural Theology*. Minneapolis: Fortress Press, 1995.

_____. *Patterns of Inner Process*. Secaucus, N.Y.: Citadel Press, 1976.

_____. *The Principle of Changes: Understanding the I-Ching*. New Hyde Park, N.Y.: University Books, 1974.

_____. *Sermons to the Twelve*. Nashville: Abingdon Press, 1988.

_____. *The Theology of Change: A Christian Concept of God from an Eastern Perspective*. Maryknoll, N.Y.: Orbis Books, 1979.

_____. *The Trinity in Asian Perspective*. Nashville: Abingdon Press, 1996.

_____, ed. *Ancestor Worship and Christianity in Korea*. Lewiston, N.Y.: Edwin Mellen, 1988.

_____, ed. *An Emerging Theology in World Perspective: Commentary on Minjung Theology*. Mystic, Conn.: Twenty-Third Publications, 1988.

Min, Anselm Kyongsuk. *Dialectic of Salvation: Issues in Liberation Theology*. Maryknoll, N.Y.: Orbis Books, 1998.

_____, William Biernatzki, and Luke Jinchang Im. *Korean Catholicism in the 1970s*. Maryknoll, N.Y.: Orbis Books, 1975.

Nagano, Paul. "The Japanese Americans' Search for Identity, Ethnic Pluralism and a Christian Basis of Permanent Identity." Rel. D. diss. Claremont, Calif.: School of Theology at Claremont, 1970.

Ng, David, ed. *People on the Way: Asian North Americans Discovering Christ, Culture, and Community*. Valley Forge, Pa.: Judson Press, 1995.

Park, Andrew Sung. *Racial Conflict & Healing: An Asian-American Theological Perspective*. Maryknoll, N.Y.: Orbis Books, 1996.

_____. *The Wounded Heart of God: The Asian Concept of Han and the Christian Doctrine of Sin*. Nashville: Abingdon Press, 1993.

Phan, Peter Cho. "The Christ of Asia: An Essay on Jesus as the Eldest Son and Ancestor." *Studia Missionalia* 45 (1996) 25–55.

_____. *Culture and Eschatology: The Iconographical Vision of Paul Evdokimov*. New York: Peter Lang, 1985.

_____. *Eternity in Time: A Study of Karl Rahner's Eschatology*. Selinsgrove, Pa.: Susquehanna University Press, 1988.

_____. "Experience and Theology: An Asian Liberation Perspective." *Zeitschrift für Missionswissenschaft und Religionswissenschaft* 2 (1993) 99–121.

_____. *Grace and the Human Condition*. Wilmington, Del.: Michael Glazier, 1988.

_____. "Jesus as the Eldest Brother and Ancestor? A Vietnamese Portrait." *The Living Light* 33:1 (1996) 35–44.

_____. "Jesus the Christ with an Asian Face." *Theological Studies* 57 (1996) 399–430.

_____. "Kingdom of God: A Theological Symbol for Asians?" *Gregorianum* 79:2 (1998) 295–322.

____. *Mission and Catechesis: Alexandre de Rhodes and Inculturation in Seventeenth-Century Vietnam*. Maryknoll, N.Y.: Orbis Books, 1998.

____. *Responses to 101 Questions on Death and Eternal Life*. New York: Paulist Press, 1998.

____. *Social Thought*. Wilmington, Del.: Michael Glazier, 1984.

____, ed. *Christianity and the Wider Ecumenism*. New York: Paragon House, 1980.

____, ed. *Church and Theology: Essays in Memory of Carl Peter*. Washington, D.C.: Catholic University of America Press, 1994.

____, ed. *Ethnicity, Nationality and Religious Experience*. Lanham, Md.: University Press of America, 1994.

Song, Choan-Seng. *The Believing Heart: An Invitation to Story Theology*. Minneapolis: Fortress Press, 1998.

____. *The Compassionate God*. Maryknoll, N.Y.: Orbis Books, 1982.

____. *Jesus and the Reign of God*. Minneapolis: Fortress Press, 1993.

____. *Jesus in the Power of the Spirit*. Minneapolis: Fortress Press, 1994.

____. *Jesus, the Crucified People*. New York: Crossroad, 1990.

____. *The Tears of Lady Meng: A Parable of People's Political Theology*. Maryknoll, N.Y.: Orbis Books, 1982.

____. *Tell Us Our Names: Story Theology from an Asian Perspective*. Maryknoll, N.Y.: Orbis Books, 1984.

____. *Theology from the Womb of Asia*. Maryknoll, N.Y.: Orbis Books, 1986.

____. *Third-Eye Theology: Theology in Formation in Asian Settings*. Maryknoll, N.Y.: Orbis Books, 1982; rev. ed. 1990.

# Contributors

**Julia Ching** is the author of many books, including *Confucianism and Christianity* (Kodansha International, 1977) and *Chinese Religions* (Orbis Books, 1993). Her forthcoming work from Cambridge University Press is entitled *Religion, Philosophy, Politics in China: Mysticism and the Sage King Paradigm*. She is active in interreligious dialogue, has taught in Asia, Australia, Europe, and North America, and is University Professor at the University of Toronto.

**Jung Ha Kim,** though academically trained in religion and theology, teaches as a sociologist at Georgia State University. She considers herself an "organic intellectual" and is a community organizer and educator at the Center for Pan Asian Community Services, Inc. Her most recent book is *Bridge-Makers and Cross-Bearers: Korean-American Women and the Church* (Scholars Press, 1997).

**Jung Young Lee** was professor of systematic theology in The Theological School at Drew University. He has authored and edited some twenty books and some fifty articles.

**Anselm Kyongsuk Min** has been a professor of religion and theology at Claremont Graduate University since 1992. He received his Ph.D. in philosophy from Fordham University in 1974 and his Ph.D. in theology from Vanderbilt University in 1989. He has co-authored *Korean Catholicism in the 1970s* (Orbis Books, 1975) and authored *Dialectic of Salvation: Issues in Liberation Theology* (SUNY Press, 1989) and over thirty articles in the areas of philosophy and theology.

**Paul M. Nagano** is director of the Council for Pacific Asian Theology.

**David Ng** was the John K. McLennan Professor of Christian Education at the San Francisco Theological Seminary, San Anselmo, California. He has written and edited three books on Christian education.

**Andrew Sung Park** is professor of theology at United Theological Seminary, Dayton, Ohio. He is an ordained minister in the United Methodist Church. Previously he taught at Claremont School of Theology, California. His publications include *The Wounded Heart of God: The Asian Concept of Han and the Christian Concept of Sin* (Abingdon Press, 1993) and *Racial Conflict and Healing: An Asian-American Theological Perspective* (Orbis Books, 1996). The latter received a Gustavus Meyers Award as an outstanding book on human rights in North America in 1997. Dr. Park received his theological education from Iliff School of Theology, Claremont School of Theology, and Graduate Theological Union. Currently he is working on doctrines for the victims of sin.

**Peter C. Phan** is the Warren-Blanding Professor of Religion and Culture in the Department of Religion and Religious Education at The Catholic University of America. He has written six books, edited some twenty volumes, and authored over one hundred essays on various aspects of Christian theology.

**Choan-Seng Song** is professor of theology and Asian cultures at Pacific School of Religion and Graduate Theological Union, Berkeley. He is also president of the World Alliance of Reformed Churches. He has authored over ten books and numerous articles.